GLOBALIZATION AND
HUMAN DEVELOPMENT

GLOBALIZATION

Series Editors

Manfred B. Steger *(University of Hawai'i–Manoa and Western Sydney University)*
Terrell Carver *(University of Bristol)*

"Globalization" has become the buzzword of our time. But what does it mean? Rather than forcing a complicated social phenomenon into a single analytical framework, this series seeks to present globalization as a multidimensional process constituted by complex, often contradictory interactions of global, regional, and local aspects of social life. Since conventional disciplinary borders and lines of demarcation are losing their old rationales in a globalizing world, authors in this series apply an interdisciplinary framework to the study of globalization. In short, the main purpose and objective of this series is to support subject-specific inquiries into the dynamics and effects of contemporary globalization and its varying impacts across, between, and within societies.

GLOBALIZATION AND HUMAN DEVELOPMENT

RONI KAY M. O'DELL
DEVIN K. JOSHI

ROWMAN & LITTLEFIELD
Lanham • Boulder • New York • London

Executive Acquisitions Editor: Michael Kerns
Assistant Editor: Elizabeth Von Buhr
Sales and Marketing Inquiries: textbooks@rowman.com
Credits and acknowledgments for material borrowed from other sources, and
reproduced with permission, appear on the appropriate pages within the text.

Published by Rowman & Littlefield
An imprint of The Rowman & Littlefield Publishing Group, Inc.
4501 Forbes Boulevard, Suite 200, Lanham, Maryland 20706
www.rowman.com

86-90 Paul Street, London EC2A 4NE

British Library Cataloguing in Publication Information Available

Library of Congress Cataloging-in-Publication Data

Names: O'Dell, Roni Kay M., author. | Joshi, Devin, author.
Title: Globalization and human development / Roni Kay M. O'Dell, Devin K. Joshi.
Description: Lanham, Maryland : Rowman & Littlefield, 2024. | Series: Globalization |
    Includes bibliographical references and index.
Identifiers: LCCN 2023044006 (print) | LCCN 2023044007 (ebook) |
    ISBN 9781538164143 (cloth) | ISBN 9781538164150 (paperback) |
    ISBN 9781538164167 (epub)
Subjects: LCSH: Globalization—Social aspects. | Sustainable development—Social
    aspects. | Sustainable Development Goals.
Classification: LCC JZ1318 .O24 2024 (print) | LCC JZ1318 (ebook) |
    DDC 338.9/27—dc23/eng/20231228
LC record available at https://lccn.loc.gov/2023044006
LC ebook record available at https://lccn.loc.gov/2023044007

CONTENTS

LIST OF FIGURES, TABLES, AND TEXTBOXES

FIGURES

TABLES

TEXTBOXES

ACKNOWLEDGMENTS

One afternoon many years ago, Roni Kay stepped into Devin's bright, windowed office at the University of Denver—his bookshelves were lined with copies of the Human Development Reports. She asked him if he would publish something with her about international development, and he said yes! That is where our collaboration began, and now with several papers already published, we are so excited that it has turned into this book. We have so many people we would like to acknowledge for making this book happen. It was not an easy process, as Roni Kay and Devin both had intense work schedules, and much of the work on this book took place during the COVID-19 pandemic. This prevented us as authors from ever meeting in person while doing the writing. Indeed, writing this book often felt like mile 25 of running a marathon, when one's buckling knees barely make it across the finish line (as a marathon runner, Roni Kay overused this analogy in almost all of our meetings). But we are thrilled that we are presenting this book to you!

Among many people who have played an important role in bringing this book to you, we would like to start off by thanking Susan McEachern, Michael Kerns, and Elizabeth Von Buhr at Rowman & Littlefield for their keen interest and support of this project. It all began thanks to the enthusiasm and encouragement of the series editors, Manfred Steger and Terrell Carver, who have greatly inspired our own thinking about the ideological dimensions of globalization.

Many other scholars have also shaped our thinking. At the Josef Korbel School of International Studies at the University of Denver where our writings on human development first began, we were fortunate in being able to work together with excellent colleagues sharing their expertise and experience on issues related to international development and international relations more broadly including Deborah Avant, George DeMartino, Jack Donnelly, Rachel Epstein, Ilene Grabel, Sally Hamilton, Nader Hashemi, Barry Hughes, Sandy Johnson, Haider Khan, Randall Kuhn, Jonathan Moyer, Martin Rhodes, Aaron Schneider, Timothy Sisk, Karin Wedig, and many others.

We also benefited immensely from feedback and conversations with colleagues from around the world. Devin would like to especially mention Jean Drèze, Jean-Philippe Thérien, K. Seeta Prabhu, and Liu Minquan who hosted his visiting scholar position at Peking University's Center for Human and Economic Development Studies, as well as Deane Neubauer who hired him many years back to work at the Globalization Research Center at the University of Hawai'i where he first came to know Manfred Steger. Devin is also grateful for receiving a Lee Kong Chian Fellowship from Singapore Management University to help him finish this project and he is grateful for the warm support he has received there and the opportunity to exchange ideas with Chandran Kukathas, James Tang, Ann Florini, Jacob Ricks, Ijlal Naqvi, Sebastian Dettman, Colm Fox, Inwook Kim, Onur Ulas Ince, Ishani Mukherjee, Hiro Saito, and many other wonderful colleagues. Roni Kay would like to thank her many outstanding and supportive colleagues at Seton Hill University (SHU). Many thanks to the institutional support from SHU's Provost Office and Provost Susan Yochum, and SHU's School of Humanities and Dean Debra Faszer-McMahon. Other colleagues to thank for the many conversations with Roni Kay on the topics covered in this book, and other library, research, or administrative support, making the finished product deep and multi-disciplinary, include Michael Cary, Kelly Clever, Christine Cusick, Susan Eichenberger, Michelle Frye, Una Henry, Jessica Lohr, David von Schlichten, and Linda Veazey, among many others. A special shout-out to Jen Jones and Sasha Breger Bush for their constant encouragement.

In putting this book together, we have had the good fortune to work with very talented research assistants. Particular mention goes to the outstanding work of Esha Nitin Doshi for her work on UN conference diplomacy and Sarah Minghini for her work on analyzing the Human Development and Capability Association. Thanks to several others who provided research support, including Ryan Dzurko, Trifol

Headman, De'Shawn McClary, Hannah Potter, Sophia Solomon, and Jarred Spellman. We would also like to thank Kathy Rosenblum at the Human Development and Capability Association for sharing much information about its past and present, some of which appears in chapter 3 of this book.

We thank the following publishers for granting us permission to reuse selected portions of some of our previous publications in this book. Parts of chapter 4 first appeared in Devin Joshi and Roni Kay O'Dell. 2017. "The Critical Role of Mass Media in International Norm Diffusion: The Case of UNDP Human Development Reports." *International Studies Perspectives* 18(3): 343–364 reused here by permission of Oxford University Press. Some parts of chapters 2 and 7 appeared earlier in Devin K. Joshi. 2021. "The Human Development and Capabilities Approach as a Twenty-First Century Ideology of Globalization." *Globalizations* 18(5): 781–791, DOI: 10.1080/14747731.2020.1842084, available at https://www.tandfonline.com/journals/rglo20. We thank Taylor and Francis for permission to reuse portions of that article. Parts of Chapters 3 and 7 draw from Devin K. Joshi. 2021. "Footprints of a Winning Idea: Three Decades of the Human Development Paradigm (1990–2019)." *Journal of Human Development and Capabilities* 22(3): 506–516, DOI: 10.1080/19452829.2021.1908240, copyright © United Nations Development Programme, reprinted by permission of Taylor & Francis Ltd, http://www.tandfonline.com on behalf of United Nations Development Programme.

Last, and most important, we express immense gratitude to our close friends and family members for encouraging us and putting up with the time we were immersed in this project. Devin is indescribably grateful for the endless love and support he has received from his wife Hyun Joo and daughter Lina and also for the kind and caring long-term support he has received from his loving parents and parents-in-law. Roni Kay thanks her husband, Matt Bates, who has not only offered immense emotional support but has acted as a desk colleague during much of the writing of this book since March 2020, when we had to work from home for months during the COVID-19 lock-down in a one-bedroom apartment, sharing space and coordinating our respective online meetings between "conference room A" (a.k.a. the living room/kitchen/office space), and "conference room B" (a.k.a. the bedroom/closet). And finally, we must thank each other, without whose constant support and fruitfully working through challenges and disagreements, this book would not have happened. We finished this marathon and crossed the finish line together!

We can't wait for you to read what we have produced. Thank you, kind reader, for indulging us and reading our acknowledgments, and now, please, continue to chapter 1!

LIST OF ACRONYMS

BWIs	Bretton Woods Institutions
CDP	Committee for Development Planning
CPD	Commission on Population and Development
CSW	Commission on the Status of Women
ECLA	Economic Commission for Latin America
ECLAC	Economic Commission for Latin America and the Caribbean
ECOSOC	Economic and Social Council
EPTA	Expanded Programme of Technical Assistance
EU	European Union
GATT	General Agreement on Tariffs and Trade
GDI	Gender Development Index
GDP(PC)	Gross Domestic Product (per capita)
GEM	Gender Empowerment Measure
GII	Gender Inequality Index
GN	Global North
GNI(PC)	Gross National Income (per capita)
GNP(PC)	Gross National Product (per capita)
GS	Global South
GSNI	Gender Social Norms Index
HD	Human Development
HDCA	Human Development and Capability Approach
HDI	Human Development Index
HDR(s)	Human Development Report(s)
HDRO	Human Development Reports Office

IBRD	International Bank for Reconstruction and Development
IDA	International Development Association
IGO	Intergovernmental Organization
IHDI	Inequality-Adjusted Human Development Index
ILO	International Labour Organization
IMF	International Monetary Fund
IO(s)	International Organization(s)
IR	International Relations
JAAIDS	Journalists Against AIDS
JHDC	Journal of Human Development and Capabilities
KOFGI	KOF Swiss Economic Institute Globalization Index
LDCs	Least Developed Countries
MDGs	Millennium Development Goals
MPI	Multidimensional Poverty Index
NAM	Non-Aligned Movement
NGO	Nongovernmental Organization
NIEO	New International Economic Order
OECD	Organization for Economic Cooperation and Development
OPEC	Organization of the Petroleum Exporting Countries
PoA	Programme of Action
PPP	Purchasing Power Parity
PQLI	Physical Quality of Life Index
SDGs	Sustainable Development Goals
UDHR	Universal Declaration of Human Rights
UK	United Kingdom
UN	United Nations
UNAIDS	Joint United Nations Programme on HIV/AIDS
UNDP	United Nations Development Programme
UNCTAD	United Nations Conference on Trade and Development
UNGA	United Nations General Assembly
UNSC	United Nations Security Council
UNU-WIDER	United Nations University World Institute for Development Economics Research

US	United States of America
USSR	Union of Soviet Socialist Republics
WB	World Bank
WDR(s)	World Development Report(s)
WHO	World Health Organization
WTO	World Trade Organization

CHAPTER 1

INTRODUCING GLOBALIZATION AND HUMAN DEVELOPMENT

It is 2020 in Gaza City, Palestine, and Abdul Rahman al-Shanti, an 11-year-old boy, posts videos of himself rapping on Instagram about the limited opportunities and the lack of complete freedom and peace in his life (Rasgon and Auheweila, 2020).[1] Two of his songs (*Peace* and *Gaza Messenger*) include lyrics that are poignant and heartbreaking: "I'm here to say that our lives are difficult. We have destroyed streets and bombs in the backyard" and "I was born in Gaza City, and the first thing I heard was a gunshot. In my first breath, I tasted gunpowder." The lyrics reveal that the mental and physical well-being of people in Gaza is hindered by political, economic, and social structures that block full and meaningful participation. The ongoing conflict with the neighboring state of Israel causes turmoil in daily life. A land, air, and sea blockade imposed on the Gaza Strip makes it challenging for the people of Gaza City to live peaceably or prosperously. The blockade—meant to limit the power of the democratically elected Hamas (party and militant group) that took control of the area in 2006—has resulted in major deprivations for the population along with "the highest unemployment rate in the world, and women and youth are disproportionately impacted by the joblessness crisis" (UNCTAD, 2018, p. 1). One report indicates that "Abdel Rahman said his music aims to convey the suffering of Palestinians in Gaza, whose economy has been devastated by a blockade by Israel and Egypt, which Israel says is to prevent the Hamas party from importing weapons or the means to build them. But he also wants to share a message of peace and equality" (Rasgon and Auheweila, 2020).

Al-Shanti's video and rap lyrics tell a story of longing for individual freedom and movement, of desiring access to a society that would help him not only survive but to thrive, of a conflict between two people groups who both want control over their own resources. The nascence of the contemporary Israeli-Palestinian conflict in which al-Shanti has been caught can be traced to the midnight Tel Aviv declaration of the state of Israel on May 14, 1948. Yet even before the 1940s, disagreements between people groups in the region periodically produced upheaval and distrust. There may be no better symbol of this than the Temple Mount (also called Haram al-Sharif), a 1,601 square foot hill in the heart of Jerusalem currently housing the al-Aqsa Mosque. The area is simultaneously claimed by (some) followers of Islam and Judaism as a holy site. Similarly, the land currently under Palestinian and Israeli control is under contention, with representatives from both Muslim and Jewish populations arguing their ownership rights. The country of Israel has been accepted into the United Nations (UN) and is internationally accepted as a state by most countries. Palestine, on the other hand, exists as a territory with a questionable international status. While Palestine is not recognized by the UN General Assembly (UNGA) as a state, the Palestinian Authority and the Hamas party control much of its territory and people.

The story to which al-Shanti speaks involves more than simply a tough situation of decades-long conflict between two people groups over control of a region. It speaks to the global paradigm of human development, the focus of this book. Al-Shanti presents his own individuality to the world showing that it is individuals (not a state government or even a people group) who must step over rubble and walk through exploded buildings to make their way to school or work. As an individual human trying to survive, al-Shanti lives in a place where some of the most familiar sites are broken concrete slabs that are tipped over and aging from what may have once been a highway or the side of a building. It is a place lacking basic resources. As al-Shanti said in an interview: "We live in a conflict area, so we don't want to live in a conflict area anymore. We want to be free. I would love to see the children here in Gaza be happy and have the same rights as the outside world . . . " (Rahman and Fayyad, 2020).

Al-Shanti's call for the chance to have meaningful life choices is one that has been made often in recent years, and it has become louder and clearer in an age of mass communication technologies. This book is about the themes that come up in al-Shanti's story, those of globalization and human development. It is about the ideals and processes that interact and change human lives, sometimes for better and sometimes for worse. The human development (HD) paradigm is a set of beliefs and ideals about human life emphasizing that humans need particular social and political structures in order to function. It also sees the expansion of human capabilities as of utmost importance to national and local policymaking and international interventions from other countries. Al-Shanti's story reflects how the HD paradigm is a major force in the way humans think about their lives on Earth, and in how they reflect on their problems. It also reveals the interdependence and interaction effects between HD and globalization. That a young boy who lives in an isolated area of the world posts an Instagram video that is viewed by millions and inspires major news stories by international newspapers reflects how human interaction and knowledge of the other has escalated and redefined human connections and consciousness in the current era of globalization.

OUR CONTRIBUTION TO UNDERSTANDING HUMAN DEVELOPMENT AND GLOBALIZATION

When we talk about globalization in the first half of the twenty-first century, we cannot fail to recognize the increasing interconnectedness of people around the planet, and a human population that has grown from less than a billion two centuries ago to roughly eight billion today. Concomitantly, economic production and consumption have been internationalizing and globalizing not only due to the development of new legislation and transportation technologies but also due to novel financial and trading arrangements. One such transformation is the installation of "export-processing zones all across the world" (especially since the last quarter of the twentieth century), which make use of lowered labor costs, nonunionized labor, weakly enforced environmental regulations, and the lure of "tax holidays, cheap access to land, power, credit, and the like" (Krishna, 2009, p. 45). While such globalization processes have raised incomes and reduced poverty in some instances, their overall effects have been highly uneven and exacerbated inequality. While many of those with wealth and power become richer, a growing gap has emerged between the relatively small share of wealthy people on the planet and the much larger share of non-wealthy people (and people living in extreme poverty), both within and between countries (e.g, Stiglitz, 2002; Piketty, 2014).

The HD paradigm first emerged in the late twentieth century as the Cold War (1947–1991) was coming to a close, a time when there was a growing "refusal to accept the linear narrative that equates the West with modernity, rationality, and modernization and the rest with irrationality, emotion, and backwardness" (Krishna, 2009, p. 154). Dissatisfaction with the trajectory of globalization led to a number of counter movements and alternative ways of thinking about global development. Fearful that globalization was largely creating outcomes that were negative for most humans, the UN championed the HD paradigm also known as the human development and capability approach (HDCA). This approach imagines and promotes a world in which globalization goes hand in hand *with* human development. The success of the HD paradigm, as detailed in this book, is an emblematic reflection of the UN's longer-term orientation and accomplishments.

A signature contribution of this book is its examination of the globalization of the HD paradigm as an ideology promoted by the UN. Employing a constructivist international relations (IR) lens, our approach is multi-disciplinary and heavily influenced by Karl Mannheim's approach to the study of ideas in the world as outlined his famous book *Ideology and Utopia: An Introduction to the Sociology of Knowledge* (1936/2015). Mannheim claimed that ideology has a profound effect on how we act and interpret the world and that the functioning of ideology always happens within a broader sociological context. Following

Mannheim's perspective, we examine the global emergence, deployment, and reception (i.e., the globalization) of the HD ideology within a broader international political sociology. Rejecting a reductionist approach, the chapters in this volume incorporate a historical and sociological focus that combine different methodologies rather than employing a single analytical lens. As Mannheim argued, "in the social realm, if we can learn to observe carefully, we can see that each element of the situation which we are analyzing contains and throws light upon the whole" (1936, p. 74). Our approach to the subject is therefore broad and sociological. In assessing how the HD ideology and its associated norms have been globalizing, we analyze the structures and functions of international organizations (especially the UN) and nation-states (particularly those of the Global South) in setting the international development agenda. The chapters of the book also assess how other important actors have contributed to spreading the HD message, including mass media, civil society, and individual critical actors (including academics and practitioners).

While examining the relationship between globalization and HD, we are interested in multiple facets of the relationship including: 1) correlations between globalization patterns and HD outcomes, 2) whether HD and globalization may be one and the same phenomenon, and 3) how the HD ideology has been globalizing to become a worldwide phenomenon (i.e., how globalization has contributed to the emergence and diffusion of HD). Departing from previous studies on the HD paradigm, we examine how HD has evolved from a counter-ideology to a possibly quasi-hegemonic ideology, deeply influencing the thinking and practice of international development in the late twentieth and early twenty-first centuries. The HD ideology refers to a particular set of ideas, beliefs, and concepts that guide policies and actions. To many observers, the HD paradigm may be seen as rather scientific, technical, and neutral, but from a social scientific standpoint, the HD public narrative is invariably ideological even if those who follow its tenets are unaware of its ideological dimension (we return to specific tenets of the HD ideology later in this chapter and in chapter 2).

As we contend in this volume, by launching the Human Development Reports (HDRs) as a rival to the World Bank's World Development Reports (WDRs), the UN subtly fired a powerful shot in the ideological battle that was destined to ensue in the post–Cold war period from

1990 to the present. And by taking a relatively quiet approach, the UN (especially those working in the UNDP) avoided losing relevance in the way that neoliberalism has, especially after the negative worldwide effects of structural adjustment programs (Stiglitz, 2002), the terrible experiences of the Asian Financial Crisis during the late 1990s, and the Global Financial Crisis starting in 2008. Furthermore, as the crises of climate change and environmental degradation have accelerated in recent years, the HD paradigm has proven its resilience and compatibility with preventing and protecting against climate change. As a result, the HD paradigm has encouraged the international community (including government officials and non-government practitioners working in international development) view and interpret their work and goals differently.

THEORIES AND HISTORY OF GLOBALIZATION

Al-Shanti's story illustrates that our global human experience is not one of humans functioning alone in reclusive areas of the world—and it likely never really was—but a world of interactions between individuals and societies on a global scale. Even reaching far back in time to the first agrarian societies, sociologists, anthropologists, and archeologists find that humans interacted with each other across cultural divides and large geographical barriers, exchanging ideas and goods (e.g., Chanda, 2007). In other words, our lives are deeply embedded in and affected by globalization defined as "the expansion and intensification of social relations and consciousness across world-time and world-space" (Steger, 2017, p. 17). What an individual does and says in their seemingly localized and small area of the world has local and global implications.

Globalization is a process involving "the intensification of worldwide social relations which link distant localities in such a way that local happenings are shaped by events occurring many miles away and vice versa" (Giddens, 1990, p. 64). This definition of globalization, like many others, represents globalization as a process or a force, an action, a verb. As a process, globalization describes the operations or actions potentially brought about by one actor or phenomenon (whether an individual, organization, government, corporation, or other) on another set of actors through the sharing or manipulation of ideas or material goods across borders and at a global level. The processes of globalization can be technological, historical, chemical, mechanical, productive, and structured or unstructured, planned or unplanned. Such processes support particular social, political, and economic human activities, such as trade, finance, governance, and communication.

The political, policy-making, and rhetorical dimensions of globalization can be confusing and make the concept seem vague or meaningless. Indeed, some have viewed the term through an exclusively political lens and found it to be what politician Clare Booth Luce once pejoratively dismissed as "globaloney" (Veseth, 2005, p. 11). Defining globalization is difficult, especially as it is a phenomenon with many processes that has multitudinous effects. The multidimensional nature of globalization is not straightforward, with its economic, political, social, ecological, and other dimensions (Dreher, 2006; Rodrik, 2011; Gygli et al., 2019). Studies focusing on outcomes of the globalization phenomenon range from those that are optimistic about its positive effects (e.g., Bhagwati, 2004) to those who are pessimistic about its seemingly negative impacts (e.g., Stiglitz, 2002), to those who reject the concept altogether (e.g., Veseth, 2005).

As numerous studies identify either positive or negative results, it seems that interpretations depend heavily on where one studies the globalization phenomenon in time and place. For instance, Atif et al.'s study on the relationship between globalization and income inequality suggests that "perhaps a simple, overarching relationship does not exist in the subject matter" (2012, p. 12). Held et al.'s work identifies three perspectives in the literature about the effects of globalization: 1) hyperglobalists see a creation of a new global age that connects humans beyond the nation-state and this creates problems for governance including challenges to sovereignty, 2) skeptics perceive a reduction of global engagement and increase in trading blocs as the main blowback or result of the negative impacts of globalization, and 3) transformationalists identify increases in unprecedented global interconnection and interdependence that can, if managed well, benefit all (1999, p. 10). Manfred Steger similarly observes a distinction between pessimistic and optimistic globalizers (2017, pp. 81–83) and in his work on globalism as an ideology identifies "three intellectual 'camps': globalizers, skeptics, and modifiers" (2020, p. 16).

Giddens' (1990) definition of globalization (quoted above) appeared in his book titled *The Consequences of Modernity*. It was embedded in a discussion of how the modern changes brought about by human activities have increased human interactions across time and space (e.g., distance) affecting all interlocutors in a dialectical process. He uses an example of how economic globalization in one area of the world has a major effect on other areas. As he states, "The increasing prosperity of an urban area in Singapore might be causally related, via a complicated network of global economic ties, to the impoverishment of a neighborhood [sic] in Pittsburgh whose local products are uncompetitive in world markets" (1990, pp. 64–65). Ironically, the two authors of this book (that you are reading right now), O'Dell and Joshi, were, while writing this book, living halfway across the world from each other in the same two places Giddens identified in his example: Pittsburgh and Singapore, respectively!

In fact, the writing of this book is itself an excellent example of globalization processes. In order to write the book, the authors made use of global communication technologies (internet, email, and online video-conferencing platforms) over several years to share ideas and collaborate across time and space. We often met weekly via video conferences to discuss the ideas and structure of each chapter, simultaneously early in the morning (cutting into one of our breakfast rituals) and late at night (interrupting one of our plans for dinners with family or outings with friends). Recognizing such human connection and influence across time and space—the very essence of globalization—allows humans to understand the political and societal implications for human life around the planet.

THE CONTEMPORARY ERA OF GLOBALIZATION

What is important for understanding the links and relationship between globalization and HD is to identify historical and contemporary globalization processes that led to creating and globalizing HD. That is, what processes contribute to actual manifestations of HD (e.g., health, education, and living standards), versus what processes globalize ideas about HD. While previous eras of globalization are important—for example, Steger (2017, chapter 2) identifies four in his review: the prehistoric, the premodern, the early modern, and the modern—it is the contemporary era of globalization that we focus on in this book. The contemporary era of globalization began after the end of the Second

World War (after 1945) and the creation of globally oriented international organizations (IOs) to facilitate international relations in a more substantial way than previously. The newly minted IOs of the 1940s supported economic and political integration between countries in areas of trade, finance, and development (especially the Bretton Woods Institutions or BWIs). They also addressed collective security, international law, and human rights through the UN, the International Labour Organization (ILO), and other organizations.

One can also divide the recent era of globalization into two, one starting at the end of the Second World War and the creation of important IOs, and the other starting in the 1970s as the BWIs lost some of their power and major changes began occurring in international finance. In the 1970s, the newly founded Organization for Petroleum Exporting Countries (OPEC) also caused changes in the price of oil, for instance, and international financial systems shifted from the gold standard to a floating exchange rate (Goldin and Reinert, 2012, pp. 21–22). Indeed, one might also identify a third shift in the changes wrought by the end of the Cold War around 1990 and the expansion of technological innovations since the 1990s. The changes and expansion in global production networks and the creation of the World Trade Organization (WTO) in 1995 provides a good example of *economic* globalization since the end of the Cold War. What is more, increased *political* integration (e.g., the European Union), and accelerating intensity of *social* integration connecting people and cultures worldwide has been occurring at a faster rate than ever since the 1990s (in increased travel, McDonald's restaurants now in almost every country, internet access, use of cell phones and associated applications, and social media, for example). We return to the multidimensional nature of globalization in the contemporary era after first briefly introducing the theory, history, ideas, and practices of HD.

A SHORT OVERVIEW OF HUMAN DEVELOPMENT

The HD paradigm, also called the human development and capability approach (HDCA), is an ideology about human interaction and human dignity that was articulated and developed by theorists and international development practitioners starting around the 1980s. The HD founders were contemplating the ideal and just society, and theorizing about the best policies and methods to achieve it. In this book, we examine how the HD paradigm functions as an ideology because it is a set of beliefs and rules about the ideal human life and societal, political, and economic structures that are meant to achieve such a life for individuals *en masse* (Mannheim, 1936/2015). While many authors have contributed to the HD paradigm, Martha Nussbaum, Amartya Sen, and Mahbub ul Haq are three good examples of intellectuals who made a huge impact on HD thinking and practice with their writings and practitioner work, particularly through the UN Development Programme (UNDP). The HD approach states that human functioning is of prime importance for policymaking and government interventions and it calls for the social, political, and economic systems of a society to be geared toward ensuring that the environment in which humans live supports their development of capabilities to function in ways that allow them to live worthwhile lives with dignity.[2] The HD paradigm is strikingly important today in the realm of governance and politics at the international level. Consider again the Israeli-Palestinian conflict and Abdul Rahman al-Shanti's vision: he raps about a world that is peaceful, where humans are able to thrive in security and belonging. That same narrative, though couched in somewhat obscure language at times, is used at the global level to guide policies meant to help societies develop. Even so, that the HD paradigm has become so influential was neither inevitable nor without difficulties in overcoming other modern ways of thinking.

Taking it a step further, HD as an ideology maintains that it is crucial for a society and its government to focus on human dignity and to provide humans with the resources necessary for humans to function and thrive. Such resources include both goods and services *and* a supportive economic and socio-political environment. As an ideology of globalization, the HDCA can be described as a *globalism* in Manfred Steger's terms. Steger (2020) identifies *market* globalism as representing how most people would think of and define globalization (i.e., the neoliberal approach to international economics, political international relations, and global development practice). But Steger also identifies ideological challengers to market globalism, including *religious* globalisms and *justice* globalism, among other possible ideologies. HD ideology is another challenger to neoliberalism that has been labeled as *capabilities* globalism (Joshi, 2021a). *Capabilities* globalism challenges other globalisms as an ideology about human life on Earth. Indeed, the idea of human freedom and thriving is compelling and age-old. Even the oldest transmitted stories regale with triumphs of humans achieving some sort of freedom and reaching for an ideal life and staving off death: Consider Gilgamesh and his exploits to find ways to avoid death, or Moses leading the Jewish people out of the Egyptian wilderness to their homeland. Seen in this light, capabilities globalism is akin to a contemporary reformulation of ancient wisdom about why everyone should live a life of human dignity.

Referring back to Abdul Rahman al-Shanti from the introduction, we see that his lyrics reveal how people think in terms of the beliefs and ideas associated with what they consider the ideal human life and how social and political systems should be set up to facilitate that life. In this case, al-Shanti's rap lyrics portray a desire for a thriving human life and living in peace without fear in such phrases as "our lives are difficult" and "we want to be free" to "have the same rights as the outside world" (Rahman and Fayyad, 2020). Humans have articulated such ideals throughout the centuries, and those beliefs and ideals are often expressed in the form of an ideology (the term *ideology* is explained in more detail in chapter 2). An ideology is a set of beliefs and values about how the world is and should be, about what an ideal human life looks like, about the kinds of ethics and morals that guide people to live the best lives possible. Such ideologies come in many forms and have particularly been codified in Western philosophy and writings: well-known examples include realism, liberalism, communism, republicanism, feminism, ecologism, conservatism, anarchism . . . and the list could go on (Freeden, Sargent, and Stears, 2013).

HISTORICAL DEVELOPMENT THINKING AND PRACTICE

Another important aspect of al-Shanti's story is that of international development theory and practice dating to the 1940s. What today we label as *international development* is a practice that began after the Second World War when countries and people were devastated by the destruction caused by war. US Presidents Franklin D. Roosevelt and Harry S. Truman lobbied for and incentivized ideas and practices that allowed the United States to become involved in reconstructing Europe. Proposals included bilateral aid packages (the European Recovery Plan of the 1940s), increases in aid through the BWIs, and eventually the creation of the US Agency for International Development (USAID) in 1961 (Norris, 2021). The BWIs refer to two organizations and an agreement established in 1944: the International Monetary Fund (IMF) to support financial integration, the World Bank (WB) to support reconstruction, and the General Agreement on Trade and Tariffs (GATT) to support international trade. The BWIs sought to enhance economic integration based on the idea that interdependence makes countries less likely to go to war with each other. The BWI founders believed that including negative economic pressures (like repayment plans or sanctions) would not lead to long-term peace, as exemplified in the economic downturn Germany took after the First World War due, in part, to the economic strictures of the Versailles Treaty (Keynes, 1919/2019). Thus, some key elements of economic globalization in the twentieth century were introduced by the BWIs starting in the 1940s (Steil, 2014).

Yet international development practice was also a combination of political intrigue and savvy guided by IR realist concerns about alliances, geopolitical control, and influence in an era of great power politics (the Cold War). From the end of the Second World War, the United States and USSR (a.k.a. Soviet Union) respectively sent funding to target countries (like Greece and Turkey) to encourage them to become their respective allies. They sought to spread a shared vision of the ideal life expressed in terms of modernization theory and capitalism for the United States, and communism for the USSR.[3] Beyond the BWIs, other government agencies and international organizations became involved in supporting various aspects of economic growth and development around the world. For instance, the UN worked on programs meant to support human thriving and reducing poverty starting in the 1950s (through the Expanded Programme of Technical Assistance, the Special Fund, and eventually the UN Development Programme) (see Murphy, 2006; Stokke, 2009). The WB controlled most of the funding that would be funneled from rich countries through IOs for development purposes in the 1960s when, after its first iteration to support post-war reconstruction, it created the International Development Agency (IDA) (Kapur et al., 1997). Disagreements about how to invest appropriately in rebuilding countries and reducing poverty abounded, with Global South countries seeking more control over how development funding was spent in their borders and Global North countries who had the funds and wanted to determine how this money should be spent. The main challenge in development practice and theory was finding the best way to promote development and support humans around the world: much of the initial funding went to supporting large projects, like building dams or other types of infrastructure, with the idea that countries needed to modernize and engage in the international economic system in order to create more opportunities for their people.[4]

The main focus of international development in the 1950s–70s was to strengthen the economic infrastructure of states and encourage economic growth as managed by states. The ideology that guided development theory and practice in these decades was a version of economic liberalism that built on modern liberalism (free market economics) and Keynesianism (concern with government regulation of the market). Keynesianism, as a theory of market functions and government relations, was named after John Maynard Keynes, a key architect of the BWIs. Keynes argued that economic crisis, depression, and recession in a capitalist system were not only to be expected but were a regular occurrence (Keynes, 1919/2019). This insight built off critiques of the capitalist system's weaknesses noted by earlier economists like Karl Marx and Friedrich Engels (e.g., Marx and Engels, 1932 [1974]). As Keynes argued, a market system would and could correct itself in some instances, but not without great suffering and pain caused to humans who lived and worked in the market system. Further, some market systems would not be able to survive crises. In order to address such problems, governments should step in to regulate the excesses of capitalism so as to prevent crises from happening or from becoming dire, and also in order to re-build after each crisis.

Shifts, however, took place in the 1970s with globalization processes including changes to the international trading system and updates to international financial currency exchange practices. Development theories and practices were reappraised and by the end of the 1970s they focused more on reducing poverty than on national economic growth. An important publication from the WB, the World Development Report (WDR), responded to increasing concerns that attachment to macroeconomic growth, guided by modernization theory, was not leading to making most humans being better off. The first WDR (1978) identified and defined extreme poverty, but it also argued that poverty could be eliminated with proper measurement and policy focus.[5] Indeed, many people working in the WB or economic bureaus in various national governments had come to realize that dominant approaches to development practice aiming primarily at macroeconomic stability or growth in overall gross domestic product (GDP) did not benefit all people. For the most part, increased GDP growth benefited a subset of the elite.[6]

In the 1980s, conservative political leaders then came to power like US President Ronald Reagan and UK Prime Minister Margaret Thatcher. Together, they proposed a new method of interacting with the world and utilized their power and influence to change the course of development practice in international development institutions. Often termed neoliberal economics (at first pejoratively, but then in common nomenclature), the new focus was on redirecting national governance policies to favor a free market economy, but with significantly less social supports than those previously supported under modernization theory or Keynesianism. The policies and practices of neoliberalism were heavily promoted by the US government during the 1980s and thus were nicknamed the Washington Consensus. The WB and IMF (both located in Washington, DC), through which much of the inter-governmental development funds traversed to developing countries, implemented *conditionalities* (later called *structural adjustment programs* in the 1980s and 90s) that less developed countries and former colonies had to fulfill in order to gain either grants and funds for development projects or financial stability loans to support international trade. New international agreements and national government policies aimed to reduce regulations on trade (reducing tariffs and non-tariff barriers, for instance) and finance (such as privatizing national firms or relying on a floating exchange rate system) (for a history of neoliberalism, see Harvey 2007).

As worldwide poverty continued to persist, despite the WB's and other interventionist policies described above, experts challenged the shortcomings of these development approaches and the neoliberal ideology by arguing that people should be the first priority in development theory and practice. Such challenges were evident even earlier in the founding documents of the UN, and in the initial practices of the BWIs and first UN funds promoting development. They were also evident in academic discussions, debates, arguments, and writings about social justice, the good life, and economic and political well-being. For instance, in the 1970s several authors put forward the Basic Needs

Approach (e.g., Streeten and World Bank, 1979), conceptualizing measurements like the Physical Quality of Life Index (PQLI) (e.g., Morris, 1979), and making suggestions about political and economic structures following a theory of justice, built on John Rawls's famous work (e.g., Rawls, 1971). Following in their footsteps, the HD paradigm and human development index (HDI) were introduced through the UNDP by, among others, Mahbub ul Haq and Amartya Sen, as a human-centered development paradigm that would become closely associated with and promoted by the UN. The HD ideology started to take hold in political thinking at the UN and among development lenders, especially in the late 1980s and early 1990s. The creation of the HD approach is one example of how the neoliberal paradigm was deeply challenged because of the negative impacts felt around the world due to the WB and IMF conditionality approach (Jolly, 2003; Hirai, 2017, pp. 8–13; 2022).

HUMAN DEVELOPMENT AS AN ALTERNATIVE THEORETICAL AND PRACTICAL APPROACH

The UNDP challenged the international development approach of the WB and its WDRs by issuing its first Human Development Report (HDR) in 1990. The report called for a novel way to approach international development practice, one that would put humans (rather than great powers, Western countries, economic elites, or men) at the center of policy creation and implementation. The HDR defined HD as "a process of enlarging people's choices. The most critical of these wide-ranging choices are to live a long and healthy life, to be educated and to have access to resources needed for a decent standard of living. Additional choices include political freedom, guaranteed human rights and personal self-respect" (UNDP, 1990, p. 1). The report also presented a new measurement that did not merely rely solely on national income to assess poverty or development progress called the human development index (HDI). The HDI was based on the notion that humans need more than just income to thrive; they need a social and political system that gives them the means to thrive. The HDI incorporates three pivotal human capabilities via four indicators: 1) Health measured by life expectancy at birth, 2) Education measured by a) mean years of schooling for those over 25 years old and b) expected years of schooling for children, and 3) Standard of living measured by gross national income (GNI) per capita.

The HDR and its message that "a person's access to income may be one of the choices, but it is not the sum total of human endeavor. HD is a process of enlarging people's choices" (HDR, 1990, p. 1) struck a chord in people's hearts and minds that reverberated across time and space. By promoting HD as more important than economic growth (as measured by gross domestic product, GDP, or GNI), the UN was subtly challenging a world in which certain people or groups (e.g., powerful states, corporations, and wealthy families and individuals) enjoy billions of dollars of surplus in their pockets and bank accounts, while hundreds of millions of people live in poverty, misery, and insecurity. It questioned a system whose laws and policies benefitted political and economic elites in rich countries at the expense of those who continued to live in abject poverty, or at least under national poverty lines. It also questioned and delegitimized classism, racism, and sexism as well as national laws and practices that limit migration and immigration. The HDRs called out social and political practices that deny people sufficient opportunities to improve their lives.

Promoted by the UN through offices like the UNDP, the HD message was promoted by delegates at the UNGA, through media reporting by journalists, and even at times through aid agencies like the WB. Almost from the beginning, journalists reporting on development prioritized the HD paradigm and the annual HDRs published by the UN over other ideologies and interpretations of development (Joshi and O'Dell, 2017, see also chapter 4 this volume). Further, the end of the Cold War had created new conditions that fostered the UN's promotion and globalization of the HD paradigm. The stand-off between the United States and USSR had temporarily ended, allowing for a change in the way those two countries funded development. While opening up space for new ideas, in monetary terms, the amount of funding for development projects dropped precipitously in the 1990s. That drop was directly related to these two empires now having significantly decreased motivation to counter, balance, or contain the other. As a result, development practitioners and even government employees in development programs and departments had to reconsider the goals of development funding, particularly in light of having less. As relates to action and behavior, the new HD paradigm changed the nature of development projects funded by major development organizations such as the UNDP. And it also influenced the WB and IMF which were still under the influence of neoliberalism, but whose language and rhetoric changed to become more focused on describing the human condition. Their language shifted to discussing individuals who would benefit from development funding and projects rather than how their loans would benefit states and governments.

By adopting the HD ideology, the UN was distancing itself from left-wing development visions championed by communists, Marxists, and the USSR's economic development model. It also distanced itself from the right-wing neoliberal capitalist economic models of the BWIs. Whereas the WB and IMF endorsed the pursuit of increasing human capital or support for strengthening human resources, which valued people's skills and knowledge primarily as an input to economic production, the HD approach instead treated humans as intrinsically valuable and as the purpose, reason, and end of development practice, not the means. Thus, although economic productivity may contribute to HD, the latter is something greater than merely increasing the production of material goods. The HD goal is to enrich human lives and "enable people to lift themselves out of poverty" (UNDP, 2001, p. 27). The first HDR focused on education and health (including measurements of these in the HDI) and later HDRs added to the discussion additional substantive concerns or needs that should guide policy such as human security (HDR, 1994), gender (HDR, 1995), and climate change (HDR, 2007).

The HD paradigm has also been highly influential in areas beyond development theory, funding and projects. Even the human rights regime as reassessed in the 1990s and beyond, benefited from and overlapped with HD in promoting the individual human as its primary unit of analysis (HDR, 2000). For example, participation and democratic deliberation are prioritized by the HD ideology, and human rights organizations like Amnesty International likewise prioritize such deliberation and discussion in creating human rights policy (O'Dell and Veazey, 2023). Additionally, part of the issue for human rights is that globalization has challenged the power of the state and governments in ways that impact and affect people's social, political, and economic life (Brysk, 2002). Human rights were originally conceived as holding states accountable for treating humans in their borders with dignity and respect, but what happens when the state is not the most powerful governing force in a territory or over a population? The HD paradigm has supported the expansion of the human rights discussion in important ways, both in theoretical and practical areas, bolstered by the changes in the international system brought on by the end of the Cold War (Thérien, 2014). Such an expansion can be seen in the 2000 HDR about how the two concepts and practices overlap: "Human rights and human development share a common vision and a common purpose—to secure the freedom, well-being, and dignity of all people everywhere" (UNDP, 2000, p. 1).

The HD ideology's influence has been perhaps most impactful in the creation of worldwide development goals set by the UN to meet specific, measurable targets. The first set of eight goals and 21 targets for the world to achieve by 2015 were the Millennium Development Goals (MDGs), passed by the UNGA in the Millennium Declaration of 2000. The MDGs called the world to, in the language of the goals themselves: 1) eradicate extreme poverty and hunger, 2) achieve universal primary education, 3) promote gender equality and empower women, 4) reduce child mortality, 5) improve maternal health, 6) combat HIV/AIDS, malaria, and other diseases, 7) ensure environmental sustainability, and 8) support a global partnership for development.

The second set of international development goals that replaced the MDGs in 2015, called the Sustainable Development Goals (SDGs), were more extensive and inclusive of environmental and sustainability concerns, featuring 17 goals, 169 targets, and 231 official indicators. The 17 SDGs cover similar territory as the MDGs, but have added on and expanded the areas of focus. The goals are to achieve: 1) no poverty, 2) zero hunger, 3) good health and well-being, 4) quality education, 5) gender equality, 6) clean water and sanitation, 7) affordable energy, 8) decent work and economic growth, 9) industry, innovation, and infrastructure, 10) reduced inequalities, 11) sustainable cities, 12) responsible consumption and production, 13) climate action, 14) life below water, 15) life on land, 16) peace, justice, and strong institutions, and 17) partnerships for the goals. The SDGs currently dominate international development thinking and practice, guiding policies and funding to focus on how to achieve the targets that are associated with each goal to make human lives on planet Earth better and more worth living.

HUMAN DEVELOPMENT GLOBALIZED

This section introduces three ways to think about the relationship between the various concepts, ideas, indicators, processes, and outcomes associated with globalization and HD. First is thinking about the causal effect between globalization and HD, that is, how one phenomenon or process affects or correlates with the other, and then investigating the outcome. The second is to consider how globalization occurred alongside and with HD, the two as inextricably linked and perhaps even synonymous with the other. The third is to consider how HD is globalizing as a process and an outcome of globalization itself, and how the HD paradigm and the ideology of capabilities globalism is extending around the globe to transcend borders, and influence individual, societal, and government behavior. Let us now review each of these possibilities.

GLOBALIZATION AND HUMAN DEVELOPMENT (CAUSE AND EFFECT)

The approach that has gained the most attention and discussion over the years is the idea of globalization as one concept with its own set of indicators, processes, and phenomena and HD as another, and then to ask what impact or affect one has on the other. From this perspective, globalization takes on the form of an economic, political, cultural, and some would add ecological process or phenomenon that has an impact or outcome on global human existence and HD in particular. Studies that specifically assess the influence of globalization on HD reveal mixed findings (using varying definitions of globalization, but specifically identifying and defining HD or using the HDI) (e.g., Akhter, 2004; Ahmad, 2005; Haseeb et al., 2019). Despite varying and sometimes contradictory definitions attempting to articulate the multidimensional elements of globalization, those studying globalization often use the KOF Swiss Economic Institute Globalization Index (KOFGI) included in Table 1.1. The KOFGI uses 43 variables under three dimensions to measure globalization under two categories: *de jure* indicators reveal what is actually happening in the world and *de facto* indicators measure legal rules or norms that identify what could happen even if not in reality (Gygli et al., 2019). An extensive review of the studies using KOFGI

Table 1.1.   Dimensions and Measures of Globalization (KOFGI)

Dimensions of Globalization Measured	*KOF Globalization Index 2022 (43 variables)*
Economic Integration	*Trade:* Trade in goods, services, and partner diversity, trade regulations, taxes, tariffs, and agreements.
	Financial: Foreign direct investment, portfolio investment, international debt, reserves, and income payments, investment restrictions, capital account openness, and international investment agreements.
Social Integration	*Interpersonal:* International voice traffic, transfers, international tourism and students, migration, telephone subscriptions, freedom to visit, and international airports.
	Informational: Internet bandwidth, international patents, high technology exports, television and internet access, and press freedom.
	Cultural: Trade in cultural goods and personal services, international trademarks, McDonald's restaurants, IKEA stores, gender parity, human capital, and civil liberties.
Political Integration	*Political:* Embassies, UN peace keeping missions, international NGOs, international organizations and treaties, and treaty partner diversity.

Source: The KOFGI website provides a review of the index: https://kof.ethz.ch/en/forecasts-and-indicators/ indicators/kof-globalisation-index.html

identified more than 100 articles showing the influence of globalization on various aspects of human existence, with at least 35 that analyzed the effect of globalization on HD themes if using a minimal definition of HD as income, education, life expectancy, or democracy (Potrafke, 2015; see also Dreher, 2006).

Perhaps the most studied, and most contentious, is the relationship between globalization and the HD component of living standard using a simple measure of per capita income (whether based on GNI or GDP). The economic dimension of globalization, connected with ideas of liberalism and neoliberalism, suggests that increased integration of trade, finance, and reduction of barriers to market and entrepreneurial forces will, in the long run if not in the short run, reduce poverty and increase incomes for all people. Statistical analyses of the relationship between globalization and the HD element of living standard mostly show—although there are some outliers—a positive relationship between the two (at least in developing countries, but perhaps not in developed countries).[7] For instance, Potrafke's review of four such studies on the impact of globalization on GDP concluded that "in developing countries, per capita income increased in the course of globalization" (2015, p. 521). The skeptical view of globalization suggests that it creates more harm than good, that it is only beneficial if growth is well-managed and that it creates higher rates of inequality. The skeptical view does not seem to hold up when considering the many studies conducted on the relationship between globalization and living standards measured in income per capita. But the assessment is a limited one and often does not account for reverse causality or endogeneity (i.e., that higher income affects level of economic integration, for example, and not the other way around).

The main negative impact of globalization that has garnered attention is its effect on inequality (e.g., Ahmad, 2005; Haseeb et al., 2019). The early publications and discussions of HD are not explicit about whether inequality is a problem, or how much inequality is acceptable to achieve positive HD. But updates to the HDI with the Inequality Adjusted HDI (IHDI), for instance, were motivated by a recognition that inequality is a crucial element to consider when assessing whether HD has improved. Breaking down globalization into its separate components helps to make effects on HD clearer. For example, Singh's qualitative analysis shows that financial globalization, or the opening up of financial markets or capital liberalization, has a negative impact on HD "if reduction in poverty is taken as a surrogate for improvement in human development" (2012, pp. 145–46), but the author does note that the overall impact of financial liberalization has reduced poverty. Similarly, Tsai's statistical assessment (2007) shows that economic globalization alone does not have a positive impact on HD, even while the three-pronged KOFGI taken altogether does show a positive impact.

Several studies show a positive association between globalization and HD, particularly those assessing local level impacts and using control variables that can account for the positive impact. Kiani et al. assessed the effects of globalization on HD in Pakistan from 1980–2014 and determined that "we may conclude that globalization overall and social, political and economic globalization have positive impact on human development index for Pakistan" (2021, p. 1). In the same line of thinking, Cieślik argues that economic development and growth have a positive and co-integrated impact (that is, as economic growth increases so does the HDI) and that "the impact of globalization on human development may be driven only by the economic dimension of globalization" (2014, p. 25). In summary, researchers studying a link between globalization and HD typically find a relationship exists between the two, especially HD and economic globalization. But more research is needed to fully understand the relationship, especially on all aspects of globalization as depicted in the KOFGI.

GLOBALIZATION AS HUMAN DEVELOPMENT (LINKING OR EQUIVALENCE OF THE CONCEPTS)

But what if we think of globalization as ineluctably and inextricably linked with HD, that the two concepts, processes, and indicators are one and the same, or at least heavily overlapping? Indeed, the issue of endogeneity (that one variable is affected by its relationship with other variables in the analysis), or that of reverse causality, is tricky and comes up quite often in the statistical analyses of globalization's impact on HD. What is more, the variables used in measuring globalization often connect with, or are the same variables that are used to measure HD (e.g., Asongu, 2014; Asghar et al., 2017; Damrah et al., 2022). For example, in Asongu's statistical analysis of the impact of globalization on corruption, the IHDI is used as a mitigating explanatory independent variable and Asongu's conclusion is that "globalization is an instrumental tool in fighting corruption through human development and good governance" (2014, p. 360). Another example is Asghar et al.'s study of the impact of globalization on gender discrimination in which the HDI is used as a measure of globalization along with the KOFGI to assess its impact on reducing gender inequality with the conclusion that the "globalization phenomenon has positive impact on reducing [Gender Inequality Index]" (2017, p. 432).

Consider the variables in the KOFGI again (Table 1.1) and how the KOFGI indicators correspond with HD indicators. For instance, like the HD indicator for living standard, a few of the economic variables for trade and financial globalization are measured with the use of GDP. Trade in goods is measured as "exports and imports of goods (percentage of GDP)," creating a problem of endogeneity for assessing the impact of globalization on living standard measured by the HDI as GNI per capita. In this case, economic globalization and HD living standard are one and the same. But the measurement of social and political dimensions of globalization shows even more cross-over between HD elements and measurements, especially when considering the KOFGI. Education as mean and average years of schooling in the HDI connects with, or is exactly the same as, measurements related to education in the KOFGI. Namely the "human capital index based on the average years of schooling and an assumed rate of education" to measure human capital as an element of cultural globalization, or the use of "ratio of girls to boys enrolled in primary education level in public and private schools" to measure gender parity (KOFGI website as cited in Table 1.1 and Gygli et al., 2019).

Indeed, the very theories and concepts of globalization seem to correlate with those of HD, particularly if considered in terms of expanding human choices and freedoms. The language of globalization suggests a breaking down of barriers and borders so that more people can access goods, services, and ideas and share cultural insights across societies. The neoclassical liberalization and neoliberal paradigms are full of references to limiting government intervention in the market system so as to expand freedom and choice (Harvey, 2007). Even one of Sen's main elements in his description of the capabilities approach is "economic facilities [which] refer to the opportunities that individuals respectively enjoy to utilize economic resources for the purpose of consumption, or production, or exchange" (Sen, 1999, pp. 38–39).

GLOBALIZATION WITH HUMAN DEVELOPMENT (CAPABILITIES GLOBALISM)

Finally, one can view HD from the perspective that it is a new theory, concept, or ideology of globalization that counters the current hegemonic ideologies (like market globalism, i.e., neoliberalism). HD has perhaps already become hegemonic in global development thinking and practice—an issue to which we will return in the book's conclusion. In considering the relationship between globalization and HD as a process we can ask how the idea of HD was and has been globalizing around the world. That is, we ask how HD conceptions of human well-being and capability—of humans as the center of the development and society-building enterprise—have proliferated in economic and political thought, taking on value and importance worldwide, and changing human, government, and whole societal thinking and behavior (see, e.g., Easterlin, 2000 for one of the first attempts).

The questions pursued in this book cover the practices and normative underpinnings of HD ideology, (i.e., *capabilities globalism*, as a particular set of processes and practices of globalization). We ask two interrelated and ineluctably connected questions: 1) how has HD been globalizing as a prominent development ideology and practice (i.e., the ideology of capabilities globalism), and 2) how have the forces of globalization impacted and influenced development practice in such a way as to promote HD initiatives and ideology above other versions or ideologies of development.

THE DIMENSIONS AND PROCESSES OF GLOBALIZATION THROUGH WHICH HUMAN DEVELOPMENT IS GLOBALIZING

Changes in human societies and global human interaction from the mid-twentieth century include an exponential increase in the international flows of goods, services, and ideas. Such changes were largely wrought because of innovations in technology, science, and ideological beliefs about human life and global human interaction. Assessing the economic, social, political, and ecological processes of globalization within and between each dimension helps us understand the multidimensional nature of the phenomenon. Globalization is not easily reduced to one particular process or indicator or even outcome. Consider Table 1.1 again, which depicts the KOFGI's various indicators to measure globalization. The KOFGI approach implies that there are multiple dimensions to globalization as an innovative, technological, scientific process of global expansion. Further, that integration occurs in different facets of human life: economic, political, and social.

When people discuss globalization they often make reference to increases in international trade and financial interactions, also known as global economic integration between people groups across nations at a macro-level that affect human life at a micro-level (Held et al., 1999, p. 4). For instance, a simple calculation of exports between countries since 1950 shows a steady increase up to 2022 so that the value of exports (in current US dollars) increased 204 times (by 20,400%).[8] The volume of international trade has also increased by 45 times (4,500%

growth) since 1950.[9] Indeed, one of the goals of the WTO (formerly the General Agreement on Trade and Tariffs, or GATT) is to reduce barriers to trade and to encourage countries to find an export specialization so that they become economically integrated and interdependent. In addition to increases in trade and financial flows across borders, economic globalization processes include the building of factories and hiring workers overseas to produce new goods and services. The creation and sharing of new technologies internationally can likewise increase competition in certain industries as an element of economic globalization.

In many ways, the economic lens or approach to globalization comes from a macroeconomic outlook about how states and their economies can and should perform so as to make the lives of their citizens better. At the state- or domestic-level, the focus is on how the government can increase gross national income (GNI), and engage in trade by selling goods to other countries after having specialized in particular ways. Al-Shanti's story of the Palestinian plight speaks volumes to the perspective of globalization as an increase in trade and financial integration. Just consider the first sentence from the UNCTAD report on its work in Palestine: "The constrained economy of the Occupied Palestinian Territory continued to *underperform* in 2017" (2018, p. 2, emphasis added). The assumption, then, is that the area should be open to global trading and exchange of goods so that it can perform like other economies but that the reason for the joblessness and the economic plight of the area is precisely because the blockade is limiting access to those trading and financial interactions that would produce better outcomes.

Advances in technology and science crucially drive the economic dimension of globalization because without them, there would be no practical way for humans to expand trade and finance across borders to the degree that they have done. Technological advances that improved global trade and financial integration in the contemporary era include the creation of oil tankers, bulk carriers, general cargo, container, and other types of ships in the international shipping fleet to move massive amounts of goods from one area of the world to another. As an example of the impact, the world shipping fleet was able to increase the amount of goods carried from roughly 681 million dead weight tons in 1981 to 2,199 in 2022.[10] The creation and expansion of maritime trade routes where ships can efficiently and easily take their cargo from one area to another has been a key technology advancing economic globalization in international trade (by creation of the Suez and Panama canals, for instance, or developing a standard trade route through waters plagued by piracy off the coasts of Somalia).

But considered in another way, al-Shanti's story represents globalization as more than just access to goods and services, it is also about human interaction and understanding, about human dialogue, connection, and social integration (the cultural and social dimension). Indeed, people who focus on the human element of globalization define it as "expansion and intensification of social relations and consciousness across world-time and world-space" (Steger, 2017, p. 17) referring to increased global human interaction and awareness of other people in multiple levels of human life. When examining social or cultural aspects of globalization, rather than focusing on the access or lack of access to goods and services, the story is about how humans interact with each other, gain consciousness of each other's lives and experiences, and develop the ability to empathize with each other. The processes of globalization in the social dimension include changes in technologies that support (or hinder) human dialogue and discussion. For example, the ability to communicate over long distances through telephone or internet has evolved and changed immensely since 1950, and even over the first two decades of the twenty-first century. For instance, the International Telecommunications Union, which collects data on internet use, has estimated a 430% increase in individuals using the internet, from 1 billion users (or 16% of the world's population) in 2005 to 5.3 billion (or 66%) in 2022.[11]

The social dimension of globalization, considered as the processes of technological innovation and creation, is one of the most important to focus on in a book that assesses how the HD paradigm or ideology, that is, the concepts and ideas associated with human life, have been globalized. HD themes and ideas in communication processes and products (whether written or in other forms) significantly impact how people think and act. Indeed, written and oral communication has blossomed extensively through journalism and newspaper reporting, in academic journal articles and discussions or presentations, and through social media in the most recent decades.

The process of globalization via faster, cheaper, and more accessible international communication devices and services has influenced human interaction and consciousness, and may even affect how people see themselves and their place in the world. Al-Shanti's lyrics show self-consciousness as well as the consciousness of the other. Consider how he points out that the children in Gaza City do not have the same rights as others. How does he know? Clearly, he has the ability to learn about and even empathize with other people's lives and experiences beyond the local area in which he lives. In an interview he makes the point about wanting to know and be like others. He encourages people to empathize with his experience and he points out that using the English language is the best way to do that since English is so widespread and utilized (al-Mughrabi, 2020). This is not just a story of a young boy trying to expand his horizons—he is compelled to use the modes and methods he has at his disposal to connect across barriers and borders with other humans, to compare his life with others, and to call on that shared humanity to compel change. Globalization has opened the possibilities for human dialogue about different ideas and cultural notions of rules, regulations, or the ideal life. Sometimes those ideas clash and sometimes they connect and find communion. When people clash over disagreements about their cultures, ideas, or their vision of the ideal life, the emotions of hatred and fear may take over, instigating negative interactions that may lead to violence (Fukuyama, 1992; Huntington, 1997). However, people also connect over shared visions and versions of reality, and find ways to empathetically view other humans.

Other interpretations of globalization focus on the political dimension because, unlike the economic and social dimensions, such approaches allow us to assess different realities and possibilities of governance, both at the nation-state level and at the international or supra-national level. For example, Hart states that "Globalization is pointing to the need for global governance . . . a re-alignment in the authority exercised by or through extra-national rules and institutions (quoted in Bambas et al., 2000, p. 113). Indeed, globalization challenges state control and authority in many ways, particularly challenging norms and understandings of border control or territoriality by which nation-states currently maintain much of their perceived legitimacy. The increase in governing resolutions, regulations, decrees, and laws as well as political integration through IOs or regional trading blocs, like those of the UN or the European Union (EU), provide important examples. The EU began as the European Coal and Steel

Community in 1952 with six member nations and a limited focus on two industries, but by 1992 it had evolved into an expansive political and economic project of integration, and it has 27 member countries as of 2023 (only losing a few on the way).[12] When so many goods, services, people, and ideas flow across borders at an increased and expanded rate, nation-states lose control of territory and borders, or even the concept of territory as *belonging to them*, to favor other concepts, like that of *human* or *global citizenship*. What is more, people begin to question the narratives that state governments have used in the past to justify the latter's legitimacy or rationale for existence.

Thus, globalization processes in the political dimension include negotiation and diplomacy at the international level through IOs, the willingness to work collaboratively in protecting against shared threats, and the practice of passing resolutions and signing treaties to hold states accountable for addressing cross-national and global-level challenges. There are currently 193 UN members (a nearly fourfold increase from the 50 countries who signed its founding charter after the San Francisco Conference in 1945). Several new countries have gained UN membership in recent years (e.g., South Sudan) and other territories continue to seek membership (such as Palestine). What is more, even while there is strong criticism of the UN by various governments and civil society organizations among its member countries, there is strong engagement in its work. For example, country delegates travel to UN Headquarters in New York every fall for the UNGA annual meeting. Exemplifying this pattern, from September 20–26, 2022, thousands of delegates gathered and they included 185 speakers (heads of state and government and other ministers of foreign affairs) in 14 opening plenary sessions, even at a time when in-person meetings were limited because of the COVID-19 pandemic.[13]

CHAPTER ORGANIZATION

This book assesses the globalization of HD. The dimensions and processes of globalization provide a conceptual lens to help determine the manner and extent to which HD ideas have spread around the world, across time and space. The chapters that follow lay out the argument and foundation for the claim that HD has become a powerful, globalizing, ideological force in the contemporary era of globalization.

The HD ideology has deeply influenced and impacted how humans communicate and empathize with each other across space and time. Chapter 2 makes the case that the HD paradigm is an ideological phenomenon. It describes how HD functions as an ideology while comparing it to rival and competing ideologies of globalization. The main purpose of the chapter is to identify the composition of HD thought and its global orientation, while presenting HD as an ideology in competition with neoliberalism and other approaches to global development thinking and practice.

Chapter 3 reviews the writings, ideas, and influence of philosophers, economic theorists, and practitioners on promoting the HD paradigm. It especially reviews and assesses the works of Mahbub ul Haq, Amartya Sen, and Martha Nussbaum. It compares and contrasts their ideas and works and assesses the extent to which their writings have been influential by analyzing the extent of their respective *oeuvres*, and also by comparing their academic works with others in similar disciplines. Overall, the chapter argues that they have been influential in their respective academic and practitioner fields, and that their positions and influence have made enormous impacts in advancing the HD paradigm. They are not alone but just significant players among a large group of people who argued that to think and practice development one should focus on the human being and their capabilities, what they can do and be in social, political, and economic life. By reviewing prominent academics and practitioners, the chapter offers further insight into *capabilities globalism*, into the discourse and practice of individual intellectuals and thought leaders, and amongst transnational associations like the Human Development and Capability Association.

Chapter 4 assess the significance of journalistic reporting and writing in promoting the HD paradigm, especially in newspaper reporting. The HD paradigm was first articulated in the 1990 HDR published by the UNDP, but the HD influence largely stems from how it was reported on and discussed in major news publications, and on whether people considered HDRs a reliable source. The chapter offers insight into the *extent* to which journalists reported on the HDRs, reports that have been published annually since 1990. Further, the chapter uses qualitative content analysis to assess *how* journalists reported on and framed HD-related ideas. Our analysis reveals that the HDRs, the HDI, and associated concepts and measures, are consistently treated as reliable and trustworthy by news media. The chapter also provides a solid research foundation for the claim that the HD ideology has become increasingly influential compared to neoliberalism as its main ideological rival.

Chapter 5 reviews the historical foundations of the HD paradigm found in international negotiations at the founding of the UN and during the Cold War, particularly in international conference diplomacy, and culminating in the publication of the HDRs at the UNDP's Human Development Report Office (HDRO). Indeed, the UNGA and other main organs of the UN were concerned, from the UN's inception, with issues of human thriving (as seen in the establishment of the UN's Economic and Social Council). The chapter shows that globalization processes allowed for HD ideas to come to the fore. For example, international conference meetings increased dramatically in the twentieth century as technologies of globalization expanded people's ability to travel and communicate easily across long distances. Such technologies allowed for increased interaction, through conferences as one mode, and increased engagement and awareness of others. What is more, the language and ideas of HD ideology can be traced in the debates, discussions, speeches, and final documents that came out of multiple international conferences investigating the human condition. In particular, the chapter reviews the conferences on the environment, women, and the least developed countries (LDCs), and discusses the current efforts and coordinating on development goals (through the Sustainable Development Goals), revealing its foundations in and connections with HD ideology.

Building on previous chapters, chapter 6 reviews development policies both toward and within the Global South. A common view is that most Global South countries are relatively powerless in international relations, but this chapter reveals how Global South countries and individuals acted as founders of HD ideas and concepts, and in turn challenged the way international development practice is conceived and implemented. It does this by reviewing the influence of the Latin American countries in the founding of the UN and the shift from the structures of the League of Nations, by assessing how Global South countries voiced dissent in the early years of development practice (and influenced the creation of the UNDP and the UNCTAD). The non-aligned movement, the new international economic order (NIEO), and the North-South roundtables further reveal foundational HD ideas. The chapter culminates by reviewing how Global South countries are doing on the measurements and metrics of HD and related development goals, like the SDGs.

The final chapter revisits the book's main arguments as presented in previous chapters, with a particular focus on the claim that HD is a global ideology that has been globalizing around the world with far reaching impact. It reviews the power of the HD ideology, and also discusses its various strengths and weaknesses. The chapter also considers the future of a more globalized, interconnected world and its implications for achieving current and future development goals while acknowledging that globalization is not a straightforward linear process.

Abdul Rahman al-Shanti's story highlights major challenges to development thinking and practice in a globalized era but also reflects the way that humans think about the ideal life. In the twenty-first century, humans share a pervasive understanding that everyone needs stability, an ideal political, economic, and social environment, and access to resources in order to function as humans. Humans are capable of great things, of creating and thriving, if only they have the ability to function as humans. The HD paradigm challenges the status quo and other development ideologies. It calls humans to re-envision the institutions that order their lives, to reorder their ways of thinking and acting in the world, and to stand up to the status quo when it does not meet people's needs. Al-Shanti's story, and his songs, offers an excellent example of the demand for a society that puts people first. His songs call for peace, and it does not matter to him that there are complicated political and historical issues to the dilemma. What he sees is the rubble at his feet; what he hears is the sound of guns or bombs going off nearby; what he smells is gunpowder and exploded cement; but what he wishes for is a political, social, and economic environment in which he can thrive. Similarly, the recent HDR (2021–2022) covers some of the major concerns and upheavals of the twenty-first century (interstate war, civil wars, the COVID-19 pandemic, to name a few) and highlights how global challenges have affected human lives. It starts out with the ominous statement: "We live in a world of worry" (UNDP, 22, p. 3). But the report goes on to highlight an important aspect of the HD ideology, that of human agency. It does not offer perfect solutions to the global challenges it discusses, but it does argue that humans are innovative and dynamic, and that they have the power to discuss, debate, and innovate: "Where we go from here is up to us. One of the great lessons of our species' history is that we can accomplish a lot with very little if we work together towards shared goals." This is the hope and belief of the HD ideology (a.k.a., *capabilities globalism* or the HDCA), and the rest of the chapters in this volume explore how HD ideas and concepts came about, and how HD impacts all our lives today.

NOTES

1. Various spellings are reported for the boy's first name including Abedalrahman, Abdel Rahman, or Abdul Rahman.

2. See Nussbaum, 2013; Sen, 1990; Haq, 1995.

3. See Rostow's 1959 *Stages of Economic Growth* on modernization theory.

4. For excellent histories of development theory and practice that cover all these issues, see Stokke, 2009 on the UN, and Kapur et al., 1997 on the WB.

5. See e.g., O'Dell and Breger Bush, 2021 for insight into the creation of the WDRs.

6. Mahbub ul Haq was one of these people who worked in the WB as well as for the government of Pakistan in formulating and implementing economic policies (Haq and Ponzio, 2008).

7. Potrafke (2015, pp. 518–521) reviewed thirteen studies that argued that either one or all three dimensions of globalization (economic, political, social integration) were the main explanatory variables that had a positive effect on people's living standard measured in terms of GDP per capita or annual GDP growth.

8. World Bank Data from https://data.worldbank.org.

9. World Trade Organization Data from https://www.wto.org.

10. UNCTAD provides overviews of statistics on merchant fleet information on its website: https://hbs.unctad.org/merchant-fleet/#Ref_62WR64FA.

11. International Telecommunications Union data available on website https://www.wto.org.

12. History of European Union available on website: https://european-union.europa.eu.

13. UN. 2022. List of Speakers: Plenary meetings for the General Debate of the seventy-seventh session - Tuesday, Sept 20 to Saturday, Sept 24 and Monday, Sept 26, 2022: https://espeakers.unmeetings.org/6320ae9f5ea20000120344dc13092022.

CHAPTER 2

HUMAN DEVELOPMENT AS AN IDEOLOGY OF GLOBALIZATION

The year 2015 was pivotal for development theorists and practitioners as the international community completed its years-long negotiations on the Sustainable Development Goals (SDGs) and approved the *2030 Agenda for Sustainable Development (Agenda 2030)* through the UN General Assembly (UNGA). *Agenda 2030* updated previous development goals by adding to them and providing an overview of a collective vision, principles, and a commitment to international development. It furthermore described what the world is like today by identifying its challenges and problems (such as the perennial problem of people living in extreme poverty), but it also went on to lay out a vision of what the world should be like (e.g., one where no one lives in poverty anywhere), and it outlined an action plan to get to that ideal world. An excerpt from the resolution is included in textbox 2.1, and some words, phrases, and sentences are italicized to show how the resolution reveals the underlying human development (HD) ideology that serves as the foundation for its descriptions, pronouncements, and predictions.

A close review of documents like *Agenda 2030* reveals an emphasis on putting people first in development thinking and actions, which is at the heart of the human development and capability approach (HDCA) also known as the HD paradigm. *Agenda 2030* and multitudinous texts, speeches, and statements like it show that HD is more than just a set of guidelines to get us closer to a better world. HD actually includes a vision of that better world within its ideational framework. In other words, HD is an ideology that has been globalizing to the world and has been taken up by many people in rhetoric if not in practice. The HD ideology prioritizes people who are dealing with problems of global significance (poverty, climate change, joblessness, domestic and international inequalities, ecological devastation, etc.). But the HD ideology, just as any other ideology, does not stop at defining problems. It goes on to claim that the world can be a different, better place where people are empowered and, as *Agenda 2030* states, " . . . all human beings can enjoy prosperous and fulfilling lives." What is more, the HD ideology provides details on how to get to such a world: by creating political, economic, and social environments in which humans have freedom of choice, meaningful opportunities, and the capabilities necessary for living decent, long, and prosperous lives.

DEFINING AND EXPLAINING IDEOLOGY

Ideologies play a pervasive role in shaping human consciousness and behavior and can have significant (negative and positive) impacts on both globalization and HD. It is important to be aware of how widespread ideologies are and the different ways in which ideologies impact our political and economic systems. Ideologies are powerful because they "shape people's thinking and actions with regard to race, nationality, the role and function of government, the relations between men and women, human responsibility for the natural environment, and many other matters" (Ball, Dagger, and O'Neill, 2004, p. 2).

The function of an ideology is to simplify the complexity of reality into an explanatory narrative that excludes other possible ways of making sense of reality. As a starting point for identifying and

TEXTBOX 2.1. EXCERPTS FROM THE 2030 AGENDA FOR SUSTAINABLE DEVELOPMENT[1]

This Agenda is a plan of action *for people*, planet, and prosperity. It also seeks to strengthen *universal* peace in larger *freedom*. We recognize that *eradicating poverty* in all its forms and dimensions, including extreme poverty, is the greatest global challenge and an indispensable requirement for sustainable development.

All countries and all stakeholders, acting in collaborative partnership, will implement this plan. We are resolved to *free the human race from the tyranny of poverty and want*, and to heal and secure our planet. We are determined to take the bold and transformative steps which are urgently needed to shift the world on to a sustainable and resilient path. As we embark on this collective journey, *we pledge that no one will be left behind*.

The 17 Sustainable Development Goals and 169 targets which we are announcing today demonstrate the scale and ambition of this new universal Agenda. They seek to build on the Millennium Development Goals and complete what they did not achieve. They seek to realize the human rights of all and to achieve gender equality and the empowerment of all women and girls. They are integrated and indivisible and balance the three dimensions of sustainable development: the economic, social and environmental.

The Goals and targets will stimulate action over the next 15 years in areas of critical importance for humanity and the planet.

People: We are determined to end poverty and hunger, in all their forms and dimensions, and to ensure that all human beings can fulfil their potential in dignity and equality and in a healthy environment.

Planet: We are determined to protect the planet from degradation, including through sustainable consumption and production, sustainably managing its natural resources and taking urgent action on climate change, *so that it can support the needs of the present and future generations.*

Prosperity: We are determined to ensure that *all human beings can enjoy prosperous and fulfilling lives* and that economic, social and technological progress occurs in harmony with nature.

Peace: We are determined to foster peaceful, just and inclusive societies which are *free from fear and violence.* There can be no sustainable development without peace and no peace without sustainable development.

Partnership: We are determined to mobilize the means required to implement this Agenda through a revitalized Global Partnership for Sustainable Development, based on a spirit of strengthened global solidarity, focused in particular on the needs of the poorest and most vulnerable and with the participation of all countries, all stakeholders and *all people.*

The interlinkages and integrated nature of the Sustainable Development Goals are of crucial importance in ensuring that the purpose of the new Agenda is realized. If we realize our ambitions across the full extent of the Agenda, *the lives of all will be profoundly improved* and our world will be transformed for the better . . .

understanding the basics of an ideology, consider Manfred Steger's definition of ideology as: "a system of widely shared ideas, patterned beliefs, guiding norms and values, and lofty ideals accepted as 'fact' or 'truth' by significant groups in society" (2009, p. 6). Ideologies simplify reality and guide people on how to make sense of their lives and their purpose by telling them three things: a) what the world is like, b) what the world should ideally be like, and c) how one ought to act so as to make the world become the way it should be. Presenting an "oversimplifying view of the world" (Eagleton, 2007, p. 3), ideologies offer explanations and solutions for social problems while providing evaluative frameworks to distinguish what is good from bad (Freeden, 1996, p. 22). Problematically, ideologies can also legitimate or justify the existence of injustices and inequalities in society by making people believe that "injustices are *en route* to being amended, or that they are counterbalanced by greater benefits, or that they are inevitable, or that they are not really injustices at all" (Eagleton, 2007, p. 27). Competing ideologies frame phenomena differently and guide or focus our attention on different events, issues, concerns, or problems we observe in the world.

Ideologies also lead humans to act in specific ways to endorse and preserve, or reconstruct and transform a given social order. Consider the difference between a conservative versus an egalitarian ideology on the topic of suffering. A conservative political ideology is likely to persuade people that the *status quo* is good and that deviations from it are bad (e.g., Mannheim, 1936/2015). It might convince people that the suffering some people experience is counterbalanced by an overall positive societal situation. It might also explain such suffering as due to people's own neglect or misdeeds (done in the past or even during a past life), and therefore their suffering is justified. For a conservative ideology, suffering might even be seen as a form of cosmic justice.

By contrast, an egalitarian political ideology might insist that *equality* is good and that deviations from it are bad. It might persuade people that the benefits some people currently experience are counterbalanced by an overall negative societal situation owing to high levels of inequality. It might also explain inequalities and suffering as due to the neglect or misdeeds of economic and political elites, either nationally or internationally, suggesting that it is a grave injustice for people to experience suffering. From an egalitarian viewpoint, there is little that is positive about stark inequalities, and nothing that is natural about the suffering inequality might cause. Rather such suffering is seen as a social injustice imposed upon the unfortunate and disadvantaged by the rich and powerful.

In some cases, the presence of an ideology may be obvious to people, as sometimes occurs with religious ideologies where followers may be fully aware of their commitment to a particular set of ideas. But ideologies may also be hidden, in the sense that people do not recognize the influence of an ideology on their thinking about what is right or wrong, proper or improper, acceptable or unacceptable, good or bad. For example, gendered beliefs and practices that privilege men in the work place and women within the household, or perhaps men in both the workplace and in the household, may be perceived as natural. Yet, in fact they result from and are reinforced by ideology. And the ideologies that guide our normative interpretation of such relationships and responsibilities are socially constructed.

Likewise, political ideologies may be either obvious or hidden. They may be obvious to a voter when they choose between electing a candidate from a party with an underlying ideology (e.g., conservative, liberal, environmentalist, socialist, etc.). But political ideologies may be hidden to their supporters if a voter never questions the meaning or arguments behind the people or parties for whom they are voting. Furthermore, the political ideology underpinning the practice of voting might also be undetected if a voter never questions whether the holding of elections to select candidates is desirable, or whether being constrained on the choice of numbers or types of candidates or parties is optimal.

As narratives suggesting a specific direction for how the world should be or how to change the world, ideologies are typically marked by a fair amount of imprecision and vagueness. They discuss proposed changes in terms of preferring (or demanding), but are lacking in specifics about when or how deeply to make changes. Ideologies are therefore not easy to hold accountable due to their slipperiness, contradictions, and countervailing claims. But ambiguity can also contribute to the impact and appeal of an ideology and helps some ideologies survive for surprisingly long periods of time, despite possible incoherence, competition from other ideologies, or other shortcomings. There are times when ideologies may fail to be persuasive but are nevertheless kept in place by elites through the use of physical coercion (Freeden, 2003, p. 10). It is also the case that sometimes because ideologies are so widely held (i.e., hegemonic) few even notice them. As an example, many societies in the twenty-first century support the practice of everyone wearing clothes, even on hot days, reflecting a belief that public nudity is inappropriate regardless of the temperature. But the clothes-wearing norm does not hold true for all societies and demonstrates that people's views of appropriate clothing vary across societies and are socially constructed. In similar fashion, the act of selecting one's own (romantic) partner "is a conscious ideological thought-practice only when put in the context of arranged marriages. Otherwise it is an ideologically unconscious practice" (Freeden, 2003, p. 23).

Given inevitable diversity in people's thinking, no ideational system ever enjoys complete dominance, even in development thinking and practice (Stokke, 2009, p. 19). There will always be some competition between ideologies even if one appears for the time being to be hegemonic or significantly more influential than its competitors. What makes ideologies distinct from each other is their *de-contestation* of pivotal concepts, referring to giving a fixed meaning to a signifier (e.g., a word that potentially has many different possible meanings) and thereby excluding all other possible alternative understandings or interpretations of that signifier (Freeden, 1996). De-contesting concepts is a process involving "prioritizing among options, of accepting or ruling out paradigms that interpret political reality, of competing over the legitimate meanings assigned to political language" (Freeden, 1996, p. 551). For example, an ideology might define the concept of *development* to mean the *elimination of hunger and starvation* to the exclusion of all other possible definitions (i.e., it de-contests the definition of development). If such an ideology were dominant (or hegemonic), people might only think of reductions in hunger and undernutrition as development and ignore alternative ways of conceiving of development. In this case, if a government were to provide electrification to more households or provide more reproductive and maternal health services to women, but the prevalence of humans experiencing hunger and undernutrition remained the same (or increased), people might not think of the government's investments in electrification or health services as *development* because they did not reduce *hunger*.

The term *ideology* sometimes gives rise to confusion because it is used in different ways. Three influential ways of using the term ideology refer to: 1) the science of understanding and analyzing ideas, 2) a tool that elites use to deceive the masses, and 3) a holistic conception of the ideas and worldview that guides the thoughts and behaviors of members of particular social groups. The first meaning of ideology concerns analyzing ideas or sets of ideas from a neutral and scientific perspective. Antione-Louis-Claude, Compte Destutt de Tracy, a French philosopher of the eighteenth century was interested in understanding the deductive origin of ideas when he first coined the term *ideology* (in French, *idéologie*) meaning "science of ideas" (Destutt de Tracy, 1776; Kennedy, 1979, p. 353). He and his followers, called the Idéologues, sought to analyze and understand the world of ideas in a similar fashion as the methods of science employed to understand the physical world: that is, through empirical observation of human behavior.

The second conception of ideology refers more pejoratively to a set of ideas that are deliberately constructed and manipulative in nature.

This perspective has often been associated with how Karl Marx and Friedrich Engels described and critiqued ideology during the nineteenth century (see, e.g., *The German Ideology,* originally published in 1865 [1965]). The subsequent Marxist tradition then used the term *ideology* to convey the way that widely promulgated ideas are often a smokescreen concocted by the elites to hide their real agenda and to benefit themselves at the expense of the masses. From this perspective, people who are wealthy owners of property would likely subscribe to and disseminate an ideology that legitimates their own wealth and others' relative lack of wealth in any society featuring major class stratification (Marx and Engels, 1965). Indeed, in the view of Marx and Engels, "the role of ideology was to smooth over those contradictions by making them appear as necessary, normal, and congruous. That way social unity could be maintained and enhanced" and "ideological illusions were an instrument in the hands of the rulers, through the state, and were employed to exercise control and domination; indeed, to 'manufacture history' according to their interests" (Freeden, 2003, pp. 5–6).

Marx and Engels would have agreed with Destutt de Tracy that our ideas about the world are shaped through our material interactions and human sensations (see Marx and Engels, 1965, section 4, para 2), but they take it a step further to say that the division of labor in society causes a division of interests (section 4, para 13) and that the elites of a given society then use ideology to keep the masses in their place (by convincing them to labor in factories, for instance) to make the elites richer or at least help maintain their riches.[2] From this viewpoint, ideologies can greatly facilitate exploitation such that "An exploited worker actually believed that it was a good idea to get up in the morning and work 14 hours for a pittance in her employer's factory, because she had internalized the ideological view that such dehumanizing work was an inevitable part of the industrial order, that it was a free act on her part, that markets gave everyone an equal chance, and that earning one's keep by renting out one's labor to others was central to one's sense of dignity" (Freeden, 2003, p. 6). As seen in this hypothetical example, ideology can potentially be a powerful force for keeping people "in a state of ignorance and suffering" (Freeden, 2003, p. 7).

A third way of employing the term *ideology* is more neutral and does not automatically assume that intentional manipulation is the primary objective of a social narrative or package of ideas. This more holistic approach understands ideology as a set of ideas, beliefs, and norms that guide the way we think and act, even if we are not aware of all its components. This more sociological perspective of thinking about ideology was developed by Karl Mannheim. The key distinction Mannheim brought to the study of ideology was to distinguish between the "particular conception of ideology" and the "total conception of ideology" (Mannheim, 1936/2015, p. 49). The *particular conception* is like that described above of an ideology being used in a given society to manipulate and control people for a specific purpose. By contrast, the *total conception* reflects ideology as being holistic, as connected to a larger society, history, culture, and people group in a given socio-historical-political context, as a set of beliefs that guide the way we think and act in the world. It concerns "the characteristics and composition of the total structure of the mind of this epoch or of this group" and stems from an awareness that "the thought of all parties in all epochs is of an ideological character" (Mannheim, 1936/2015, pp. 49–50, p. 69). What these two conceptions of ideology have in common, however, is that neither one "relies solely on what is actually said . . . opinions, statements, propositions, and systems of ideas are not taken at their face value but are interpreted in the light of the life-situation of the one who expresses them" (50).

Mannheim's insights on ideology have been incorporated into the international relations (IR) perspective (that guides this book) of "theory-as-ideology" (Martill and Schindler, 2020) which has exposed how theories about IR, international development, and global practices are not free of ideology nor are methods of science or social inquiry (also see Marcuse, 1964/1991). Instead of pretending that such methods and theories are impartial, we can develop a much better understanding of theories and approaches in all fields of IR (including global development) by becoming aware of their ideological attributes. As Robert Cox famously stated, "theory is always *for* someone and *for* some purpose" (1981, 128). The point here is that it is important to be aware that all theories, paradigms, and perspectives are influenced by ideology. "Theory is never only concerned with objective knowledge. Instead, theory always expresses a particular perspective. It is always partial and cannot be otherwise" (Martill and Schindler, 2020, p. 7).[3] With this in mind, the next section examines several ideologies of globalization.

COMPETING IDEOLOGIES OF GLOBALIZATION

Ideology shapes how people view life in general and also influences specific aspects or domains of human life. Political ideologies (such as social democratic, conservative, or anarchic) shape how we think about power and governance. Religious ideologies (such as Buddhist, Islamic, or Christian) give us insight into ontology, metaphysics, and soteriology. Economic ideologies (such as statist, capitalist, or communist) provide a basis for understanding and organizing the production and consumption of goods and services. Likewise, ideologies of globalization shape how humans understand the world around them. Such ideologies allow humans to interpret and direct international interactions and interdependencies that impact human life. Ideologies of globalization are narratives about how human life across the whole world is, how it should be, and they include plans and ideas for making a particular conception of the global become reality. Any ideology can become global, or say something about globalization, but not all do. Those that make specific references or connections to the global, and the processes of globalization, are the ones we are most concerned about here.[4]

Probably the most well-known and influential ideology of globalization is neoliberalism, also known as *market globalism* (e.g., Steger, 2020, p. 45). At its core, neoliberal ideology maintains that capital (including financial investments), raw materials, consumer products (and materials made to use those products), and data should be able to move freely across national borders without restrictions (or with as little impediments as possible). Some of its most famous proponents in the twentieth century included Friedrich Hayek, Milton Friedman, and James Buchanan, all of whom accepted the nation-state framework of individual countries having their own separate governments but championed limited state intervention in a free market, capitalist economy (e.g., Hayek, 1944/2007; Buchanan, 1969; Friedman and Friedman, 1980). Under the neoliberal ideology, the free market is expected to enhance the profits that accrue to the owners of capital and to increase overall global economic growth which will eventually reduce poverty around the world. As a global ideology, neoliberalism emphasizes the formation of a single global market, the role of commercial businesses (i.e., those not owned by governments), and technological innovations playing the dominant role in the world economy (for an explanation of neoliberalism as a theory that is not only technical and economic but also highly political, see Harvey, 2007 or Biebricher, 2019).

Neoliberalism as a theory and practice has strongly influenced global capitalist organizations and corporate media in much of the Western world since the 1940s. It became especially ascendant in the early 1980s after the departure of the initial Bretton Woods System during the 1970s that was built in the 1940s on Keynesian economics. The ideology of neoliberalism aims to create a global business-friendly utopia. As a market-oriented globalism, its goal is to open up commercial business opportunities around the world for those who can afford to invest in them and it endorses bringing much of human activity under the domain of the market system, even if this requires doing so by using force (i.e., using non-market forces to impose commercial or capitalist models) (Harvey, 2007, p. 4).

As an ideology, as opposed to an objective assessment of reality, neoliberalism sets up a dichotomy between the state and the market, viewing them as separate institutions of society that should be kept apart from each other. Neoliberalism's claim is that the state should not have a role in regulating the market beyond setting up institutions to support markets: "State interventions in markets (once created) must be kept to a bare minimum because, according to the theory, the state cannot possibly possess enough information to second-guess market signals (prices) and because powerful interest groups will inevitably distort and bias state interventions (particularly in democracies) for their own benefit" (Harvey, 2007, p. 2).

Perhaps not surprisingly neoliberalism, a.k.a. market globalism, and its slogan of promoting free markets, has been controversial because some see it as advancing the interests of large business corporations at the expense of everyone else. Much has been written by critics about how neoliberal policies have contributed to fueling environmental degradation, conflict among peoples, and increased inequality, as well as racial and gender injustice (e.g., Sandbrook et al., 2007). Nevertheless, market globalism has been popular with major private property holders in the Global North, multinational corporations, and international capitalist institutions like the World Trade Organization (WTO), World Bank (WB), and International Monetary Fund (IMF) (see Steger, 2009 or Stiglitz, 2002).

The term *neoliberalism*, as we know and use it today, derives from a critique of the policies promoted by the powerful Anglophone states in the West (i.e., the United States [US] and United Kingdom [UK]) in the 1980s, particularly through the World Bank and IMF (Peters, 2021). Although first used pejoratively, it came into fashion as a way to promote and articulate the development theories and policies of the 1980s. It has been identified as a right-wing and relatively conservative ideology that is essentially a variant of libertarianism, an ideology that broke away from the more mainstream and centrist ideology of liberalism. "The revival of free-market [ideology], or neo-liberalism has, after all, recently appeared under a conservative protective mantle. It has always characterized libertarianism, which has broken away from liberalism . . . In this case liberty is associated with unlimited consumer choice while crowding out or demoting other liberal core concepts" (Freeden, 2003, 95). As this ideology has heavily influenced globalization patterns and trends over the past half-century, we return to it at the end of this chapter to tease out its similarities and differences with HD ideology.

In contrast to neoliberalism (a.k.a. *market globalism*), a number of competing globalization counter-ideologies have emerged over the past few decades, in part to counter what they see as negative outcomes caused by neoliberal thinking, policies, and practices. These ideologies include, but are not limited to, what Steger terms *justice globalism*, *religious globalisms*, and *national populism* (e.g., Steger, 2020). Justice globalism refers to the ideology of the Global Justice Movement (GJM) founded in the 1990s, which included many different social movements challenging neoliberalism largely through transnational civil society and activist networks (Steger et al., 2012; Steger, 2020, p. 81). A key slogan of the GJM reflected the view that market globalism is neither inevitable nor desirable: "Another World is Possible" (Scerri, 2013). Recognizing that most people are deliberately shut out of the discussions and institutions that make the rules of the global economy, the GJM has worked to organize public awareness, public gatherings, street demonstrations, and peaceful protests outside of international economic summits (such as the alternate to the World Economic Forum called the World Social Forum). Large-scale demonstrations in the United States against the IMF in Washington, DC, in 2000 (Rupert, 2000, xi), or those in Seattle against the WTO in 1999 (Murphy and

Pfaff, 2005) offer clear examples. The GJM goal, however vague and transient, is to transform global economic governance from prioritizing corporate profits to improving the well-being of workers, consumers, and the environment (Steger, 2009, p. 119). In contrast to the objectives of neoliberalism, a major contribution of the various GJM organizations and movements has been promoting "citizen participation, grassroots democracy, racial and gender equality, ecological balance, community-based economics, and distributive justice" (Steger, 2009, p. 123). Justice globalism, as an ideology, also aims to eliminate war and usher in an era of global peace and non-violence.

Another category of globalization ideologies are those that center around religion, or *religious globalisms* (Steger, 2020, p. 106). Since these are sometimes deeply irreconcilable, they have been seen as contributing to a global "clash of civilizations" (Huntington, 1997). Broadly speaking, religious globalisms describe an ideological family with particular reference to those religions that have a global agenda or which seek to evangelize to a global audience in order to gain more converts or to struggle against "false belief" (Steger, 2009, p. 148). Unlike *market globalism* and *justice globalisms*, which are more secular in orientation, religious globalisms typically make claims about the role of God, divinities, or the supernatural in calling for certain global changes and arrangements. Examples include religiously inspired ideologies which call for a global reuniting or homeland for the members of a particular faith or which seek to enlist followers or "disciples into a global crusade or campaign against unbelievers. The ideological family of religious globalisms is not limited to any single religion and includes, for example, both Christian and Islamic variants. A radical example of the latter is the Jihadist globalism ideology of the international al-Qaeda terrorist network and its former leader Osama bin Laden who sought to promote radical Islam as an alternative to market globalism (Steger, 2009, p. 145).

Another ideological approach to globalization is *nationalist populism*. Nationalist populist movements in many countries have been on the rise during the first quarter of the twenty-first century. Although nominally rejecting and opposing globalization, nationalist populism comprises a "mounting anti-globalist wave [that] is itself a globalizing phenomenon that is sweeping across all continents" (Steger and James, 2019, p. 257; see also, Rupert, 2000, p. 119). Nationalism, which can be defined as "a doctrine of popular freedom and sovereignty" (Hutchinson and Smith, 1994, p. 4), has been a challenge to globalization from the start since it presupposes giving priority to the nation or state (through citizenship), or to the people group closely connected with one's identity (through bloodline, custom, or religion, for instance). National populist ideologies speak to concerns people have with what they perceive to be the overreach of transnational corporations that seem to take away their livelihoods (when they lose their jobs) and limit their access to goods or services: "Fearing the loss of national self-determination and the destruction of a circumscribed national culture, [national populists] pledge to protect the integrity of their nation from those 'foreign elements' that they identify as responsible for unleashing the forces of globalization" (Steger, 2009, p. 132).

The ideological structure of national populist movements tends to rely on pronouncing, creating, and reifying "political differences" to create opposing identities of "us" versus "them" as well as employing emotionally powerful techniques including "demonizing, scapegoating, and the spinning of conspiracy tales" (Steger, 2020, p. 134). As Steger elaborates on this dichotomous construction: "Hence, (good) ordinary people (who are imagined to be homogeneous) supposedly radiate honesty, purity, piety, resourcefulness, resilience, quiet wisdom, willingness to play by the rules, fondness for religion and tradition, and hard work" and are portrayed as major victims of the (evil) establishment elite's decisions to allow their community to be "infiltrated" by (bad) "immigrants, guest workers, ethnic minorities, or foreign radicals" (2020, p. 134). A prominent example of a political leader promoting this kind of ideology was former US president Donald Trump (2016–2020) but Trump is not an isolated case (Steger, 2020, p. 143).[5]

As Steger notes, national populist ideologies tend to "denounce free trade, the increasing power of global investors" and "unpatriotic practices" of transnational corporations that have "contributed to falling living standards and moral decline. Fearing the loss of national self-determination and the destruction of a circumscribed national culture, they pledge to protect the integrity of their nation from those 'foreign elements' that they identify as responsible for unleashing the forces of globalization" (2009, p. 132). Alarmingly (and resembling Jihadist globalism), a number of these "populists have been reluctant to endorse the rules of representative democracy" and in some cases they endorse violating or altering constitutional provisions "as necessary measures to carry out 'the will of the people' against the power interests of corrupt social elites" (2009, p. 133).

While there is no global agreement over which ideology of globalization is most desirable, many civil society groups (whether formal or informal) have joined to challenge the dominance of market globalism and its associated policies. Indeed, new ideologies always emerge as challengers or counter-ideologies to dominant and influential ideologies (of globalization or otherwise). Another globalization ideology that has received less scrutiny, but also become prominent since the late twentieth century, is that of *capabilities globalism,* also known as the human development (HD) paradigm or the human development and capability approach (HDCA), examined in the next section.

HUMAN DEVELOPMENT AS AN IDEOLOGY OF GLOBALIZATION

The HD paradigm, also called the human development and capability approach (HDCA), functions as an *ideology* of both globalization and development. It functions as an ideology because it communicates a set of beliefs, ideas, and norms about how the world is and how it should be.[6] The HD ideology has also been labeled as *capabilities globalism* (Joshi, 2021a) in line with Steger's nomenclature as a contrast to *market globalism, justice globalism,* and *religious globalism.* The HD ideology has its own particular set of guiding principles, foundational ideas, and vocabulary. Unlike religious globalisms, it is secular and contains no references to the divine or supernatural. It also does not champion markets, justice, or the nation above all else. Rather, the HD ideology is committed to concepts of individualism and freedom found in classical liberalism, and it has been connected to the theory and practice of human rights (UNDP, 2000). HD ideology reorients global development thinking and practice away from macroeconomic thinking and policy, away from income generation for its own sake, and away from thinking of humans as means to development. It focuses instead on the well-being and capabilities of the individual human. As with all ideologies, the HD ideology emphasizes a unique set of vocabulary (Table 2.1).

At its core, the HD ideology promotes the idea that *development* is and should be about individuals having maximal agency, discussed in terms of capabilities and functionings. The concept of *capabilities* is central to understanding HD. It implies not only achieved end-states of well-being, or *functionings*, but also human potential (i.e., the ability to achieve such functionings). Capabilities are the potentials that humans have to act in the world (whether that be the ability to survive, to obtain an education, or to reproduce, for example).

The primary unit of analysis in the HD ideology is the *individual* human being who should be treated as a *subject* (with agency) as opposed

Table 2.1. Key Concepts in the Human Development Ideology

Key Concepts	Definition
Agency (Human)	Ability for a human to control their lives, to live lives they have reason to value, to make choices as regards functioning, and to be able to change their lives as they see fit.
Capability/ies	Potential that each individual person has to act in the world, to gain what they need or want to survive, to be and do what they desire to live their best life (see Sen, 1999, p. 75).
Choice	Ability to decide to do one thing over another, to function in the way that best meets one's individual idea of the best life.
Democratic Engagement and Dialogue	The freedom, capability, and functioning to participate in open dialogue and discussion with fellow citizens about what policies or laws will best support all citizens in a society so that they are able to enjoy capabilities and to choose how to function.
Development	Theories and practices of social and economic growth supported and implemented by governments (sometimes in conjunction with IGOs and NGOs) to support the well-being of the nation-state and the population.
Functioning/s	The way in which people act in the world to gain what they need or want to survive, to be and do what they desire to live their best life.
Individuals	The human being as the primary unit of analysis (not the nation-state, the group, or the family), and the individual is conceived as the final focus, as the end of all policy and discussion (rather than the means of obtaining something else).
Well-being (Human)	How well an individual is doing in society as regards access to capabilities, the choices to function in particular ways if they would like.

Source: Main concepts and key ideas of the HDCA (or to which the HDCA approach speaks) that are covered in this chapter. The definitions provided are derived from the works of Amartya Sen, Martha Nussbaum, and Mahbub ul Haq as well as from publications on the HDCA, especially the Human Development Reports (HDRs).

to being treated as an *object* (or passive recipient) of development, or even as a means (mechanism by which to obtain something) to achieve economic growth. Thus, individuals take precedence over the nation-state, household, planet, divinities, moral precepts, and non-human species. Saying that the human being is an *agent* means that people should be able to make changes to their own lives and have choices in how they live and act in the world. The HD ideology's normative vision posits that the aim of human agents is to expand and enjoy their own *capabilities,* referring to their ability to be and do whatever they value or have "reason to value" in the course of their life (Sen, 1999, p. 18). The HD ideology also prioritizes the concepts of freedom, equitable access to goods and services, and the well-being of the individual in society.

The HD ideology stresses the *multi-dimensionality* of humans and HD outcomes in contrast to development approaches or theories of justice that aim to maximize a single item (such as income in neoliberalism, military power in IR realism, or happiness in utilitarianism). Notably, the dimensions that matter for HD are not always interchangeable. For example, both health and wealth can facilitate human well-being but neither can be directly substituted for the other: someone may have lots of money, but terrible health and even if they were to gain more money, it would not improve their well-being as much as being in better health.[7]

Resembling Mannheim's perspective, the HD ideology insists that value judgments are inevitable and ought to be made explicit instead of hidden. As Alkire notes, "capabilities include only possibilities that people really value. Having some options matter more than others of course—it is usually more valuable that a young man is physically safe than that he can choose between rival brands of toothpaste" (2005, p. 2). As different people value different things, the HD approach generally maintains that society should allow for and support diversity and pluralism.

How one approaches HD is of course heavily influenced by culture. Given differences across cultures, the promotion of global HD requires some basic consensus on which dimensions are essential. Three of these stipulated in the HD paradigm as articulated in the 1990 HDR are "1) to lead a long and healthy life, 2) to acquire knowledge, and 3) to have access to resources needed for a decent standard of living" (UNDP, 1990, p. 10). Thus, while there are still on-going debates over which other dimensions of HD are essential, what is largely agreed upon is that HD is inescapably multi-dimensional and that at the very least it comprises education, health, and income.[8] Among major promoters of the HD paradigm, one point of disagreement is over whether other essential dimensions of HD are universal (i.e., the same for everyone), or whether they are open for interpretation and should be decided upon collectively and democratically by the members of a community (e.g., see Robeyns, 2005, 2017 on this debate). The next two sections review arguments for both these positions, for particularism and participation at the local level, and for universalism at the global level.

PARTICULARISM AND THE CONCERN FOR CAPABILITIES, FREEDOM, AND DEMOCRACY

One of the most important concepts of the HD ideology is that of freedom in human lives supported by the ability for people to engage in debate and deliberation about what freedoms and capabilities are most important to their particular society. *Freedom* is championed by the HD paradigm in the sense of both *positive* freedom (ability and permission to do things one values) and *negative* freedom (absence of interference) and influential proponents of this paradigm have talked at length about the meaning of freedom to HD (e.g., Sen, 1999; Nussbaum, 2011). A comprehensive conceptualization of freedom (i.e., championing both negative and positive freedom) reveals an affinity between HD ideology and liberalism in its "developmental" variant (Freeden, 1996), while also distancing the HD approach from and opposing it to the libertarian ideology of neoliberalism.

Expanding on a comprehensive idea of freedom, one of the main proponents of thinking about freedom as a major component of HD (as a core concept) is Amartya Sen (we return to his ideas in chapter 3). As he proclaims in the opening lines of his book titled *Development as Freedom*: "Development can be seen, it is argued here, as a process of expanding the real freedoms that people enjoy. Focusing on human freedoms contrasts with narrower views of development, such as identifying development with the growth of gross national product, or with the rise in personal incomes, or with industrialization, or with technological advance, or with social modernization" (Sen, 1999, p. 3). Originally trained as an economist, Sen famously criticized traditional welfare economic models by suggesting that policies should promote individual capabilities instead of focusing solely on resource distribution and allocation from governments (Atkinson, 1999; Hamilton, 2019, pp. 1–22). Sen's criticism of neoclassical economics also tied into his thinking about social contract theory and theories of justice, engaging with eminent thinkers on the issue—like John Rawls, for instance—who sought to identify how societies could be set up to be as just as possible. At issue was the lack of choice and freedom in people's lives, not the lack of resources. Sen compares instrumental to constitutive freedoms, arguing that freedom is necessary as a means (instrumental) as well as an end (constitutive) of development (Sen, 1999).

In Sen's view, individual freedom and social arrangements (economic policies, welfare measurements and distribution, etc.) are deeply intertwined, leading him to view "development as a process of expanding the real freedoms that people enjoy" (Sen, 1999, p. 36). This means that if a society does not guarantee particular freedoms to its people, those people will be unable to function in ways that would support their well-being. In particular, Sen highlights the importance of political freedom, economic facilities, social opportunities, transparency guarantees, and protective security (for more on this, see chapter 5, table 5.2). As Sen argues, without freedoms people not only are unable to meet their basic needs but also cannot "lead responsible lives" (1999, p. 284).

Sen's fundamental claim is that an individual's freedom is contingent upon having various capabilities (a term that may alternatively be conceived of as potential or potentiality, that is, what a person has the possibility of doing and being rather than what they can do and be) (Hamilton, 2019, p. 51; Sen, 1993). A person's capabilities enable them to live a life that they believe is valuable or worthy of living, and most importantly, capabilities provide people with the ability to choose the life they desire (Sen, 1993, 1999). Sen illustrates this point by using the example of inequality between two people who do not eat a meal. If a wealthy person chooses to fast, they are making a decision to under-nourish themselves whereas if a person in poverty cannot eat and is therefore malnourished it is not because of a decision they have made. Rather, it is because they do not have the choice to eat: "the first can choose to eat well and be well nourished in a way the second cannot" (1999, p. 75).

Additionally, certain freedoms or capabilities are *fertile* building blocks that allow people to obtain other capabilities and freedoms. Education and health feature prominently among such capabilities because they are enablers of other functionings. Therefore the early stages of a person's life are especially important. When the HD ideology was solidified in the first Human Development Report (HDR) issued in 1990, and measured by the Human Development Index (HDI), it was these two freedoms (education and health) that stood out to the creators as particularly important for guiding government policy (along with poverty reduction measured through income). Other capabilities that the HD ideology prioritizes include gender equality, participatory and deliberative democracy, human rights, and human security because of the role they can play to enhance human freedoms.

The theme of choice (participation, or democracy) comes up regularly in the HD ideology, and Sen's writings and arguments reveal choice as central to his concern for capabilities. In his view, social structures, rules, and norms that guide economic or development practices must be "open for deliberation" (Sen, 1999, p. xiii) and he welcomes reasoned, inclusive, and pluralist discussion on such issues to achieve solutions. For Sen, participation in decision making "must be wide open for people in the society to address and join in deciding" (Sen, 1999, p. 32). Sen thus adamantly rejects the traditional conservative claim that one should keep doing things the same way as done in the past. The reason why is because it denies people their participatory freedom to have a say over whether or which things done in the past should be continued or discontinued. Thus, in the HD paradigm, *democracy* refers to a complex and ideal political system entailing respect for human rights, protections of liberties and freedoms, widespread actual participation, and free discussion involving the give and take of opposing arguments with all sides having an adequate opportunity to present their case so that people are able to exercise their agency and make a difference in the world (Deneulin and Crocker, 2006, p. 1). From this perspective, democracy has intrinsic, instrumental, and constructive value (see Sen, 1999; Drèze and Sen, 2002).

UNIVERSALISM, HUMAN FLOURISHING, AND CAPABILITIES

Another major contributor to the human development and capability approach (HDCA), Martha Nussbaum, places comparatively less emphasis on deliberation and discussion than Sen, although does not categorically oppose it. She proffers a specific list of human capabilities, though concedes that it is just one of many interpretations of what a list of capabilities might look like based on the HD ideology. Nussbaum argues that a list of key capabilities can be universal by drawing on a foundational analysis of what it means to be human. And she argues that the basic capabilities that matter for HD and human flourishing are essentially the same for everyone, everywhere. To this end, Nussbaum promotes a list of ten "central capabilities" that she argues are universal and applicable to all humans (see Table 2.2), but can also be "contested and remade" by individuals or communities as the situation necessitates (1999, p. 40). The question from which the list is derived investigates the very meaning of *human*, that is, "What activities characteristically performed by human beings are so central that they seem definitive of a life that is truly human? In other words, what are the functions without which (meaning, without the availability of which) we would regard a life as not, or not fully, human" (Nussbaum, 1999). In her view, the key role of governments is to make sure all citizens meet a minimum threshold level on all ten central capabilities.

Nussbaum defends her list of ten universal capabilities by stating that in contrast to mainstream capitalist economic thought, her approach "is not based on the satisfaction of existing preferences" (2011, p. 35). Rather, the ten central capabilities were selected based on observation of human life and because they uphold human dignity. Nussbaum supports translating the idea of capabilities into social arrangements through government decisions, as this creates "policy choices that protect and support agency, rather than choices that infantilize people and treat them as passive recipients of benefit" (2011, p. 30). Nussbaum also maintains that governments (rather than the for-profit or non-profit sectors) must take responsibility for ensuring that humans can live at least a "minimally flourishing life" by removing obstacles to their ability to flourish as well as setting up the social arrangements in which they can function and achieve capabilities (2011, p. 33, p. 65).

Table 2.2.   Martha Nussbaum's List of Ten Central Capabilities

Ten Central Capabilities	Definition of the Capabilities (from Nussbaum, 1999, pp. 41–42)
1. Life	Being able to live to the end of a human life of normal length, not dying prematurely . . .
2. Bodily health	Being able to have good health, including reproductive health . . .
3. Bodily integrity	. . . to move freely from place to place . . . to be secure against violent assault . . . having opportunities for sexual satisfaction . . .
4. Senses, imagination, and thought	. . . to use the senses . . . to imagine, to think, and to reason . . . informed and cultivated by an adequate education . . .
5. Emotions	. . . to have attachments to things and persons outside ourselves . . .
6. Practical reason	. . . to form a conception of the good and to engage in critical reflection about the planning of one's own life.
7. Affiliation	. . . to live for and in relation to others, to recognize and show concern for other human beings . . . having the social bases of self-respect and non-humiliation . . .
8. Other species	. . . to live with concern for and in relation to animals, plants, and the world of nature.
9. Play	. . . to laugh, to play, to enjoy recreational activities.
10. Control over one's environment	Politically: being able to participate effectively in political choices that govern one's life . . . Materially: being able to hold property . . . having the right to seek employment . . .

In line with human rights theory (and practice) and political liberalism, Nussbaum insists that the HD paradigm is a universal theory that identifies and supports all people to attain a quality of life that all humans have reason to value (2011, p. 55). As she states, the capabilities approach " . . . begins from a commitment to the equal dignity of all human beings, whatever their class, religion, race, or gender, and it is committed to the attainment, for all, of lives that are worthy of that equal dignity" (2011, p. 186). The importance of the individual human being is central to the HD approach in that social arrangements should be concerned with supporting individuals, not necessarily groups, to function and flourish as human beings (2011, p. 35).

Nussbaum's critique of the differences in how genders experience the world is particularly damning when considering whether women are able to function in the same ways as men in their societies. Circumventing arguments that suggest that wealthy countries have overcome gender disparities, Nussbaum notes that wealthy countries can be just as culpable in infantilizing women and turning them into dependents (2011, p. 55), and in devaluing family life and work in the household (2011, p. 38). Indeed, as Table 2.2 illustrates, gender is one of the important concepts in the HD ideology because it denotes that a specific category of individuals (females) may not be able to access capabilities, or if capabilities are available in society, social norms may be such that they limit females from functioning accordingly.

All the major HD theorists explore the challenges of female access to capabilities and their ability to function. Sen discusses the "missing women" of societies that devalue the female gender (1992) and the importance of giving women agency, not just being concerned with their well-being (1999, p. 189). Nussbaum addresses more specifically the issues of sexual justice, including reproductive rights and bodily integrity in the face of social practices that allow violence (such as rape) against women to go largely unpunished, or continue to support practice such as female genital mutilation (1999, p. 118). Reiterating the importance of gender, the 1995 HDR focused exclusively on gender concerns, highlighting the "equal enjoyment of human rights by women and men [as] a universally accepted principle" while asserting that the HD approach supported equality of opportunity, sustainability, and empowerment for all genders (UNDP, 1995, p. 1).

In comparing the views of Sen and Nussbaum, it is evident that both agree that HD requires a multidimensional approach, but they differ on their willingness to identify a list of capabilities around which governments could or should create policy in an effort to ensure that all humans globally can achieve a good, decent, dignified human life. Sen references certain capabilities in his work, but mostly as examples in explaining the approach such as "being able to survive," or "the ability to read and write" (Sen, 2003b, p. 11). Sen also identifies a set of freedoms, but notes that the process of identifying specific provision of and kinds of freedoms and capabilities requires public deliberation and discussion to ascertain (since they may differ across contexts or societies) (e.g., Sen, 2003a, p. ix). Nussbaum, on the other hand, identifies 10 capabilities that she finds are necessary for all governments to implement in order to meet basic pre-conditions for human flourishing.

LOCATING THE HUMAN DEVELOPMENT
PARADIGM AS AN IDEOLOGY

The HD ideology is unique and departs from older ideological families, while simultaneously overlapping with the established Western ideologies of liberalism and humanism. As defined by Edward Said, "humanism is centered upon the agency of human individuality and subjective intuition, rather than on received ideas and approved authority" (2003, p. xxix). Similarly, the HD ideology focuses on human agency and individuality though it places less emphasis on subjective intuition. The HD approach with its general targets but no specific demands and very little focus on laws or coercion is unlike conservatism. As Mannheim explains, from the liberal viewpoint "the 'should' is accentuated in experience, in conservatism the emphasis shifts to existing reality, the 'is' . . . what in liberalism is merely a formal norm, in conservatism acquires concrete content in the prevailing laws of the state" (1936/2015, pp. 209–211). In this respect, HD ideology is much closer to liberalism as it places much greater focus on aspirations (e.g., targets, goals, resolutions, recommendations, etc.) than on specific demands for restructuring power or the bestowing of rewards and punishments.

The HD ideology is also somewhat hidden in that it is usually not described as an ideology, and therefore is able to escape some of the typical criticisms ideologies naturally attract. What perhaps makes HD seem natural is that it resonates with common understandings of basic and seemingly inevitable biological, psychological, and social processes. From the perspective of developmental psychology, HD proceeds through the healthy and natural unfolding of different stages across the human lifespan. But such healthy unfolding does not always happen as it also requires the right kinds of conditions to occur in each phase. Beginning with conception, the early stages of life are fundamentally important for HD. Not only does a person need proper care and nutrition while in the womb, but infancy is likewise a critical phase as 90% of human brain development happens within the first two years of life (Ghosh, 2006). As Martha Nussbaum explains, "a great deal of human potential is being wasted by the failure to intervene early" both *in utero* and after birth since what happens "at a very young age" strongly influences later development (2011, p. 194). The entire pre-adolescent years are likewise essential for a person's physical and intellectual development both in and out of school. As Jean Drèze and Amartya Sen argue, "elementary capabilities" including "the ability to avoid undernourishment and related morbidity and mortality," as well as the mastery of reading, writing, and arithmetic are essential components of HD (1989, p. 12). These are also prerequisites for achieving "more sophisticated social capabilities such as taking part in the life of the community and achieving self-respect" (Drèze and Sen, 1989, p. 12).

As for which ideological family the HD paradigm belongs to, Martha Nussbaum, describes it as a "form of political liberalism" while also arguing that "it is not a comprehensive doctrine of any sort" (2011, p. 92). Nussbaum does not see the HD paradigm as cosmopolitanism. Rather, she conceptualizes HD as affiliated with liberalism, albeit tangentially, and makes the point that if an approach to life (like the capability approach that she created with its list of ten capabilities) is offered to a wide audience in the broadest terms possible, it will be more palatable to them and they will be more likely to accept it (Nussbaum 2011, 90). Nussbaum's conception of the HD paradigm is that of a thin, overlapping consensus, of a political conception of justice that can be applied universally. Her pronouncements suggest that the producers and promoters of the HD approach have indeed been strategic in architecting, designing, and marketing the ideology.

COMPARING HUMAN DEVELOPMENT TO NEOLIBERALISM

Neoliberalism (a.k.a. market globalism), as discussed in a previous section of this chapter, has been a highly influential ideology of globalization from the late twentieth century to the present. The HD paradigm acts as a counter-ideology to neoliberalism in several ways, three of which we consider here (for more details, see Jolly, 2003). Firstly, the HD approach rejects a simplistic reliance on economic growth to conceptualize development as measured through gross national income per capita (GNI) or some other macroeconomic measure. Secondly, the HD paradigm opposes the idea of humans serving only (or primarily) as the means to economic growth or development. Thirdly, the HD ideology does not accept inequality or divisions between humans as inevitable or preferable. Hence, HD ideology proposes a different set of national and international economic and social policies than neoliberalism, as the HD paradigm prioritizes the creation of enabling environments in which humans have freedom, choice, and the ability to function as they wish to live their best lives.

In contrast to neoliberalism, the aim of HD differs significantly from merely trying to raise GNI in a country or expanding worldwide commodification. As many critics have pointed out, a major limitation of using GNI as a single measure or goal of development, or even to measure reduction in poverty, is that human poverty is a function of multiple deprivations, not just lack of income (e.g., Max-Neef, 1992). Even Aristotle, writing in the fourth century BCE (roughly 2,400 years ago), pointed out that "wealth is evidently not the good we are seeking; for it is merely useful and for the sake of something else," a statement oft-quoted, especially in writings on the HDCA (e.g., Sen, 1999, p. 14). Writing in support of an HD focus with a concern for what people are able to do and be in society, or as Sen would have it, with a concern for capabilities, HD authors point out the limits of income. For example, income is not the only variable that would support a person who needed nourishment. To properly nourish oneself requires decent healthcare and other such social institutions. Human functioning needs a multidimensional approach, not just a reliance on income generation (Drèze and Sen, 1989, p. 13).

Over reliance on GNI as a measure of development by neoliberalism is arguably short-sighted and incomplete (e.g., Haq and Ponzio, 2008, p. 23; Sen, 1999, pp. 13–14; Stewart et al., 2018: pp. 1–25, pp. 19–20; UNDP, 1990, p. 1). Several reasons are self-evident: when an economy grows, average per capita income increases automatically, so long as GNI growth exceeds population growth. But growth does not mean that people will necessarily live longer, be healthier, or that income poverty will necessarily decrease, as growth does not always accrue to those who are poor. Even if an economy expands, certain population groups may experience a decline in their standard of living while others gain. Economic growth may also occur at the expense of poor people's life opportunities, health, and education. For example, an economy may grow rapidly through the hard work of young children and teenagers toiling in mines, factories, and brothels for twelve hours a day, seven days a week. Treating children and young adults so poorly goes against HD ideas (when, for example, they have no time to attend school, they receive low wages, and when they develop serious physical and mental injuries) even if the owners of the mines, factories, and brothels may walk away with a handsome profit and therefore contribute to the GNI.

Paul Streeten, one of the proponents of the basic needs approach to development, and a major contributor to the founding ideas of the HD paradigm, critiques the neoliberal focus on economic growth, or GNI. He points to productive labor that is not included in GNI accounting, and the myriad ways in which GNI benefits (i.e., increases) from terrible events that occur in human societies. His points are worth quoting at length concerning GNI as a flawed measure of development and poverty reduction because, in his words, GNI per capita sums up:

> . . . only goods and services that are exchanged for money, leaving out of account the large amount of work done inside the family, mainly by women, and work done voluntarily for children or older people or in communities. Public services are counted at their cost, so that doubling the wages of all public servants appears to double their contribution to welfare or development. National income accounting does not distinguish between goods and regrettable necessities, like military or anti-crime expenditure, products needed to combat "bads." Addictive eating and drinking is counted twice: when the food and the alcohol are consumed, and when large sums are spent on the diet industry and on cures for alcoholism. Environmental degradation, pollution and resource depletion are not deducted, so that the earth is treated, it has been said, like a business in liquidation . . . Increasing the production of whisky, bought by rich men, counts for much more than increasing the production of milk that would have gone to a starving child. (Streeten, 2003, pp. 78–79)

In other words, the type and distribution of economic growth around the world is much more important than its rate of increase. In place of the simplistic measure of GNI per capita, the first formal report promoting HD offered a compromise, the Human Development Index (HDI), which still used GNI per capita as one measure of HD, but added two crucial measurements of education and health to create a simple, yet powerful index (HDR, 1990). Measuring education and health outcomes builds on the HD core idea that focusing on human capabilities (what humans can do and be in society) are essential markers of development. Focusing on how much money humans can accumulate or spend does not provide enough information on human lives. Indeed, humans could be living in extreme poverty and misery while the GNI per capita might indicate (i.e., suggest) that all is well (Sen, 1999, p. xi).

A second difference is that neoliberalism is premised upon individualism in such a way that humans are conceived as cogs in a machine, as the human capital or human resources that are needed in order for society at large to grow and develop. Neoliberalism is built on "the idea that society is comprised of atomistic individuals whose worth is dependent on what their skills can command in a competitive market" (Krishna, 2009, p. 157). While HD is also an ideology that considers the human as the primary unit of analysis, it does so in a different way than neoliberalism. The HD paradigm sees humans as the end goal and reason for development and growth, not the means to such an end (HDR, 1990, p. 1). The distinction is a tricky one and quite difficult for some people to grasp, but it has enormous implications for the ways in which international development and national policies are created and implemented. A related issue is that neoliberal globalization might fuel a *race to the bottom* in which public policies favor corporations or wealth maximization at the expense of human laborers. Indeed, neoliberal policies often incentivize corporations to set up (or subcontract to) factories in countries where they will have the lowest expenses so as to maximize profits. A possible result is that:

> The difference in wages compared to the West, alongside the lowering of what are called transaction costs (due to transportation, tariffs, time required from production in faraway sites) under globalization, allows for the making of profit. In effect, the working or laboring classes of different parts of the world are pitted against one another, and as various poorer countries compete with one another to make themselves more attractive to foreign investment, wages are driven down further, environmental and other regulations weakened further, unions are busted and/or prevented from organizing, and, ironically, tax breaks and incentives are used by the poor to entice the rich to invest in their countries. (Krishna, 2009, p. 161)

Contrastingly, the HD paradigm contends that goals like maximizing human empowerment and ensuring environmental sustainability should not be sacrificed on the altar of corporate profits.

A third area of difference is that neoliberalism supports unfettered international movement of capital, but does not support an enabling environment for human freedom, and indeed, it benefits from imposing restrictions on human movement across borders. Neoliberal policies support the opening of trading borders and lifting of restrictions against trade (following certain points of classical liberalism first laid down by Adam Smith and David Ricardo). But states typically concomitantly impose restrictions on migration of people across borders and limit freedom of movement for those who labor to make and consume goods. Thus, "the economic profits and gains of neoliberal globalization rest to a significant degree on the relative immobility of unskilled and semiskilled labor," as people from the Global South find themselves confronted by "energetic policing of immigration" in countries of the Global North (Krishna, 2009, p. 160). Critics like David Harvey likewise argue that neoliberal policies actually serve to create or re-create class divisions and inequality between people groups, especially at the international level (Harvey, 2007, p. 16). Thus, Harvey maintains that neoliberalism is an ideology aiming to enrich the wealthy at the expense of the poor. The HD ideology, on the other hand, aims to benefit and empower all humans and encourage the maximum freedoms possible, including freedom of movement and choice.

Indeed, the policies that the HD paradigm supports tend toward promoting human freedom and empowering humans in every capacity, as seen in the first HDR report of 1990, which enumerates recommended policy changes to improve HD (Table 2.3). HD does not abandon the goal of promoting economic growth, recognizing as Aristotle did, that growth and income are important to humans for what it can do for them. The main shift in policy orientation is a return to the Keynesian idea that the market needs to be properly managed, but more to the point, that "what matters is how economic growth is managed and distributed for the benefit of the people" (UNDP, 1990, p. 3). The first HDR further stated that governments and development policies need to put more resources into social services, like health and education, and less into military spending noting that "developing countries as a group spend more on the military (5.5% of their combined GNP) than on education and health (5.3%). In many developing countries, current military spending is sometimes two or three times greater than spending on education and health" (UNDP, 1990, p. 4).[9] The HD vision

Table 2.3. Restructuring Government Budget Priorities to Support Human Development

Reallocate resources from	Reallocate resources to
Curative medical facilities	Primary health care programs
Highly trained doctors	Paramedical personnel
Urban services	Rural services
General education	Vocational education
Subsidizing tertiary education	Subsidizing primary and secondary education
Expensive housing for the privileged groups	Sites and services projects for the poor
Subsidies for vocal and powerful groups	Subsidies for inarticulate and weaker groups
The formal sector	The informal sector and programs for the unemployed and underemployed

Source: UNDP, 1990, p. 4.

calls on governments to restructure their budget priorities as displayed in Table 2.3 to ensure an enabling environment for humans, guaranteeing access to capabilities so that all humans have the ability to function in ways they see fit for decent and flourishing lives.

As Table 2.3 illustrates, the HD vision is visibly dedicated to enabling all humans to have more choices and opportunities, especially those people of a lower socio-economic class and who have less income or wealth. This contrasts with business as usual in international politics and the international economy, where one often sees the gifting of economic benefits, political favors, skewed laws, and special opportunities to those who are already affluent, privileged, or advantaged.

HUMAN DEVELOPMENT AS A FORWARD-LOOKING IDEOLOGY

This chapter revealed that ideology is an important concept that guides how humans live, think, and behave in their political, economic, cultural, and other dimensions of life. Ideologies (over)simplify reality and help people interpret how the world is and how it should be. Ideologies that have a global vision may be called ideologies of globalization, of which there are many (such as capabilities globalism, market globalism, justice globalism, and various religious globalisms). Indeed, ideologies are everywhere and in everything humans do, from local to global governance, in implanting and negotiating power politics, to dictating the very intimate actions of our lives.

Among these competing ideologies, *capabilities globalism* (i.e., the HD ideology) represents an important but largely under-examined ideology of globalization, one that contests the supremacy of the nation-state while simultaneously offering an alternative vision inclusive of global humanity. The HD ideology is normatively grounded, explicitly critical of real world injustices, and represents a distinct and conscious effort to establish a new paradigm for globalization, global development, and global policy-making in contradistinction to other globalisms. Much like liberalism, the intellectual roots of the HD ideology lie in the middle strata, meaning that while the ideology offers a way forward on achieving a more just world (connected to its vision of human freedom and agency), it has mostly championed gradual reforms and has not challenged the status quo as sharply as some of the other globalization counter-ideologies.[10]

The HD ideology is a paradigm of its own, a set of beliefs, norms, and ideals, that guide human thinking and action on how the world is and should be. Prominent authors of its core texts also include men from the Global South (such as Amartya Sen and Mahbub ul Haq) and women from the Global North (like Martha Nussbaum), thus reflecting a more diverse (and global) composition of authors than many competing ideologies of globalization. The next chapter takes a look at the role of such intellectuals in creating and promoting HD as a new development paradigm.

NOTES

1. UNGA. 2015. "Resolution Adopted by the General Assembly on 25 September 2015. Transforming Our World: The 2030 Agenda for Sustainable Development" Resolution A/RES/70/1. Minor formatting changes have been made to allow for better readability in the text. Italics have been added by the authors of this book.

2. This is a simplistic version of the Marxist interpretation of ideology from Marx and Engel's book *The German Ideology* and which was taken up by later Marxists and re-interpreted and utilized in different ways (by Vladimir Lenin, for instance). Indeed, it is more in the interpretation of Marx and Engels than in the text itself that we see the use of ideology, but it nevertheless has influenced

society's interpretation of ideology as manipulative. For more on Marx and Engels and ideology, see, e.g., Geuss (1981) or Elster (1985).

3. As Martill and Schindler (2020, p. 11) argue, "All true theory is distinct from ideology, and all true theory is ideology. This fundamental paradox is, on the one hand, unacknowledged by positivist science." Hence, they highlight the importance of applying reflexivity to "understand the ideological credentials of one's own tools of analysis" (6).

4. There have been several attempts to catalogue and compare the different ideologies of globalization. At a general level, there are studies which have identified ideological differences between the political left vs. political right when it comes to globalization (e.g., Noël and Thérien, 2008). Others have made distinctions between ideological approaches which are pro-rich vs. pro-poor or top-down vs. bottom-up. Other taxonomies of globalization ideologies can also be found, for instance, in Rupert (2000), Backer (2005), and De Wilde (2019).

5. Similar ideological viewpoints have been found in "Viktor Orban's Hungary, Norbert Hofer's Austria, Marine Le Pen's France, Matteo Salvini's Italy, Jaroslaw Kaczynski's Poland, Nigel Farage's United Kingdom, Pauline Hanson's Australia, Ivan Duque's Colombia, Rodrigo Duterte's Philippines [and] Jair Bolsonaro's Brazil" (Steger 2020, p. 143).

6. This section, in which we describe what we call the HD ideology draws from Joshi (2021a).

7. While some people can use money to buy better healthcare, many people are excluded from healthcare systems or specific treatments in the real world due to discriminatory practices and rules governing "eligibility," "citizenship," or "pre-existing conditions."

8. The HD approach has since grown to become a prominent paradigm for approaching global development and the HDCA has further evolved into new variants taking into consideration more and more nuanced factors as seen in the Socially Embedded Intersectional Capabilities Theory (SEICT) (Khan, 2021).

9. One reason why military spending is so high is to protect against invasions not only from neighboring states but also from countries in the Global North.

10. As Mannheim similarly contended, with respect to the ideology of liberalism in his day, "Socially, this intellectualistic outlook had its basis in a middle stratum, in the bourgeoisie, and in the intellectual class. This outlook, in accordance with the structural relationship of the groups representing it, pursue a dynamic middle course between the vitality, ecstasy, and vindictiveness of oppressed strata, and the immediate concreteness of a feudal ruling class whose aspirations were in complete congruence with the then existing reality" (1936/2015, p. 199).

CHAPTER 3

THE ROLE OF INTELLECTUALS IN GLOBALIZING HUMAN DEVELOPMENT

The HD ideology promoted by the UN is rooted in the Human Development and Capability Approach (HDCA). The HDCA has a strong grounding and foundation in academic and philosophical circles, among development practitioners, and with groups and organizations devoted to identifying what it means to live the best human life. While it is difficult to identify the origins of ideas and ideologies, this chapter reviews how intellectuals contributed to the development of the HDCA and it assesses how individual academics and academic organizations contributed to globalizing the HD ideology worldwide.

Individual academics have been theorizing, practicing, and promoting HDCA ideas in the twentieth and twenty-first centuries. What is more, in contrast to the dominance of Western men in creating and promoting the mainstream international development approaches that the UN and World Bank endorsed during the Cold War, many of the key academic figures involved in advancing the HDCA paradigm are brilliant non-Western intellectuals. Such men and women offered differing standpoints, perspectives, and experiences, influencing how people understand and practice international development today. The lives, philosophies, publications, and influence of key academics and practitioners reveal that it is not just governments or public policies that have the power to shift societies and transform the way that humans think about their place in the world.

The spread of new development ideas was also enabled by processes of globalization, such as new communication technologies acting as magnifiers for their views. The social dimension of globalization involves increases in the speed and volume of communication between people across time and space. The main processes covered in this chapter that led to globalizing the HD paradigm are those of written and oral communication mainly through published books, journal articles, and networking and presentations facilitated by academic organizations and institutions. The technologies that allowed for such communication include broadcasting, digitization, the internet, and other technological inventions in communication and transportation providing the very means to travel and meet worldwide. Such technologies allowed academics and practitioners to communicate their ideas about the HDCA to a global audience. One of the prominent associations supporting such intellectual activity is the Human Development and Capability Association. Through academic associations and other organizations, and in their individual work, academics and practitioners prioritized and emblemized HD concepts and ideas as a new development paradigm, suggesting that it should be the guiding force for policy or practical interventions in human lives.

Ultimately, many academics, practitioners, public servants, and international civil servants have contributed to the HDCA. Three famous contributors and founders of the ideas that we examine in this chapter are Amartya Sen, Martha Nussbaum, and Mahbub ul Haq. But they were not alone in their endeavors, and below we also mention some of the others whose contributions have been important to expanding and globalizing the HDCA framework and paradigm.[1] Perhaps most important for globalizing the HD paradigm was the United Nations Development Programme (UNDP), under the aegis of its former Administrator William H. Draper III. In the 1980s, Mahbub ul Haq convinced Draper to invite a team to work on formulating a new publication and index to measure and to think of development practice in a new way. That publication became known as the Human Development Report (HDR), published almost annually since 1990. The 1990 report not only presented the HD paradigm as a new way of thinking about international economic and social arrangements between states and people, but it also introduced the Human Development Index (HDI), a simple metric for measuring the well-being of people that was not based solely on average income levels in a society.

The HDCA is not the first or only paradigm of development to be influential. The history of development has been marked by overlapping arrivals and departures of development ideas which became prominent for a while before eventually getting sidelined by new ways of thinking about, framing, and conceiving development (e.g., Rist, 2008; Pieterse, 2010). Since development ideas are always in flux and competing against each other, there is no guarantee that any newcomer will succeed or remain in a position of influence in the intellectual marketplace (e.g., Alkire and Ritchie, 2007; McNeill, 2007). In this struggle among competing ideas and ideologies of development, the HDCA was refined and promoted through the HDRs and HDI, and it has actively challenged other development ideas and paradigms, particularly those that promote priorities such as state-based or privatized infrastructure building or economic growth over more individual-centered and human-based needs (e.g., Joshi and O'Dell, 2015 and 2017; Hirai, 2017).

ACADEMICS ON THE HUMAN DEVELOPMENT AND CAPABILITY APPROACH

The rest of this chapter explores the ways in which particular individuals and intellectual institutions have been promoting and globalizing the HDCA. It reinforces how and why intellectuals and practitioners created and latched on to the HDCA as opposed to subscribing to other development paradigms.

AMARTYA SEN

One of the most important academics to develop HD as a new framework is Amartya Sen, an economic philosopher who has written voluminously on economic development and human capabilities from the 1960s to the present. Sen is well known for challenging traditional notions of social choice theory, welfare economics, and historic rationalizations for why famines occurred. His large *oeuvre* (i.e., collection of writings) heavily emphasizes ensuring that economic policies are concerned about what people are able to do or be (their *capabilities*) rather than what people have (as in, how much wealth or income).[2]

One of Sen's first and most influential memories as a child was his encounter with a man who had been stabbed with a knife in the street and who bled to death after seeking work one day in Dhaka, then a city in India that is now in Bangladesh (as Sen describes in his book *Development as Freedom*, p. 8). Sen was only 10 years old then and was sitting in his garden where the man, Kadar Mia, rushed in upon him one evening, bleeding profusely. Kadar Mia, a Muslim, was stabbed by a Hindu nationalist in one of the many instances of communal violence occurring in India at the time. The reason Sen relates the story multiple times in his writing is because the reason Kadar Mia was on the street that fateful night was because he had to leave the safety of his house and neighborhood in search of a job. Since his options were so few, he was forced to put himself in harm's way by venturing into parts of the city that were unsafe for someone of his background, and he paid for it with his life. Sen points to this story as one of those moments in time that changed his view and set his life on a new course. What this experience helped Sen understand—and helps us remember today—is that it does not always matter what is going on in the national economy, how much national income is being made at the aggregate level, or even how much money individuals can obtain, if there are no or very few job opportunities or freedom in the society.

Sen's writings on the themes of capabilities, freedom, and choice are numerous. The ideas are well summarized in his book *Development as Freedom* (1999), published as a culmination of many of his shorter articles and presentations. Sen's publications challenge standard Western notions of economic progress and development, re-center the focus of development on human lives, and in the process have contributed to creating, disseminating, and globalizing the HD ideology. It is significant that Sen's education and career was motivated by the goal of identifying how governments and society could pursue policies that would ensure human well-being (and avoid such losses of life or unfreedoms that Sen observed firsthand as a child). Sen obtained his tertiary education (two BA degrees, an MA, and a PhD) in economics. He then spent most of his career as a Professor of Economics in universities in India, England, and the United States from the 1950s to the 2010s (as of 2023 he is the Lamont University Professor at Harvard University) while also spending time in government and working with inter-governmental organizations (IGOs) and other intellectual institutions.

It was not only Sen's experience meeting Kadar Mia but also the foundational family support, education, and challenges that his society was facing during his childhood that pointed him to a career in which he investigated how changing economic policies might better meet human needs. Sen was born in 1933 in Santiniketan, a city in West Bengal in India, near the border of what is now Bangladesh, an area under British rule until independence in 1947. He grew up in a family and a society that was dealing with enormous changes to the political and economic systems under which they lived, and Sen benefitted from the discussion and dialogue to which he was exposed early on, considering that his parents were heavily involved in politics and his father was an academic (Sen relates these discussions and influence in his 2021 autobiography *Home in the World: A Memoir*).

The challenges facing India during his childhood were grave: religious violence and social upheaval, economic dependence and resistance against colonialism, political stalemates, independence movements, and inequality. One of the most challenging issues was that of famine. Sen's introduction to famine was one of personal experience since 3 million people died of starvation in the West Bengal famine of 1943 when Sen was still a boy. Sen later studied and wrote much on the topic of famine for which he is famous (for example, in his 1981 book *Poverty and Famines*). In his writings, Sen argued that famine is not a matter of lack of goods (in this case, food). Rather, it is a lack of choice or ability to gain the goods (in economic terms, entitlements) and therefore the fault of the government policies and politicians by not creating a supportive and free environment in which people have the necessary capabilities to obtain what they need.

MARTHA NUSSBAUM

Martha Nussbaum is another prolific intellectual who has transcended academic boundaries and borders and overcome typical limits to academic writing and research by combining multiple disciplines in her work. Nussbaum, who has been writing extensively from the 1960s to the present, is currently the Ernst Freund Distinguished Service Professor of philosophy and law at the University of Chicago (from 1999 to the publication of this book in 2023). She is well known for her analyses (and novel interpretations) of Ancient Greek philosophical plays, writings, and ideas (particularly Aristotelian notions of human welfare), culminating in her concern with exploring human and animal functionings and human flourishing, investigating what humans need, desire, and do that makes their lives worth living. But in HDCA circles, she is best known for her philosophical attempt to create a list of capabilities that are necessary for humans to access in order to thrive, and which could ultimately be used to guide government policies to make human lives better (especially beginning with her book *Sex and Social Justice*).

Nussbaum's education (in American universities where she obtained a BA, MA, and PhD, the last from Harvard), and early career, were devoted to analyzing how ancient Greek poets, playwrights, and philosophers conceptualized the good life, and what that could mean for our understanding of human and animal life today. Nussbaum peppers her work with true stories about people facing specific limiting conditions, of women she met in developing countries who were not able to live well or enjoy a decent quality of life. The aforementioned book, *Sex and Social Justice* (1999b), is a culmination of several previously published essays. In the first few pages, Nussbaum writes about Seleha Begum, a Bangladeshi woman who defied gender norms to work on her farm and save herself and her family from losing their livelihood when her husband became disabled (1999b, pp. 3–4). Later, Nussbaum mentions another example of an Indian woman she met named Metha Bai, who, after her husband's death, could not leave her house because of gender and caste restrictions, meaning she was at the mercy of those around her for survival (p. 29). Confronting and being moved by women's lived experiences like Begum and Bai, along with her work together with Amartya Sen at the United Nations University World Institute of

Development Economics Research (UNU-WIDER) in the 1980s and '90s, encouraged Nussbaum to consider and expand upon basic philosophical questions about quality of life, human flourishing, women's rights and opportunities, and in essence, what makes a human life worth living.

Her critical and novel approaches to analyzing Greek literature before working with UNU-WIDER created a foundation for what she would pursue related to philosophizing about human flourishing through her writings, presentations, and support of intellectual institutions during her illustrious career. Nussbaum's position as professor at prestigious American universities (Harvard, Wellesley, Brown, and the University of Chicago) from the 1970s to the present acted as a boon for her to be able to devote time to researching and writing about human flourishing as well as other topics. As with Sen, Nussbaum's publications on human functioning and capabilities have been widely cited and used as a foundation for how to think about humans living the good life. In essence, Nussbaum's philosophical considerations of a list of capabilities that humans would need to be fully human (along with investigating whether functioning is a necessary component of capabilities), add to and illuminate Sen's analysis of human freedoms and capability (or potentialities) undertaken from a more economic standpoint.[3]

MAHBUB UL HAQ

In a similar way that Amartya Sen and Martha Nussbaum were central developers of the HD paradigm, Mahbub ul Haq (1934–1998), another intellectual heavyweight, was one of its central promoters. He was a development practitioner working on international trade, economic governance, and negotiations for the government of Pakistan, the World Bank, and the UN. He acted, in a way, as an organizational manager who brought the HDCA from philosophy into practice by envisioning policies, measurements, and practices that would be acceptable to governments and politicians and that would better meet human needs. Haq spent most of his life and career in the Pakistani government creating and implementing economic policies, conducting policy analysis, and engaging with development practice at the World Bank and later at the UNDP. He was also a prolific writer (for an excellent edited volume that reviews Haq's work and influence, see

Haq and Ponzio, 2008). Haq's experience and knowledge led him to provide leadership in creating the first HDR published by the UNDP which included a then controversial new development measurement, the Human Development Index (HDI).

Like Sen, Haq was born in India before the country gained independence from the United Kingdom (UK) and he was well aware of the challenges to human thriving evident in his own community. As the independence movement in India matured, political leaders rose to promote nationalism and statehood and create political parties to run the new government. Muhammad Ali Jinnah led the Muslim League while Mahatma Gandhi and Jawaharlal Nehru led the Indian National Congress Party. The latter was a secular party with a strong Hindu following. Although these leaders were able to discuss, negotiate, and work together on gaining independence as achieved by India on August 15, 1947, they were unable to bridge the religious and social divisions between the Hindu and Muslim populations. Thus, India claimed independence as a secular but Hindu majority country, while Pakistan claimed independence as Muslim dominated (later, in 1971, East Pakistan seceded from Pakistan and gained independence as Bangladesh). After India's independence in 1947, mass migration occurred with millions of Muslims relocating to Pakistan and millions of Hindus relocating to India. The unimaginable sectarian violence carried out in the aftermath of the mass population resettlement has continued into the 2020s, sometimes lying dormant for years and then reigniting. India and Pakistan still struggle with the challenges of sectarianism, nationalism, and religious movements, much like how many Western countries still suffer from problems of discrimination and violence against individuals who follow the Muslim or Hindu religions.

The experience of social division and sectarian violence as a child led Haq to become deeply concerned about economic growth, poverty, and nation-state building. After graduating at the top of his class at Cambridge University, Haq worked in the Pakistani government to build and strengthen its fledgling economic institutions by creating and implementing economic policies. Serving .as Chief Economist under General Ayub Khan's Administration in the 1960s led him to question traditional economic models of macroeconomic growth centered around maximization of Gross National Product (GNP) (Jillani and Bano, 2008). In fact, a speech he delivered in Karachi, Pakistan, in 1968, known as the "22 Families Speech," incited angst in domestic Pakistani politics and may have sparked the revolution that followed (2008, pp. 23–24). In the speech, he challenged traditional economic methods such as import-substitution policies and concentration on macroeconomic growth. He argued that such traditional economic methods had grossly enriched the wealthy without benefiting most of the rest of the population, in effect, keeping them in poverty. The Pakistani revolution that followed, and the change in government, gave Haq the opportunity to find employment elsewhere and he moved to the World Bank where he worked for 12 years. He then served a second stint in economic policy-making in Pakistan under the General Zia ul Haq administration in the 1980s (for which he was much criticized) causing him to turn back to international development policymaking, this time at the UNDP.

Haq deeply influenced development thinking and practice at the World Bank and UNDP. He supported policy changes and encouraged the World Bank to shift its focus from infrastructure development to assessing and discussing poverty alleviation along with President Robert McNamara (President of the World Bank from 1968–1981). Yet, Haq also realized the World Bank would not be the best international organization to facilitate a change in the focus and practice of development. The World Bank was too much connected to the wealth of developed countries and subservient to their ideologies. It favored a focus on traditional macroeconomic growth theories and policies (which also became known as neoliberalism in the 1980s and which supported conditionalities on government loans, called structural adjustment programs). Haq thus turned to the UNDP, then run by his friend William H. Draper III. Haq had also developed a long-standing friendship with his college peer and academic rival from Cambridge, Amartya Sen. What a pair they were, Sen and Haq: both economists, but Sen pursuing a philosophical and academic career while Haq was deeply embedded in practical policy development and implementation. Haq reached out to Sen to ask him to consult with his team that was working on an alternative economic development paradigm at the UNDP in the 1980s, and after much cajoling and pressure, Sen agreed.

The UNDP team worked together under Haq's leadership on "developing a new paradigm—a human development philosophy—that would change the conventional wisdom about concentrating on GNP growth" (Haq and Ponzio 2008, pp. 37–38). The result was the first Human Development Report (HDR) published in 1990. Its contents were inspiring and controversial, for it offered a framework and a way forward that had been missing in mainstream development arguments, practice, and thinking (albeit the ideas had been latent and forming for decades in international discussions, conferences, and negotiations on development as discussed in chapter 5). Just as Haq had done in his Karachi speech, the first HDR challenged status quo traditional economic thinking. The report argued that while income was important, income alone did not give insight into what a human was able to do and be in society and did not offer practical measurements or guidelines for supporting individual human functioning and capabilities. For perhaps the first time since the World Bank eclipsed the UNDP as the primary multilateral development agency in the 1960s, the UNDP reemerged as a thought-leader in international development and once again forged its preeminence and respected standing in the development community.[4]

ASSESSING THE ACADEMIC GLOBALIZING OF THE HDCA BY SEN, NUSSBAUM, AND UL HAQ

This section provides an analysis of the cumulative impact and relevance of Amartya Sen, Martha Nussbaum, and Mahbub ul Haq, specifically focusing on their academic research and publications. A common way to assess the influence of an academic is by identifying the number of publications—the extent to which the author wrote and published their work—compared with other similar or more influential writers, and to assess where their work is published (such as by widely read, disseminated, and respected publishers and publications). Several analytic databases give researchers the ability to search abstracts and citations, making connections between and within academic journal articles and books to understand the impact of particular works.[5] The databases offer data on measurements that assess academic influence such as the H-index (Hirsch, 2005), the G-Index (Egghe, 2006), the i10-index (Google Scholar), and the Impact Factor (IF) of a journal. One of the most widely used, even with its flaws, is the H-index which we use in the following discussion of academic influence.[6] The index combines an author's quantity of publications and their impact as measured by citations. According to its creator, the H-index aims to "quantify the cumulative impact and relevance of an individual's scientific research output" (Hirsch 2005, p. 165).

As mentioned earlier, Sen published and presented his research widely during his academic career. His curriculum vitae lists 21 books, 407 journal articles, and numerous other writing pieces and speeches, many of them on social choice theory, welfare economics, economic measurement, and economic development. Searches on bibliographic databases produce thousands of results,[7] and even though many of the sources included in such searches are reprints or perhaps redundant citations or translations of his works, the sheer volume gives a strong indication of how much Sen wrote and published.

But merely listing the number of Sen's publications does not tell us enough about the influence or extent of his work, so it is useful to compare him to his intellectual peers. In 1998, Sen received a Nobel Prize, also known as the Sveriges Riksbank Prize in Economic Sciences in Memory of Alfred Nobel. The prize recognized Sen's "contributions to welfare economics."[8] As of 2023 the Nobel Prize in Economic Sciences has been awarded to 92 individual economists with 53 prizes awarded (some awards were shared between two or three laureates). Only 25 people received the award individually, Sen being one of them.[9] The Nobel Prizes include a major ceremony, a bespoke diploma for each prize, and major news coverage. In all, only 615 prizes over all the Nobel Prize categories have been awarded since inception in 1901 after Alfred Nobel committed his wealth to honor "those who, during the preceding year, shall have conferred the greatest benefit to humankind" through their work in such disciplines as physics, chemistry, physiology, or medicine, literature and peace, and later economics was added as a category.[10]

The list of Nobel laureate economists for the 10-year period from 1991–2000 are compared in Table 3.1 using their H-index, number of citations, and number of publications listed on Scopus (as of June 2023). The table is sorted by the H-index to show the laureates' relative influence. As shown by the highlighted row, Sen was second from the top in influence (both when compared by the H-index and total publication numbers) and only surpassed by James Heckman (2000 laureate) who won a dual award "for his development of theory and methods for analyzing selective samples."[11] When sorted by total citation numbers, Sen comes in fourth, surpassed by Robert Merton (1997 laureate),

Table 3.1.   Amartya Sen's Academic Influence Compared to Nobel Prize–Winning Peers

Nobel Prize Laureate and Year	Publications Listed	H-Score	Scopus Author Identifier
James Heckman (dual award 2000)	245	93	7102737699
Amartya Sen (1998)	**218**	**61**	**7401592846**
Daniel McFadden (dual award 2000)	95	44	56260191600
Reinhard Selten (triple-person award 1994)	74	33	6602907525
Douglas North (dual award 1993)	69	26	7102197724
Robert C. Merton (dual award 1997)	61	27	7003952399
James Mirrlees (dual award 1996)	61	20	6505807247
John Harsanyi (triple-person award 1994)	57	21	6603833317
Robert Lucas Jr. (1995)	53	33	7201704033
Gary Becker (1992)	53	25	7401553445
Robert Fogel (dual award 1993)	50	19	7005348741
Robert Mundell (1999)	36	9	7004487955
Ronald Coase (1991)	29	16	6506602060
William Vickrey (dual award 1996)	25	8	16416384200
Myron Scholes (dual award 1997)	15	10	24548407600
John Forbes Nash (triple-person award 1994)	12	7	7202698543

Source: Elsevier's Scopus database. Search conducted June 2023.

Robert Lucas Jr. (1995 laureate), and once again, James Heckman (2000 laureate). It is clear from this peer-comparison that Sen's work is highly influential on account of the number of works he published, the total number of citations of his work, which is higher than most of his peers, as well as how he outranks all but one of his laureate peers with the H-index score.

Sen's top 10 works with the most citations listed on Scopus include his books: *Poverty and Famines: An Essay on Entitlement and Deprivation* (16,351 citations), *Inequality Reexamined* (16,059 citations), *The Idea of Justice* (15,547 citations), *Commodities and Capabilities* (12,956 citations), *Capability and Well-Being* (7,882 citations), with the next two being translations of *Development as Freedom* into Portuguese (11,310) and Spanish (9,439). Google Scholar shows similar results except that it lists the English language edition of *Development as Freedom* as Sen's top-cited book with 52,970 citations and Google Scholar author profile reports 333,974 citations in total for Sen's work.[12]

Sen's journal articles and speeches have also been widely cited and reprinted, and one especially worth noting is a speech he gave at Stanford University on May 22, 1979 (in the Tanner lecture series). That speech tipped the balance of traditional international development thinking and practice, and it challenged moral philosophical theories of utilitarianism and Rawlsian social justice. Using an example of how such theories distribute resources among individuals in society, Sen showed that a person who is already not doing well would be worse off under most conceptions of justice. He asks how such a situation would be appropriate under any real-world circumstances, and then offers an alternative that would focus on capabilities (Sen, 1979). The lecture has been discussed and cited enormously and reprinted in multiple formats.

Finally, in considering how influential Sen's ideas have been, we can assess not only the number of citations of a given work, but how that work has been taken up and discussed by peers and presented to the general public. Sen's most cited book, *Development as Freedom,* is a culmination of many of his previously published articles and lectures given at the World Bank in 1996. The book was written to inspire public discourse and reconsider public policy on development and poverty issues, as Sen relates in the preface to its first edition (1999, pp. xi–xiv). The book inspired dozens of book reviews written by well-known academics, journalists, and cultural critics, and has been mentioned in the title of hundreds of works.[13] The book reviews reveal that Sen's book was widely praised and inspired intense debate and discussion, which was exactly what Sen sought. As he says in the introduction: "If my arguments arouse any interest, and lead to more public discussion of these vital issues, I would have reason to feel well rewarded" (1999, pp. xiv) and indeed, he has been.[14]

Some reviews of *Development as Freedom* conveyed that Sen did not go far enough in his criticism of the reigning development paradigm by arguing that he either missed an important part of the framework that would make it more practically applicable (Deneulin, 2005; Rosati, 2018), lacked a geographical analysis (Rosati, 2018), or did not offer policy prescriptions for how to adequately bring about human well-being (Cooper, 2000; Flaurbaey, 2002). Another concern was that Sen's work was missing a more plausible assessment and discussion of the community environment in which people make choices or pursue the functioning of their capabilities (Deneulin, 2005, p. 508). Sen delighted in and actively engaged in the debate, thereby mirroring the emphasis he has placed on the importance of dialogue and discussion throughout his career.[15]

Nussbaum is likewise widely read with publications in multiple disciplines including philosophy and legal studies, but also in the areas of literary criticism, development economics, feminism, human rights, and cultural criticism. A *New York Times Magazine* article called her "the most prominent female philosopher in America" (Boynton, 1999), and one might say "the most prominent philosopher regardless of her gender" considering her extensive publications, the impact of her work across multiple disciplines, and the clarity with which she has brought deep philosophical problems to the American and global public. One reason for her public acclaim (as well as intense criticism from her opponents) is that she has always been willing to discuss challenging topics where she saw the need for social justice. For instance, her work addresses topics of gay and lesbian rights, women's rights, the rights of sex workers, pornography, female genital mutilation, female objectification, and many other provocative topics that inspire both admiration and vitriol from her peers and critics. But perhaps most controversial of all, Nussbaum argued in many of her works for a universal list of capabilities that could be used to create socially just public policies and laws. Her curriculum vitae lists 28 books in English (some of which have also been translated into other languages), 504 journal articles published between 1972 and 2022, and 70 review articles. Bibliographic database searches reveal thousands of results that include shorter articles, speeches, op-eds, etc.[16]

The major concept that Nussbaum contributed to the HDCA was the discussion of how capabilities relate to women. Indeed, Nussbaum began building her version of the capability approach through early books, particularly *The Fragility of Goodness* (1986), and journal articles in which she analyzed Aristotle's ideas on human well-being and the good life. Those ideas eventually became the substance of her books. The specific books about the capabilities approach gaining the most notoriety include *Sex and Social Justice* (cited 3,638 times according to Google Scholar), a collection of essays that she had previously written and published in various forms. Excerpts from that book have also been published in multiple other works since 1999, for example, in Micheline Ishay's (2023) *Human Rights Reader*. More influential books by Nussbaum then followed up on and expanded upon the idea of a universal list of capabilities including *Women and Human Development: The Capabilities Approach* published in 1999 (cited by 13,875) and *Creating Capabilities: The Human Development Approach*, published in 2011 (cited by 8,952).

Nussbaum received dozens of honors and prizes for her philosophical work associated with the HDCA (her CV lists 65 Honorary Degrees, the last one from Harvard University awarded in 2022 where she had also received her MA and PhD and was among the Society of Fellows in the 1970s, as well as 62 other honors and awards that include fellowships and book awards). The Holberg Prize awarded to Nussbaum by the government of Norway for Philosophy and Culture in 2021 honors academics with a goal "to increase awareness of the value of academic scholarship in the humanities, social sciences, law and theology."[17] A comparative analysis of 10 Holberg peer laureate winners (2012–2021) as shown in Table 3.2 reveals that Nussbaum is ahead of most of her

Table 3.2. Martha Nussbaum's Academic Influence Compared to Holberg Prize–Winning Peers

Holberg Laureate and Year	Publications Listed	H-Score	Scopus Author Identifier
Cass R. Sunstein (2018)	354	69	7006153931
Martha Nussbaum (2021)	**234**	**39**	**7102451262**
Bruno Latour (2013)	140	41	6603524164
Griselda Pollock (2020)	93	12	37079415800
Onora O'Neill (2017)	92	26	7003475713
Manuel Castells (2012)	69	28	7005236804
Jürgen Kocka (2011)	58	13	22234000400
Paul Gilroy (2019)	57	17	6603830966
Stephen Greenblatt (2016)	49	8	26035655300
Michael Cook (2014)	13	5	56572031700
Natalie Zemon Davis (2010)	12	12	26631742700

Source: Elsevier's Scopus database. Search conducted June 2023.

peers in influence and dissemination of her ideas when it comes to comparisons of H-index scores and number of publications. Nussbaum is second when considering the number of publications recorded in Scopus database and when sorted by H-Index score and number of citations, Nussbaum only trails Cass Sunstein (2018 laureate) and Bruno Latour (2013 laureate). While not everyone in the Holberg Laureate list is from the same academic discipline (they range across philosophy, literature, history, and more), the 10 included in Table 3.2 are similar in the way that academics cite each other's work in their own work, which tells us something about the level of influence.[18] Clearly, Nussbaum's works are widely cited and discussed compared to her peers across multiple disciplines.

It is not only that Nussbaum has published widely, been astoundingly honored with awards and prizes, and been extensively cited by peers in her field, but the depth and controversy of her ideas has raised an immense amount of discussion and dialogue on issues associated with human well-being. Considering the response to two of her books about capabilities (*Sex and Social Justice* and *Women and Human Development*, both published in 1999) will help us better understand Nussbaum's influence and the extent to which she helped to globalize the HD ideology. Prominent reviews of her works range from those that offer high praise along with mixed and technically oriented discussions of weaknesses in her argument (Fricker, 2000; Young, 2001; Kamtekar, 2002), to pointedly *ad feminam*, vitriolic attacks (Harpham, 2002), to those who take up specific ideas presented in her text, such as how the book fits within the feminist literature (Fair, 1999), or assessing the essentialist claims that underpin the capabilities approach (Heberle, 2000).

The main praise of her work is the breadth and depth with which she analyzes and criticizes utilitarianism and Rawlsian theories of justice, and supports universal, international, essentialist versions of liberalism with a list of 10 capabilities (Fricker, 2000; Fair, 1999), although the same sources criticize her for being disjointed, unbalanced, and covering too many disciplines. Heberle suggests that Nussbaum's work does not have enough to say about "the structural imperatives of competition and the market" (2000); and Kamtekar—while praising her work on the whole—takes issue with the lack of significant and foundational grounding for the 10 capabilities, even questioning the rationale for the list in the first place (2002, p. 267). Despite such criticisms, her work has inspired dozens of articles that pursue the capabilities discussion further by debating their content, or assessing whether the capabilities approach is the best framework for improving human life.[19]

Nussbaum did not limit her time and attention only to researching and writing for academic purposes, she also worked on practical endeavors with IGOs and NGOs to apply the philosophical notions of the good life to actual analysis of people's lived experiences. In the 1980s and '90s, while working as an advisor for UNU-WIDER, she co-edited a volume with Sen, based on a conference at the institute titled *Quality of Life* (Nussbaum and Sen, 1993, cited by 5,184). Indeed, it was in the context of UNU-WIDER that Sen and Nussbaum worked together "to develop a universal cross-cultural concept of basic standards of human well-being that can be used by international organizations and governments to assess how well people are doing in particular locales" (Young, 2001, p. 820). Sen and Nussbaum both authored their own texts on the subject of capabilities, and worked within international organizations to promote their ideas as foundations for policy (and not just as abstract philosophical concepts). They also set up academic associations to promote further discussion and debate (like the Human Development and Capability Association to which we return below).

But perhaps the most influential person in making the capabilities approach become a practical policy project was Mahbub ul Haq. As noted previously, Haq's influence was more practical than academic, but he may be the most influential of these intellectuals considering how, after earning his PhD in Economics from Yale University, he strategically worked through the Pakistani government, the World Bank, and the UNDP to promote a vision of development that would change the trajectories and policies of international development practice. Indeed, Olav Stokke calls Haq "the main architect in this silent revolution in the perception of development" (2009, p. 652, fn 6). The creation of the Human Development Reports (HDRs) and their annual publication (as discussed in chapter 5) attest to Haq's significant influence on global development. Another one of Haq's major contributions is his book *Reflections on Human Development* (cited by 1,846 according to Google Scholar), a 1995 publication that discusses some of the history and challenges associated with the HD approach and the HDRs. Seeking to add to the missing evidence of Haq's academic work after he died, his widow Khadija Haq and Richard Ponzio edited a volume that reviews his life and impact called *Pioneering the Human Development Revolution: An Intellectual Biography of Mahbub ul Haq* (2008). As the preface claims: "Mahbub ul Haq profoundly changed the way development policies were framed and practiced. Haq questioned the prevalent development philosophy and pioneered the concept and practical application of the human development model, thus revolutionizing economic and social development policies" (2008, p. xiii).

To sum up, specific individuals who had the courage to take risks, the discipline to study hard, and the willingness to challenge the prevailing way of thinking about development have been influential in promoting and globalizing the HD ideology and what the authors themselves would call *a concern for capabilities* (Sen), *functioning capabilities and human flourishing* (Nussbaum), and *human development* (Haq). They wrote about and published extensively on HD ideology concepts, ideas, and philosophies. Their works have been cited and discussed by thousands in the academic world, and reviews of their work reveal how bold, how novel, how controversial, how scintillating, and how revolutionary their ideas were. What is evident is that these intellectuals were not afraid to share their ideas, to challenge outdated ways of approaching development, and to argue for a new global development paradigm to eradicate many forms of global injustice.

THE HUMAN DEVELOPMENT AND CAPABILITY ASSOCIATION

Intellectual associations building off the work of Sen, Nussbaum, Haq, and other likeminded scholars have been pivotal to promoting the HD paradigm. The Human Development and Capability Association established in 2004 (hereafter called the Association) is a prime example, as it has helped to globalize the HD approach in several important ways. First, it lends authority and legitimacy to HD ideas through committed and thorough publication and dissemination of research and reports on HDCA topics. Second, it provides networking possibilities for academics, theorists, philosophers, and practitioners to gain insight from and work with each other on expanding HDCA theories and practices, particularly in influencing government and development policies. Third, it acts as a platform for further discussion, dialogue, and democratic

engagement—both within the institutions, and among the general public—on HDCA topics.

The Association's goal is "promot[ing] high quality research in the interconnected areas of human development and capability."[20] Intellectual
work shared in various formats through the Association interrogates
the HDCA's foundational ideas and encourages intellectual exchange
about updates to HDCA theories, measurements, and practices. Its first
two presidents, Amartya Sen and Martha Nussbaum, led the Executive
Council in its formative years. The Association's interdisciplinary work
is also evident in leadership choices as well as in the thematic networking groups available to members and non-members alike (Table 3.3).
Members create the thematic groups to support research and collaborate on particular HDCA issues, as shown in column 2 of Table 3.3.
Thousands of people have signed up at one time or another (including
this book's authors) to be included, showing the extent and reach of
the Association.[21] The thematic groups meet to plan conference panel

Table 3.3. HDCA Association Presidents (2004–2023) and Thematic Groups (as of 2023)

HDCA Presidents, Years Served, and Main Academic Discipline (listed in chronological order)	HDCA Thematic Groups (as of 2023)
Amartya Sen (2004–2006) Economics	Children and Youth (C&Y)
Martha Nussbaum (2006–2008) Philosophy	Education (E)
Frances Stewart (2008–2010) Development Studies	Empowerment and Collective Capabilities (E&CC)
Kaushik Basu (2010–2012) Economics	Ethics and Development (E&D)
Tony Atkinson (2012–2014) Economics	Foundational Issues in the Capability Approach (FI)
Henry Richardson (2014–2016) Philosophy	Gender and Sexuality (G&S)
Ravi Kanbur (2016–2018) Economics	Health and Disability (H&D)
Ingrid Robeyns (2018–2020) Philosophy	Horizontal Inequality (HI)
Jay Drydyk (2020–2022) Philosophy	Human Rights (HR)
Melanie Walker (2022–2024) Higher Education	Human Security (HS)
	Indigenous Peoples (IP)
	Participatory Methods
	Quantitative Research Methods
	Sustainable Human Development (SHD)
	Technology Innovation and Design (TI&D)
	Work and Employment (W&E)

Source: HDCA website: https://hd-ca.org

presentations, presentations for members and non-members through-out the year, and to engage in general networking.

The Association supports the *Journal of Human Development and Capabilities* (JHDC) (since 2009, formerly the *Journal of Human Development* 2000–2008) published by Taylor and Francis, Routledge publishing house, with 24 volumes published as of 2023. One measure of journal influence is its impact factor (IF), a measure calculated to indicate the extent to which various articles are read or considered important by scholars. The JHDC impact factor for 2021 was 2.094 (calculated from 277 citations divided by 116 documents over a four-year period from 2018–2021). The JHDC was ranked by the Web of Science at 101 out of 287 (or 64th percentile) among "development studies" journals while also being ranked among the top twenty journals in "development economics" by Google Scholar.[22] Submissions to the journal have also increased, revealing that academics have great interest in publishing on HDCA topics, with a high of 218 submissions to the journal in 2021 and an average of 145.6 submissions per year (2008–2022).[23] The journal publication rate has remained roughly the same since 2008, publishing an average of 27.4 research articles, 9.8 book reviews, and 4.4 other published content per year. In total, the journal has published 543 original research articles (January 2000–April 2023).[24]

It is useful to know what types of substantive issues the JHDC covers in order to understand how it has been helping to globalize HDCA concepts through its publications. As noted above and in Table 3.3, Association members create thematic groups to facilitate networking opportunities through list-serves, and through organizing conference panels and other types of presentations for Association members and a wider audience. Using these themes as a guide for coding JHDC publications shows the types of HDCA issues most often published.[25] Foundational issues in the capability approach (FI) constitute the topics most often published by the journal between 2000–2022, including issues such as how to measure HDCA, empirical findings and outcomes of HDCA programs or development interventions, or philosophical and conceptual ideas (top three cited articles in this category are Robeyns, 2005; Alkire, 2005; and Anand and Sen, 2000). The second most published category of articles falls under the gender and sexuality (G&S) theme, which review HDCA impacts and outcomes on varying gender groups, primarily female (top three cited articles in G&S are Folbre, 2006; Nussbaum, 2000; and Chant, 2006). The third most published theme is in empowerment and collective capabilities (E&CC), covering issues of voice and accountability, democratic engagement and dialogue, and the ability for people to work collaboratively to make their lives better (the top three cited articles in E&CC are Ibrahim, 2006; Stewart, 2005; and Cleaver, 2007).

The Association also strives to engage scholars in interdisciplinary dialogue and research and offers multiple avenues of networking and engagement through conferences, networks, groups, and membership offerings. Every year the Association creates a list of recent publications about the Capability Approach, pooling information from its members as well as records of publications. Between the years 2005 and 2013, the bibliographies were published in the JHDC with specific guidance from the publisher that the source "may be used for research, teaching, and private study purposes" (JHDC, 2005, p. 421), and in subsequent years (2014–2023) have been compiled and made available for download on the Association website.[26] The bibliographies reveal an interest in publishing on HDCA topics in English and non-English languages (including Dutch, French, German, Italian, Japanese, Lithuanian, Portuguese, Spanish, and Turkish) outside of the JHDC. They include a total of 129 books, 120 book chapters, and 485 (non-JHDC) journal articles in English plus 38 books, 46 book chapters, and 109 journal articles in languages other than English.[27]

Each year the Association hosts a conference where academics and practitioners apply to present their research in panels, share the benefits of their work and ideas through discussion and dialogue, hear speeches, and gain general networking benefits. They are a truly global organization as can be seen in the locations of the conferences (Table 3.4). Twenty conferences have been held since 2004. They have taken place in major cities around the world, including being held in Global South countries (not always true of academic conferences that are traditionally hosted by Global North associations and also held in Global North countries). Their membership is also extremely diverse, representing multiple disciplinary approaches and geographical diversity, as shown in the online member database map, reproduced in Figure 3.1. The map represents members who have signed up to share their information, discipline, and expertise to facilitate networking,

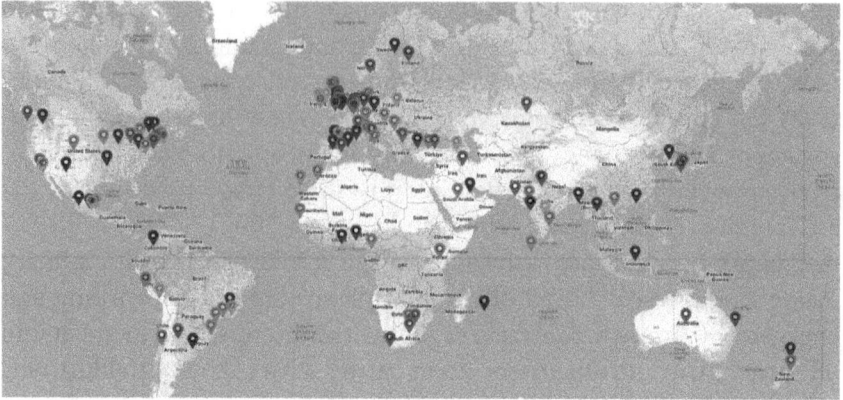

Figure 3.1. Map of HDCA Association Global Membership (2023) (2008–2022).
Source: Information provided by HDCA and Taylor and Francis. Personal communication with HDCA Representative Kathy Rosenblum on May 26, 2023.

but does not represent all Association members. Membership numbers have risen from roughly 300 in initial years, to an average of 697 from 2011–2023.[28] What is more, Table 3.4 provides additional information about the processes and mechanisms by which the Association engages in globalizing knowledge of the HDCA. People become members of the organization in order to maintain access to certain privileges, such as the ability to see and connect with other members through the website, and to gain access to journal articles from the JHDC. Membership numbers are highest toward the end of conferences since people usually obtain membership by signing up to attend an annual conference and

Table 3.4. HDCA Association Conferences (2004–2023) and Member Numbers

Conference Theme	Year	Location	Number of Attendees	HDCA Members
Enhancing Human Security	2004	Pavia, Italy	182	287
Knowledge and Public Action	2005	Paris, France	220	547
Freedom and Justice	2006	Groningen, Netherlands	204	519
Ideas Changing History	2007	New York, USA	298	548
Equality, Inclusion, and HD	2008	New Delhi, India	229	825
Participation, Poverty, and Power	2009	Lima, Peru	220	678

Human Rights and HD	2010	Amman, Jordan	180	N/A
Innovation, Development & Human Capabilities	2011	The Hague, Netherlands	373	782
Revisiting Development: Do We Assess It Correctly?	2012	Jakarta, Indonesia	320	602
HD: Vulnerability, Inclusion, and Well-Being	2013	Managua, Nicaragua	370	513
HD in Times of Crisis; Renegotiating Social Justice	2014	Athens, Greece	295	760
Capabilities on the Move: Mobility and Aspirations	2015	Washington, DC, USA	525	850
Capability and Diversity in a Global Society	2016	Tokyo, Japan	330	735
Challenging Inequalities: HD and Social Change	2017	Cape Town, South Africa	285	676
HD and Social Inclusion in an Urbanizing World	2018	Buenos Aires, Argentina	292	676
Connecting Capabilities	2019	London, United Kingdom	437	741
New Horizons: Sustainability & Justice	2020	Online due to COVID-19 Pandemic (planned location was Auckland, New Zealand)	408	706
HDCA Global Dialogue	2021	Online	830	705
Capabilities and Transformative Institutions	2022	Antwerp, Belgium, and online as hybrid conference	398	619
Vulnerability, HD, and Cooperative Re-Building in Turbulent Times	2023	Sofia, Bulgaria	N/A	706

Source: Personal communication with HDCA Representative, Kathy Rosenblum, May 26, 2023.

are financially supported to do so through professional development funds from their universities, although practitioners also attend the conference.[29]

The Association and its members create novel and innovative ways to engage scholars and practitioners on the issues, including through new modes of interacting, like the Global Dialogue Day (GDD) that took place in lieu of the 2021 annual conference, and continued in subsequent conferences.[30] The innovation was inspired by the challenges of the COVID-19 pandemic that made meeting in-person impossible and meeting online difficult. Thus, for the year 2021, the Association leaders decided to host GDD as a more accessible online experience which then was subsequently included in the 2022 and 2023 conference plans, adding another element to engagement. The GDD is an example of a process of globalization, with the organization leaders and members engaging in innovation to encourage participation. As a newsletter to members explained on September 14, 2022: GDD "is a free online event open to all. It includes parallel sessions and webinars bringing together academics, leaders, and practitioners of human development and diverse voices from across the world to discuss the most pressing global challenges and emerging challenges to human-centered development." As an example of impact, the 2021 GDD included 50 speakers with roughly 830 attendees, and the 2022 GDD included roughly 530 attendees.[31]

In sum, it is intellectual institutions like the Human Development and Capability Association that have contributed significantly to globalizing the HD paradigm. There are also other academic organizations that offer similar support to researchers on human development and capability-approach topics, some more focused on the specific issues, and others including them as a thematic area or within a larger focus on international development studies or human rights in general. These include, but are not limited to, the Academic Council on the United Nations (ACUNS), the Cambridge Capabilities Conferences (CCC), and the International Studies Association (ISA).

THE DRAMATIC RISE IN ACADEMIC PUBLICATIONS ON HUMAN DEVELOPMENT

The academic intellectuals and organizations discussed thus far in this chapter have produced massive amounts of publications over the years on HDCA topics.[32] We can assess the extent to which the HD ideology has been globalizing through academic publications and other popular writings (book publications of all types and scholarly academic work) by quantitatively examining the number of such publications over time through comparative bibliometric analysis (see Joshi, 2021b).

PUBLICATIONS ON THE HUMAN DEVELOPMENT REPORTS AND HUMAN DEVELOPMENT INDEX

Academics, journalists, researchers, IGOs, NGOs, and government agencies produce research and reports about many things, including the HD ideology. Their social influence can be felt in how government policy is made, where researchers focus their time and attention, and how development practice and implementation occurs at the international level. The human development reports (HDRs) published by the UN promote a different ideology than the World Development Reports (WDRs) produced by the World Bank. The HDRs focus on putting people at the center of analysis and expanding people's choices whereas

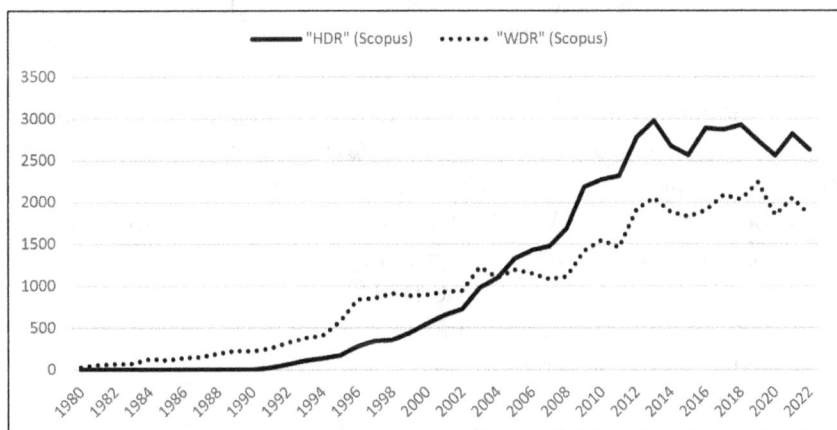

Figure 3.2. Academic Publications Mentioning Development Reports (1980–2022). *Source:* Authors' searches for "Human Development Report" and "World Development Report" in all fields by publication year on Scopus on June 15, 2023.

the WDRs tend to focus more on promoting a neoliberal economic ideology of development, poverty reduction, and improvements in infrastructure and technological capacity.[33]

Counting the number of publications referencing the HDRs over time serves as a useful proxy for ascertaining their public influence and the extent to which the HD ideology has been globalizing. Figure 3.2 demonstrates that publications citing the WDRs received slightly more attention than the HDRs during the 1990s, but the HDRs surpassed the WDRs starting in the early 2000s. This reveals that the influence of HDRs has not only been increasing over time but they have also outpaced the influence of the WDRs, a major ideological competitor, in the academic world. As studies have found, this is not only the case for academic publications but also in worldwide newspaper publications (See Joshi, 2021b; Joshi and O'Dell, 2017; and chapter 4 of this volume).[34]

Aside from the HDRs, another prominent contribution of the HD approach is the Human Development Index (HDI) which aggregates indicators of health, education, and income into one simple numerical indicator). The HDI was designed with the specific intent of challenging unidimensional metrics that treat national income as the main indicator of success in economic development (Haq, 1995; Fukuda-Parr and Shiva Kumar, 2003). The composite HDI measurement has rapidly traveled from obscurity to mainstream over the past three decades. The analysis of citations of the HDI illustrate how it has challenged neoliberal economic ideas, and how the HDI has been globalizing as a new way to measure human well-being. HDI now appears much more often in academic publications than either gross national product (GNP) or gross national income (GNI).[35] HDI still does not appear as often as the search term Gross Domestic Product or "GDP" but the search term "human development index" does appear more frequently than the search term "per capita GDP." And the ratio of mentions of GDP to HDI have decreased significantly from 6:1 in 2000 to less than 2:1 in 2020. As shown in Figure 3.3, whereas the HDI did not exist in the 1980s, it rose dramatically in popularity and already overtook "per capita GDP" in academic scholarship by the late 2000s.

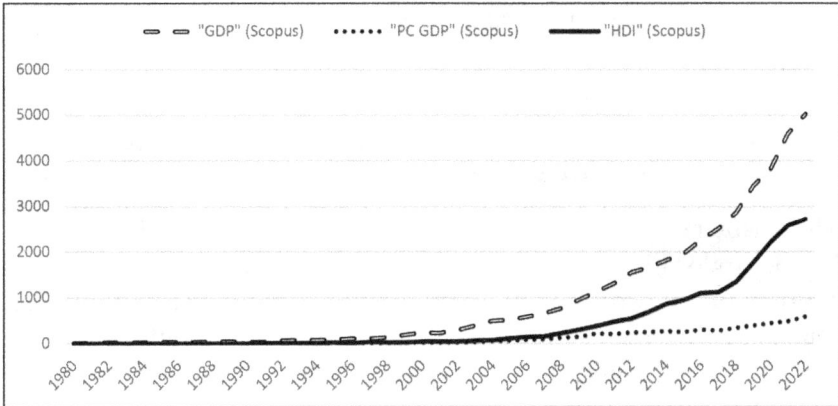

Figure 3.3. Academic Publications on HDI, GDP, and Per Capita GDP (1980–2022). *Source:* Authors' searches for "Human Development Index," "Gross Domestic Product," and "Per Capita GDP" in all fields by publication year on Scopus on June 15, 2023.

PUBLICATIONS ON HDCA THEMES AND DEVELOPMENT CONCEPTS

Another major component of the UN's approach to HD has been its promotion of large-scale global *development goals* like the 2000–2015 Millennium Development Goals (MDGs) and the 2015–2030 Sustainable Development Goals (SDGs). The UN has also linked HD to international security via the *human security* concept which it first launched in the 1994 HDR (UNDP, 1994; Thérien, 2012b). To see whether these innovations have succeeded in public discourse, we counted how many publications in the Scopus database on "development goals" and "human security" have appeared vis-à-vis those addressing the "free market," a term closely connected to neoliberalism, a prominent rival paradigm to the HDCA (see Jolly, 2003). We found that since the early 2000s, academic publications on "development goals" have overtaken the "free market," and in 2022, there were more than 10 times as many on "development goals" (34,371) than on the "free market" (1,758). The concept of "human security" (2,608 publications in 2022) has also gained considerable attention over time, now appearing more often than works on the "free market." Thus, it is quite evident that especially since the turn of the millennium, the HDRs, HDI, and "development goals" have all fared impressively well vis-à-vis the WDRs, "per capita GDP," and the "free market" in academic publications.

THE SIGNIFICANCE OF INTELLECTUALS IN GLOBALIZING THE HUMAN DEVELOPMENT IDEOLOGY

This chapter shows the extent and significance of how the HD paradigm has been globalizing among intellectuals in the academic world from 1990 to the present. The paradigm has been promoted by individual scholars and philosophers and by intellectual organizations like the Human Development and Capability Association. Although the influence of a development approach can be difficult to measure, the frequency of books, journal articles, and newspaper reports published on given development topics and approaches can give us a practical sense of which development ideas and concepts are more salient than others at a given point in time. Correspondingly, our comparative bibliometric analysis also offers considerable evidence to support the assertion that the human development paradigm has indeed been very successful in capturing international attention among intellectuals through its increasing prominence in published writings. The next chapter assesses whether the HD paradigm has had similar success influencing the discourse and practice of global mass media.

NOTES

1. The authors of this book apologize in advance if we have unintentionally left out reference to an important academic, practitioner, author, or work that should have been included.

2. See, e.g., Sen, 1979, 1981, 1999, 2009, and 2018.

3. Indeed, Sen and Nussbaum's work can be considered collectively as two sides of the coin of HDCA developed in conjunction (Crocker, 1995; Nussbaum, 1999a, 379, fn 26), as revealed in their 1993 co-edited book, *The Quality of Life,* a project they pursued together at UNU-WIDER.

4. For a good history of the UNDP's transformation over time see Murphy (2006).

5. Globally oriented information-gathering and analytic organizations (like Elsevier or Clarivate) have worked to create academic databases (such as Scopus and Web of Science), using advances in technology to combine and offer valuable insight into knowledge production (Google Scholar also offers a freely accessible database).

6. As explained on Google Scholar the "H-index is the largest number *h* such that *h* publications have at least *h* citations."

7. For example, a search for au= "Sen, Amartya Kumar" on WorldCat database January 5, 2023 found 699 results; similar searches on Scopus and Google Scholar, respectively, brought up 13,702 documents and 2,003 works.

8. Information about Amartya Sen can be found on https://www.NobelPrize .org.

9. Information on Nobel Prizes and specifically "Facts on the prize in economic sciences" can be found on https://www.NobelPrize.org.

10. Quote from Nobel's last will and testament setting up the Nobel Prize, as related on Nobel Prize. "The Man Behind the Prize—Alfred Nobel." can be found on https://www.NobelPrize.org.

11. Information about James J. Heckman can be found on https://www .NobelPrize.org.

12. Search for *Development as Freedom* on Google Scholar conducted on June 5, 2023.

13. A search on EBSCO Host and WorldCat on June 5, 2023, produced 209 sources that mention the book and the author in titles.

14. For instance, Fareed Zakaria, a well-known political commentator, reviewed the book in the *New York Times* (1999) and Richard Cooper, a Harvard University Professor of government and economics, entitled his review "The Road from Serfdom" in *Foreign Affairs Magazine* (2000), thereby comparing Sen's book to the renowned and acclaimed book *Road to Serfdom* by Friedrich Hayek.

15. In one response to what he calls the "perspicacious essays" that reviewed his work he says "I am grateful to them not only for their kindness, but also for the care with which they have examined, extended, criticized, and developed what I have tried to do" (Sen, 2002, p. 78).

16. A search on the WorldCat database for au= "Nussbaum, Marth C." January 5, 2023, returns 1,800 works; a Scopus search lists 234 works, and Google Scholar 2,310 works.

17. Information about the Holberg Prize can be found on the website "About the Holberg Prize." https://holbergprize.org.

18. In order to conduct a similar comparison, only those peers who won the Holberg award for a 10-year period (from 2012–2021) and who were in academic fields that rely heavily on citations of each other's work were included. Thus, though extremely influential in their own disciplines, the following were excluded from this analysis: Holberg laureates Marina Warner (literature), Paul Farmer (health and science), and Ruth Bader Ginsburg (legal practitioner).

19. For instance, studies have applied the capabilities approach to interpretations of the Bible (Classens, 2016), the rights of ecosystems (Crescenzo, 2013), higher education (El Khayat, 2018), and corporate responsibility (González-Cantón et al., 2019).

20. The quote is a specific statement found on many HDCA publications, including their 990 tax-exempt forms filed with the US Government Internal Revenue Service.

21. Personal communication with the HDCA Association leaders, March 30, 2023. Roughly 5,000 people are signed up through the HDCA website for the thematic or regional groups.

22. Scopus CiteScore info accessed on website: https://www.scopus.com.

23. Information provided by HDCA and Taylor and Francis. Personal communication with Kathy Rosenblum May 26, 2023. The journal has access to data going back to 2008 because that is when it started using Scholar One for submission. Total published content includes research articles, book reviews, other published content types like editorials, introductions, errata, replies, and other.

24. Authors' original analysis of each volume and issue number through Volume 24, Issue 1 (2000–2023) with research assistance from Sarah Minghini (main research assistant on this section), also supported by Ryan Dzurko and Trifol Headman.

25. Author created database, see fn 24.

26. The bibliographies were compiled by—as reported in the documents— Ingrid Robeyns (2004–2005, 2005–2006, 2006–2007), Solavia Ibrahim (2008–2009), Andrea Vigorito (2009–2010, 2010–2011, 2011–2012), Graciela Tonon (2014, 2015), Sammia Poveda (2016–2022), Matthias Kramm (2023), and HDCA representative (2007–2008, 2013).

27. This initial analysis was conducted by combining all the documents from the HDCA website and those published in the JHDC, coding for English, Non-English, whether the work was a journal article, book, or book chapter, and excluding those published in the JHDC, then finally reviewing for any repeat citations.

28. Personal communication with the HDCA Association leaders, March 30, 2023. Membership has stayed relatively stable, ranging from year to year between 650 and 825 members.

29. The membership numbers reported in Table 3.4 are point in time data provided by the HDCA administration. Records on conference attendees are close to accurate from 2007 on (before then, approximates are reported). The 2012 and 2013 conferences had a high number of attendees from the hosting country population (130 Indonesia participants out of 320 in 2012, and 189 Nicaraguan participants in 2013 out of 370).

30. Information on the Global Dialogue Day inception and initial plans was provided in personal communication from the Association administration on June 1, 2023.

31. Information gathered from the "Global Dialogue Day Programme" shared with HDCA members in the HDCA email newsletter in PDF format on September

14, 2022. Information on attendance gathered from communication with HDCA representative.

32. This section includes and builds on the analysis first published in Joshi and O'Dell, 2015 and Joshi, 2021b.

33. Several sources capture the difference in the ideology and foundation of the HDRs and WDRs (e.g., Joshi and O'Dell, 2013). On differences between the human development paradigm and the neoliberal paradigm, see Jolly, 2003.

34. Information on newspaper reporting is discussed and reviewed in chapter 4.

35. Measurements of national income sum up the final amount of goods and services bought or sold within a country, or globally by nationals of a country, and include Gross Domestic Product (GDP) for sales within the country's borders, and Gross National Product (GNP) or Gross National Income (GNI) for global sales by nationals of the country. These macroeconomic indicators of wealth are then divided by the population (per capita) to ascertain the average amount of wealth each person might be gaining in the country. The challenges with using such limited measurements to assess economic growth as well as human thriving are well documented (for example, Haq, 2003) and the HDI was created specifically to reveal such limits and offer an alternative.

CHAPTER 4

THE ROLE OF MASS MEDIA IN GLOBALIZING HUMAN DEVELOPMENT

In all political interactions, whether domestic or international, individuals or organizations that are able to shape the beliefs, values, and attitudes of others have an advantage over those who cannot.[1] Following this basic insight into the nature of human relations, international actors including mass media outlets (such as newspaper organizations or television stations), nation-states, international organizations, multi-national corporations, and transnational advocacy networks regularly use strategic political communication to persuade international target groups to change their thinking and behavior. This chapter focuses in particular on how news media reporting can promote or globalize a particular event, message, or ideology by looking at how journalists have promoted the HD ideology.

Part of the reason why the HD ideology has gained influence since the 1990s is because of the way news media have taken an interest in reporting on the Human Development Index (HDI) and Human Development Reports (HDRs) issued by the HDR Office (HDRO) of the United Nations Development Programme (UNDP). Such reporting also includes expansive coverage of the development goals agreed upon by the United Nations General Assembly (UNGA), the 2000–2015 Millennium Development Goals (MDGs), and 2015–2030 Sustainable Development Goals (SDGs).

We find that mass media generally endorses and echoes the positions and recommendations made by HDRs. Mass media is a term that refers to both the methods of communicating messages to large audiences and the organizations or actors who communicate messages.[2] One clear example of mass media endorsement of the HDRs occurred in 1997 on the front-page of the *Montreal Gazette* (see textbox 4.1), a major Canadian newspaper founded in 1778, serving as the only English language newspaper in the Québec area since 1989 (Potter, 2014). The article, written by journalist Julian Beltrame, treats the HDR as an authoritative source of development thinking, conveys core messages advocated by the UN, and expounds on HD themes that resonate with Canada's mass audience and political elites. The article first discusses the HDI as a way of measuring development and then draws the reader into a more complex understanding of international development involving the removal of impediments to human capabilities and moving beyond income as a sole measure of progress. As with many media reports citing an HDR, Beltrame's article highlights Canada's HDI ranking and explains the multidimensional concept of HD, based on a core nucleus of health, education, and living standard. The article also gives space for the UNDP's external affairs director to elaborate further on HD, and it discusses how prime ministers from two different Canadian political parties positively cited the HDR's findings to support their public policy preferences.

As seen in Beltrame's article, political communication through mass media reporting helps to promote the HD ideology as a global set of norms about international development influenced by the human development and capability approach (HDCA).[3] Journalists reporting on the HDRs and HDI around the world have thereby made an important contribution to globalizing the HD message. Indeed, in order for the ideas and norms embedded in the HDRs to be accepted and relevant, endorsement and dissemination from the mass media plays a critical

TEXTBOX 4.1. EXCERPT FROM A 1997 *MONTREAL GAZETTE* NEWSPAPER ARTICLE COVERING THE HDR[4]

For the fourth straight year, Canada is ranked as the world's best country in a United Nations report . . . This year's UN Human Development Report finds Canadians heading all others in an index meant to measure people's well-being as a function of health, educational opportunities and living standards . . . Both former prime minister Brian Mulroney and current incumbent Jean Chretien have cited the annual assessment as reason Quebecers should think twice about separating from a country others judge the world's best place to live . . . Normand Lauzon, external affairs director for the UN bureau that compiled the report, said Canada's relatively healthy and well-educated population gives it a consistently high ranking. On average incomes, Canada ranks eighth in per capita gross domestic product at $ 21,459 US. "We believe that income above a certain amount does not say it all about how people live," Lauzon said. "If we ask people in many countries, 'Would you rather have an additional $ 2,000 a year income or be healthy and have education?' most will choose health and education.

role in legitimizing them. And mass media reporting and attention to details of the reports has been crucial in getting the HDI and other content of the HDRs—in essence the HD ideology—to a global audience of the general public—basically anyone working outside of UN offices.

WHO'S REPORTING ON HUMAN DEVELOPMENT? COVERAGE OF THE HDRs AND HDIs

Daily and weekly newspapers published both in print and online are important vehicles of news media reporting. In fact, newspaper reports regularly provide a significant amount of worldwide news reporting on the annual HDRs and on HDI rankings of different countries. Newspapers and other mass media are powerful in how they shape public opinion. Studies conducted on the effects of news reporting and campaigns show significant impacts on the resulting norms and behaviors of those who are exposed to the messages. For instance, studies on mass media messages and campaigns aiming to reduce smoking and tobacco use have found these messages to have a positive effect on reducing tobacco use (Durkin et al., 2012).

Among media sources, newspapers—as private and publicly owned organizations—hold a prominent and powerful place in disseminating information to the public.[5] Newspaper methods of sharing and reporting news have faced increasing competition from broadcast media (e.g., radio and television) and online media (e.g., internet, blogs, and social media) over the past decades, which have challenged the primacy of newspaper reporting (Kovach and Rosenstiel, 2021, p. xxi). While such changes have brought about declining revenues and reduced circulation for some newspapers, it has also prompted many outlets to publish stories online through newspaper internet websites.

When assessing the influence of news media on the public, an important issue is whether or not potential audiences trust their news sources, as some people may turn away from media outlets that they perceive as biased or partial. A related issue is that changes to mass media and internet access in the contemporary era of globalization now offer some people easier access to multiple news sources and an overload of information. This has brought about changes in perceptions of news sources with some studies finding trust in mass media organizations to have declined precipitously over the course of the twentieth and into the twenty-first centuries. However, trust varies across countries and might be related to access to or competition from other news reporting mechanisms. For instance, according to one study conducted in the United States, trust in media, no matter what source, has dropped significantly from a high point (in 1976) when 72% of those polled said they had a great deal or fair amount of trust in mass media to a low of 34% (in 2022) (Brenan, 2022). Similarly, Democrats in the United States are much more likely to report trust in the media (70%) compared to independents (27%) or Republicans (14%); and only 16% of US respondents reported having a great deal or quite a lot of confidence in newspapers specifically (Brenan, 2022). A study conducted in Brazil, India, the United Kingdom, and the United States, also found that minority groups had low trust in media: "Most saw news media as not only out of touch but at times an especially harmful force that did real damage to their communities, either through neglecting them altogether or exploiting them, reinforcing harmful stereotypes, or sensationalizing in divisive and polarizing ways" (Arguedas et al., 2023). However, public opinion polls about trust in news media often do not distinguish between different media sources and therefore their results might not necessarily apply to newspaper content (Daniller et al., 2017; Tsfati et al., 2023). Indeed, a Reuters Digital News Report (the tenth edition) reveals an increase in trust in news sources worldwide after the COVID-19 pandemic "with 44% of our total sample saying they trust most news most of the time" (Newman, 2021).

Since the HDRs and HDI were first launched in 1990, newspapers have been reporting on them to the public. Table 4.1 shows results of the authors' search of the Factiva archive for news articles with the term "human development report" (HDR) or "world development report" (WDR) among major world newspapers over the period from 1990 to 2022.[6] The search found 21,965 articles mentioning an HDR in comparison to only 8,913 articles mentioning a WDR, thereby revealing that mass media outlets have covered HDRs much more actively than the HDRs' main competitor, the WDRs. Meanwhile, the "human development index" (HDI) appeared even more often in 39,764 articles. As Table 4.1 reveals, news sources from around the world consistently reported on the HDI and HDRs more frequently than on the WDRs. This

Table 4.1. Global News Reports Mentioning HDR, WDR, or HDI (1990–2022)

Selected News Sources	Region/Country	HDI	HDR	WDR
All Africa	Africa	2,941	1,815	513
Times of India	India	1,222	656	167
CE Noticias Financieras	Latin America	1,112	249	47
Agence France Presse (AFP)	France	810	264	45
Reuters	UK	750	715	455
Hindustan Times	India	486	326	70
Xinhua News Agency	China	387	385	84
Jakarta Post	Indonesia	377	161	45
Associated Press (AP)	USA	279	213	72
Globe and Mail	Canada	274	127	50
Total	World	39,764	21,965	8,913

Source: Factiva search conducted by the authors on July 6, 2023.

is consistent with our previous study which provided a breakdown of 75 major English language world newspapers and wire services by region, revealing that news articles mentioning the HDR exceeded those mentioning the WDR in Africa (2,289 to 671), East Asia (988 to 293) Europe (1,815 to 516), North America (1,089 to 449), Oceania/Pacific (242 to 60), South Asia (252 to 46), and West and Central Asia (112 to 7) (Joshi and O'Dell, 2017).

POLITICAL COMMUNICATION AND THE HD IDEOLOGY (FRAMING AND AGENDA SETTING)

Beyond just shaping or sending a message, mass media organizations strive to create and maintain an audience in the way in which they share or report on a message (Potter, 2013, p. 17). For those working in mass media—as owners, staff, or journalists of organizations that produce news content—enticing people with a message is important to gain readership and profit. As Yee (1996) notes, the ability of ideas to impact policy is contingent upon carriers who keep ideas alive by sustaining, spreading, amplifying, and endorsing them through language. Ideas that are spread through mass media can impact many people, even those who do not watch or read news programs or content: "Since mass media messages reach large audiences, changes in behavior that become norms within an individual's social network might influence that person's decisions without them having been directly exposed to or initially persuaded by the campaign" (Wakefield, Loken, and Hornik 2010, 1262).

Mass media is pivotal to the global diffusion of norms and ideas not only by making information available to the public but also through the critical role that media plays in *framing* and *agenda setting*. Like all political actors, mass media outlets do not simply relay messages but they also engage in the process of *framing* which means "selecting and highlighting some facets of events or issues, and making connections among them so as to promote a particular interpretation, evaluation, and/or solution . . . To frame is to select some aspects of a perceived reality and make them more salient . . . frames call attention to some aspects of reality while obscuring other elements." (Entman, 2004, p. 5, p. 52, p. 55)

When newspaper editors and journalists report on events or issues, they focus on or highlight certain aspects of the event over other
aspects. When they do so they are motivated by a variety of reasons
including, but not limited to, catering to their likely audience, crafting
the story based on their own perspective or biases (even when they
might try to avoid bias), and meeting the requirements of their news
organization or the goals of its owners. Thus, the writers and editors
of newspaper articles and other mass media publications choose which
messages to relay and whether to do so in a way that is favorable or
oppositional.

It is not only that journalists, editors, and newspaper owners (or
other creators of messages produced by mass media) frame an issue,
but that their audiences may be enticed or convinced to accept the way
that the event or issue is framed and then take on the interpretation for
themselves (Chong and Druckman, 2007). Mass media publications
frame an event or issue by connecting it to their audience's worldviews
(i.e., how they think and understand the world around them in "familiar categories" (Norris, 1997, p. 2). Framing an event or issue can
change the perception of the audience, encourage them to think more
deeply or shallowly about an event, support misinterpretation, or cause
changes in behavior (Chong and Druckman, 2007). Through framing,
media has the power to define effects or conditions as problematic,
identify causes, convey moral judgments, and to endorse remedies or
improvements, all of which are key to a message's receptivity (Entman,
2004, pp. 5–6).

Thus, when considering the political communication provided by
mass media on an event or issue, it is crucial to understand two elements about 1) framing, or presenting a message to an audience, and
2) audience reception, or how an audience will perceive the message.
The first element is asking how the message is framed so as to influence
and increase interest in the message and to change outcomes. In other
words, does the mass media present the message in such a way as to
gain support, trust, and influence perceptions and behaviors of an audience? The second element is crucial to understand in order to identify
how an audience perceives the message or source; does the message
confirm or change perceptions of the audience on the issue or event?
Several facilitating mechanisms by which a norm promoter can share
their message through the media, and reduce the risk of it becoming

distorted, muffled, or silenced, include: a) credibility, b) persistence, c) resonance, and d) decentralization. The first of the four mechanisms is credibility. The credibility of a news source stems from its perceived expertise, trustworthiness, reputation, and accuracy. Studies find credibility of a news source strongly influences the extent to which an audience is persuaded by its message.[7] Psychological experiments also demonstrate that people are more persuaded by messages coming from sources they find credible.[8]

A second mechanism is persistence. The more a message is presented to an audience, the more it is perceived as an important part of reality, leading audiences to put more focus on and gain more respect for that message. A message gains both agenda-setting and preference-shaping power when it is presented consistently and credibly to the public, thereby making those themes appear salient, familiar, and even as shared beliefs (Cohen, 1963; McCombs and Shaw, 1972). As McCombs notes, "those elements emphasized on the media agenda come to be regarded as important by the public . . . for all the news media, the repetition of a topic day after day is the most powerful message of all about its importance" (2004, p. 68, p. 2). A consistent message regularly delivered to the public through mass media can make an impact on the behavior of individuals as well as on collective organizations, like governments.

The third mechanism, resonance, reflects the way a message conforms to an audience's belief systems and how it is crafted by media to fit with the local culture. Resonance is important for dissemination and for eventual public acceptance of a norm or ideology (Coleman, 1990; Checkel, 2001; Epstein, 2006). A message is more likely to have an impact and community acceptance when it fits with a recipient's pre-existing values, perceptions, and understandings (Petty and Wegener, 1998; Acharya, 2004), thereby giving credibility to the message and its promoter. By shaping messages to resonate with media consumers' pre-existing beliefs, mass media can influence how big, serious, or relevant an issue appears to the audience. As scholars have noted, people "pay particular attention to the familiar, the culturally similar . . . an event with a clear interpretation, free from ambiguities in its meaning, is preferred to the highly ambiguous event from which many and inconsistent implications can and will be made" (Galtung and Ruge, 1965, pp. 66–67).

A fourth mechanism important to the analysis of framing and agenda-setting by mass media for an audience is that of decentralization. In political science, decentralization refers to the distribution of power among different levels of authoritative structures and the greater involvement of the public in decision-making procedures (Cheema and Rondinelli, 2007, pp. 3–4). This concerns the ways in which audience members themselves take up the messages they receive in mass media and further perpetuate and disseminate them through other more localized means.

To summarize, political communication through mass media—both as a method of communicating a message to a large audience as well as a name for the actors that communicate the message—allows us to have insight into how a message has been or is globalized. It provides a way for us to assess how the HDRs and HDI are reported on. It gives us insight into how the HD message is framed by mass media, perceived by audiences, and either ignored or ingrained in the way that humans worldwide perceive and interpret their reality. Further, assessing news reporting on the HDRs and HDI through the mechanisms of credibility, persistence, resonance, and decentralization gives further insight into the influence of the HD ideology and whether it has gained a place on the global public agenda (both in the eyes of the public at large as well as for well-positioned policy-making actors).

THE DRAMATIC RISE IN MEDIA REPORTING ON THE HDRs AND HDI

Building off the discussion above regarding the media's role in framing and agenda setting, and the identification of four mechanisms used by mass media to influence how an audience interprets a message, this section analyzes how mass media has presented the HDRs and HDI. It also gives some insight into how global audiences have perceived and interpreted media messages about the HD ideology. Analyzing newspaper reporting on HD, both quantitatively and qualitatively, we examined the mechanisms of credibility and resonance to assess the extent to which mass media presents HDRs as credible sources. The more the HDRs are presented as credible, the greater likelihood there is that the HD ideology will be disseminated to, and well received by, the global public. Assessing the level of local resonance of the HD ideology—by analyzing the way that media frames the HDRs and HDI for different local audiences, and the way the media reports local people accepting tenets of the ideology—reveals how the HD ideology has been globalized. The mechanisms of persistence and decentralization, which is both the consistent and continual reporting on the HDRs and HDI from year to year, as well as in reference to the multiplicity of HDR producers and news outlets from global to local levels, also helps to reveal the extent to which the HD ideology is globalizing worldwide. Examining the decentralization of reporting on HDRs and HDI provides further insight into whether the HD ideology has become widely disseminated and normalized (McCombs, 2004).

CREDIBILITY AND RESONANCE IN MEDIA REPORTING

The mechanism of credibility helps us identify the extent to which mass media presents the HDR as a reliable source. To assess credibility, we reviewed newspaper articles published about the HDRs and HDI and conducted an analysis of the language used to describe and frame them.[9] To do this, we randomly selected 50 news articles about the HDRs per year for 1992, 1997, 2002, 2007, and 2012 for a total of 250 articles. From this sample, we found an overwhelming majority of the articles (241 out of 250) assigned high levels of credibility to the UN and HDR, with only nine articles questioning their credibility as a source. This finding is consonant with earlier work asserting that HDRs are seen as highly credible and as products of a high degree of intellectual autonomy and professional integrity (Haq, 1995, p. 43; Murphy, 2006, p. 242; McNeill, 2007, p. 11). In the news article titled "We're No. 1—Still: UN Report Finds Canada Is Tops for 4th Straight Year" as mentioned at the beginning of this chapter, we find a representative example of a media source bestowing credibility on the HDR and the HD ideology. That article conveys the HDR's credibility by mentioning how leaders take the report's findings seriously. It also legitimizes HD norms by drawing the reader into a more complex understanding of how the HD paradigm is based on removing impediments to human capabilities. A more recent article from a Swiss news source in 2022 provides a similar message by exuberantly proclaiming that "Switzerland has ranked first in the [HDI] in 2021, mainly due to a rise in life expectancy and a rebound of its income per capita . . . " (Mangin, 2022). The article is accompanied by a picture of a young girl joyously jumping into the Rhine River, hands raised high with hair defying gravity. The message is one of approval and pride.

In other news articles, journalists and op-ed writers often conveyed a high-level of credibility to the HDRs not only because of how they are associated with the UN but also because the HDRs disseminate data and development indicators on issues of relevance to mass publics (textbox 4.2 includes examples of excerpts from newspaper articles in different countries). For example, media coverage citing an HDR regularly highlights a country's HDI ranking and how it compares to other countries. Media reports likewise indicate that political elites in developing countries take HDI scores seriously and will contest them when the scores are lower than expected. On this point, Rwanda has criticized the UN for using outdated figures to calculate its HDI, and Cuban diplomats have expressed dismay over Cuba's exclusion from the HDI, as occurred in the 2011 HDR, despite scoring among the top Latin American countries in the past: "Cuba was included in 2009 HDI but excluded from 2010 HDI supposedly due to technical issues calculating its PPP per capita income which the World Bank doesn't do for Cuba due to the US 49-year old blockade of the island" (Deen, 2011). Yet even in the small number of cases where the HDR's credibility is questioned, journalists have rarely amplified such dissenting opinions. For example, in the following excerpt taken from global monitoring reports of the British Broadcasting Corporation (BBC, 2012), there is

TEXTBOX 4.2. FRAMING HUMAN DEVELOPMENT IN NEWSPAPER ARTICLES

"The [HDR] report ranked Korea above France and the UK . . . However, when adjusted for inequality, Korea dropped from 15th to 32nd place. The other country to see such a significant drop in the inequality adjusted HDI rankings was the U.S., falling from 4th place to 23rd . . . The adjusted index takes into account economic and social inequalities within the general development index, enabling a more comprehensive assessment of a society's well-being." ("Korea Ranks 15th in 'Human Development Index,'" *Korea Times*, November 8, 2011)

"Pakistan has been ranked 146th among 187 countries in the Human Development Report 2013 compiled by the United Nations Development Programme . . . The report also pointed out that Pakistan's expenditure on social sectors is lower than some of the poor African countries such as Congo which spends 1.2 percent of GDP on health and 6.2 percent on education. Pakistan spends 0.8 percent of GDP on health and 1.8 percent on education . . . Around seven million children were out of school of which 60 percent were girls. Pakistan has already seen societal conflicts and tension arising out of unequal distribution of and access to resources." (Zaheer Abbasi, Pakistan Sinks to 146th in HDI: UNDP, Business Recorder [Karachi], March 29, 2013)

"The Abu Dhabi Department of Economy and the United Nations Development Programme on Tuesday unveiled the first Human Development Report of the Emirate of Abu Dhabi 2011/2012 . . . 'We hope that the Human Development Report for the Emirate of Abu Dhabi would be part of a series of regular reports, intended to widen its spread and frequently partake in the government and media circles, universities, schools, research centers and NGOs discussions and decisions' . . . The report endeavors primarily to broaden the base of the national debate on human development beyond the traditional financial growth." ("Abu Dhabi Unveils 2011–2012 Human Development Report," *Khaleej Times* [Dubai], October 9, 2012)

"Chuluun Togtokh, writing in the journal Nature, said the U.N.'s annual Human Development Index is flawed because it fails to take into account sustainability. 'Worse still, the index celebrates gas-guzzling developed nations. It is time this failure—hidden in plain sight—was exposed and corrected,' he said of the index released earlier this month . . . Under his Human Sustainable Development Index, Australia slides from 2nd place to 26th; the United States drops from 4th to 28th; and Canada falls from 6th to 24th. 'If the U.N. continues to encourage countries such as Mongolia to aspire to the U.S. lifestyle, we will all be in serious trouble,' Togtokh wrote." ("Scientist Says Development Index Wrong," *United Press International [UPI] Newswire*, November 16, 2011) no effort to bolster the credibility of the government minister critiquing the HDR: "UNDP launches Kosovo Human Development Report 2012; Nenad Rasic, labor and social welfare minister, says report findings relating to unemployment level, average salary 'unrealistic.'"

The excerpts in textbox 4.2 are representative of many global newspaper articles reporting on the HDRs, indicating just how seriously mass media takes the findings of HDRs and HDI rankings. The excerpts also highlight how countries of the Global South consider HDRs credible. Reports consistently take the measurements presented in the HDRs seriously (like the HDI). The HDI is globally influential, in one way evident because it is critiqued for giving favorable ratings to countries of the Global North while ignoring their detrimental impacts on other countries' development due to things like environmental degradation (as expressed in the textbox 4.2 excerpt profiling a Mongolian scientist).

Furthermore, textbox 4.2 includes several excerpts from newspaper reporting that show how HD themes are reported and framed while also revealing the extent to which HD themes are considered credible. The news article excerpted in the textbox from a 2013 Pakistani newspaper contains the country's ranking compared to neighboring countries, additional information from a UN spokesperson, evidence that Parliament members are aware of the report's findings, and the citing of extensive data. The article echoes the HDR's framing of issues like inequality, homicide, out-of-school children, and low health care spending as high priority problems. Overall life satisfaction, social expenditures, and trust in people are contrastingly portrayed as positive and desirable goals. As with the Canadian news article discussed above, the article from a Karachi news organization uses the HDR to justify public policy choices by advocating for an income support program.

The United Arab Emirates (UAE) news organization article in the textbox likewise provides strong evidence that the UN is treated as highly authoritative. In this case we see the production of a local HDR incorporating input from the local level. Residents in the UAE created this particular report (i.e., the report was not created by a team in Washington, DC, New York, or Geneva). Clearly on display in the UAE article is the notion of local ownership and priorities. The UN's trademark emphasis on data collection and bench-marking is highlighted as well, and the article further discusses the signature HD issues of education, health, and standard of living, plus references to gender equality and treating migrants like citizens. All of these development issues represent central tenets of the HD ideology.

What also comes across in media coverage of the HDRs is a notion that there are multiple pathways to HD rather than a simple, standardized formula (for more on this point, see Joshi, 2012). The work of the UN, in developing regional, national, and subnational reports to weigh in on relevant local development issues and social problems has also been extremely helpful in channeling dialogue and providing data over prominent social crises. Such is evident in this short statement found in an article from a major Indian newspaper: "A 'perception survey', the Delhi Human Development Report 2013, released earlier this year, confirmed that women's safety is still a priority" (*Hindustan Times*, 2012).[10]

Our analysis of media reporting on the HDRs also observes an important change over time. In the 1990s, newspaper articles were careful to explain the HDR and give information specific to its publication and development indicators. Explanation was often provided in order to validate the report's authenticity as a source for data on income inequality, poverty, and the relative status of countries on the HDI. However, the authority of the HDR and HDI later solidified to the extent that most reports (that we analyzed from 2000 onward) did not describe the HDR or HDI. Reporters seem to have taken it for granted that readers knew about them and would accept them as authoritative sources.

PERSISTENCE IN REPORTING

The persistence mechanism concerns the frequency of media reporting on the HDRs and the HD paradigm. The idea of persistence also relates to consistent messaging that does not change over time. In order to analyze persistence in media coverage, it is insufficient to merely take a snapshot from a particular year, or to summarize the number of times articles have cited the HDRs, since "there needs to be a longitudinal element to 'mass' media research in order to establish a pattern of media use" (Potter, 2013, p. 19).

Examining the persistence of media coverage in every world region shows that the HDRs are mentioned in significantly more newspaper articles than its main competitor, the WDRs (see Figure 4.1). What is more, Figure 4.1 shows how even when the WDRs were being

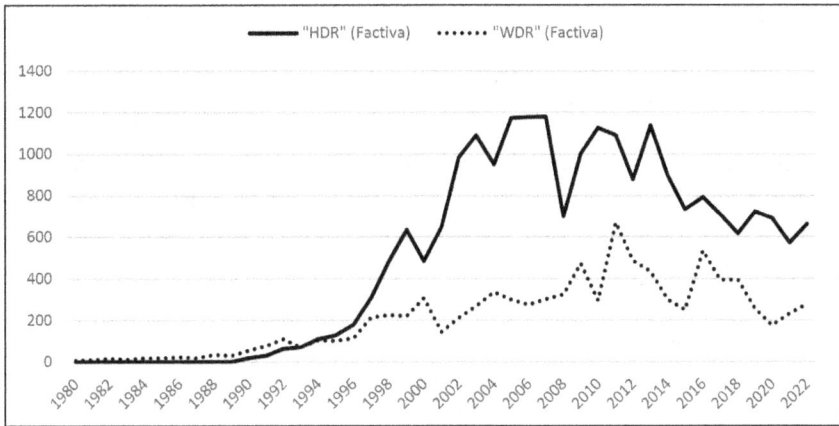

Figure 4.1. **HDR and WDR Reporting in Newspapers (1980–2022).** *Source: Author's searches of number of news publications produced each year mentioning "human development report" or "world development report" (search terms in quotes) from all news sources and in all languages with no duplicates from 1980 to 2022 in Factiva. Data search updated on July 10, 2023.*

produced (since 1978) they gained little attention in the news until the HDRs came on the scene to act as their rival starting in 1990. The total number of newspaper articles covering the HDR each year also grew exponentially from 19 in 1990 to a high of about 1,200 in 2006, and then to around 662 in 2022.[11] By contrast, annual articles covering the WDR increased only from 53 to 276 over the same time period. This is a substantial transformation: whereas HDRs were mentioned less than half as often as WDRs three decades ago, HDRs are now mentioned more than twice as often.

What is more, Global South countries have been very active in reporting on the HDRs and HDI. As shown in Table 4.1 above, African news services have reported on the HDI and HDRs more than any single news service from any other continent. Likewise, among all news sources in the LexisNexis archive, another database of global newspapers, that which has given the most coverage to the HDRs is the Africa News wire service (Joshi and O'Dell, 2017).[12] This illustrates the degree to which journalists in Africa, as in other regions, treat both the HDR and HDI as credible. Even though there has been a decline in reporting on development reports in Africa since the Global Financial Crisis in 2008 there is still much more reporting on the HDI and HDR compared to the WDR.

It is not only in Africa that the HDI has become a widely used measure of development. Whereas the HDI did not exist in news reporting prior to 1990, it has rapidly traveled from obscurity to the mainstream. For instance, globally, we found mentions of HDI (2,792 times) almost as often as per capita GDP (3,046 times) in news reporting in 2022 (see Figure 4.2) which is rather impressive given that articles mentioning the HDI often also discuss per capita GDP as it is one of the HDI's components.

Persistence has also contributed to the legitimization of HD ideology in the way the HDI is covered and explained as a global norm in the mass media. In the early years, newspaper articles mentioning the HDI usually explained it as rooted in a multidimensional approach to development based on a core nucleus of health, education, and living standards. For example, in 1992, 18 out of the 50 articles in our sample explained the HDI in this way. However, by 2012 the HDI was so well-known and almost taken for granted such that few articles (only 3 out of 50) bothered to explain it. In fact, ten years after the introduction of the HDI, most of the twenty-first century articles we analyzed (11 out of 150) did not explain either the HDI or HDR. Reporters presumably took it for granted that readers knew about the HDR and

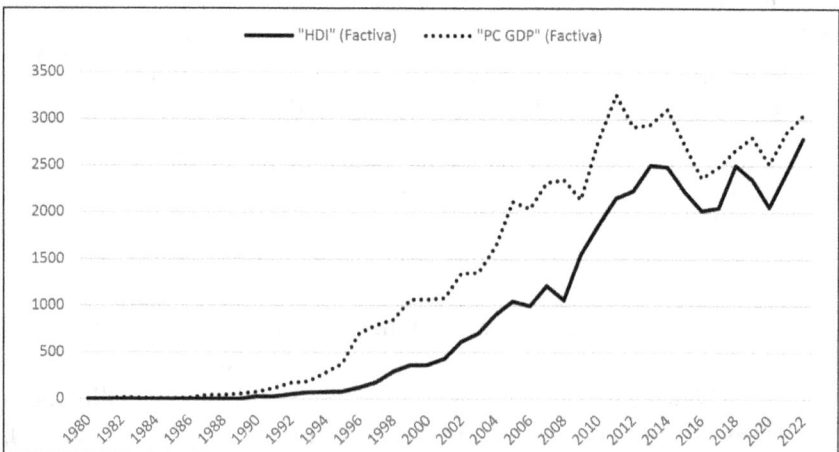

Figure 4.2. HDI and Per Capita GDP Reporting in Global Newspapers (1980–2022). *Source: Author's searches of number of news publications produced each year mentioning "human development index" or "per capita GDP" (search terms in quotes) from all news sources and in all languages with no duplicates from 1980 to 2022 in Factiva. Data search updated on July 10, 2023.*

HDI and would accept them as authoritative sources. Hence our analysis here bears out what other scholars like Jean-Philippe Thérien have argued, that "the *Human Development Reports* consistently underscore two objectives: the increase of well-being and the empowerment of people. Twenty years on, the core of the UNDP's approach has remained remarkably stable" (2012a, p. 3).[13]

DECENTRALIZATION IN REPORTING: LOCAL AND GLOBAL NEWSPAPER AUDIENCES

Next, we assessed the degree to which media reports found the HDRs to resonate with local audiences. Three powerful ways in which the HDRs aim to do this are through a) data analysis, b) visual symbols, and c) discussion of gaps between reality and ideals. In many cases, all three of these are combined in powerful ways. As Entman (2004, p. 104) argues, visual images are especially powerful because they can convey a message more strongly than mere words. The HDRs noticeably put much effort into this strategy by producing a number of startling visual displays. One prominent example from the 1992 HDR is the image of a champagne glass reflecting global income inequality, which was subsequently discussed heavily in the media. The champagne glass pictures a distribution of world GDP in 1989 showing that the richest 20% of people in the world control 82.7% of the wealth, and contrariwise, that the poorest 20% control a mere 1.4% of the wealth. Such shocking visual displays can provide more impetus for change than statistical tables.

Another example from the 1998 HDR is a comparison of actual global spending patterns with estimated costs of meeting global needs (Table 4.2).[14] The table reveals the lack of governmental or even consumer or civil society concern, for development and poverty. It compares spending on unnecessary consumer items with spending on important social services. Thus, in 1998 consumers spent more on cosmetics (in the United States) than what it would cost to provide basic education worldwide. They spent more on ice cream (in Europe), than the estimated cost of providing safe drinking water and sanitation worldwide. The list and comparison go on, and like the champagne glass image reflecting global inequality, the spending comparison provides an insightful way to think about global development spending and priorities.

Table 4.2. HDR Comparison of the World's Expenditures and Priorities (in mid-1990s)

Actual Expenditures	Cost in USD Billions
Cosmetics in the USA	8
Ice cream in Europe	11
Perfumes in Europe and the USA	12
Pet foods in Europe and the USA	17
Business entertainment in Japan	35
Cigarettes in Europe	50
Alcoholic drinks in Europe	105
Narcotics drugs in the World	400
Military spending in the World	780
Global Priorities	
Basic education for all	6
Water and sanitation for all	9
Reproductive health for all Women	12
Basic health and nutrition for all	13

Source: This table is an adaptation of Table 1.12 in the 1998 HDR (UNDP, 1998, p. 37).

Finally, we assessed whether national and local media replicated the HD content presented in HDRs to determine how the decentralization mechanism contributes to the diffusion of the HD ideology. The HDRs have explicitly pursued this strategy. They have been translated into many languages and being decentralized in the form of HDRs written for regional, national, and sub-national audiences. In fact, according to the UNDP's website, during the HDRs' first twenty-five years (1990–2014), at least 737 HDRs were published at four different levels: global (23), regional (32), national (657), and sub-national (26).[15] As the director of the office responsible for overseeing dozens of sub-national HDRs in India explained in an interview, the aim of the UN was to expand HD thinking and make it a norm by having people at local levels put together their own HD reports.[16] Not only is replication via imitation and hybridization evident in national and sub-national HDRs, but such reports are also frequently cited by the media. For example, among the sample of 250 articles we analyzed, all HDR references in 1992 news articles were to the global HDR whereas less than 40% in 2012 mentioned the global HDR and most instead discussed regional, national, or subnational HDRs. National and regional level reports each made up over 20% of references to HDRs and articles referring to subnational HDRs comprised nearly 10% of the articles in 2012.

Concerning the impact of the HDRs on norm diffusion, we found a high correlation in each of our sample years between the annual themes discussed in HDRs and content reported in the newspapers. Some of the most cited themes among our sample articles were income inequality (1992 and 1997), poverty reduction (1997), quality of life (1997), the importance of democracy (2002, 2007, and 2012), and climate change (2007 and 2012). Thus, components of HD ideology that came across in the reports mirrored those themes promoted by the UN in the HDRs. More specifically, five particular ideas of importance to HD were covered in some depth (gender equality, rights of migrants, democracy, foreign aid, and the Millennium Development Goals, or MDGs) in news reporting. Among these, the most discussed issue was gender equality followed by foreign aid and democracy. By contrast there was much less discussion of the rights of migrants or the MDGs. Thus, it appears that norms involving commitments by the Global North (such as treating migrants better and properly funding the MDGs) are less amplified by the media than advocacy of democracy and gender equality, issues on which the North might claim to be doing better than the South.

Among major norms emphasized by the HDRs, gender equality, income inequality, and the reduction of poverty were influential in multiple HDRs, but seemed to make the most media impact in the 1990s. Newspaper reporters and op-ed columnists were shocked at the income inequality reported in the HDRs and reacted strongly to the champagne glass image featured on the cover of the 1992 report. They also used data and statistical analysis from the HDRs to launch a call for action on norms the UN was promoting. As one journalist at a financial newspaper wrote, "the [HDR] concludes that 'political commitment not financial resources is the real obstacle to poverty eradication'" (Balls, 1997, 54). In another example, from an Australian newspaper, the article was positive about the outlook on poverty reduction: "But the [HDR] carried a message of hope, backed up by an array of charts, statistics and case histories, 'that poverty is no longer inevitable'" (The Mercury, 1997). Further, the focus of the HDRs on human freedom versus simply accounting for income resonated with many reporters and op-ed columnists. In one opinion piece, the author pointed out how

"The UNDP [HDR] 1997 argued that income is not the total sum of well-being; therefore, lack of income cannot be the total sum of poverty. Human poverty does not focus on what people do or do not have, but on what they can or cannot do" (Bwiire, 2012).

News reports about the HDRs in the 2000s focused on political events such as the fight against terrorism, the US invasion of Iraq, and the negative and positive impacts of globalization and climate change on specific countries around the world. A major theme that stuck out in 2002 was the HDR's support for democracy, and tellingly, the HDR for that year was entitled *Deepening Democracy in a Fragmented World* (UNDP, 2002). The global HDR 2002 made waves around the world in that it was controversial, but it was still deeply supported by almost all reporters who wrote about it. Likewise, the regional Arab HDR 2002, which promoted democratic institutions for the Arab world, was depicted in a favorable and respected light. Support for democratic institutions came up repeatedly with a diverse amount of quotes taken from the HDRs, especially in the 2000s. For instance, "The 2002 [HDR] contends 'politics matter for human development because people everywhere want to be free to determine their destinies, express their views and participate in decisions that shape their lives. These capabilities are just as important for human development . . . as being able to read or enjoy good health" (Sabaratnam, 2002, p. 11).

REFLECTIONS ON THE HUMAN DEVELOPMENT PARADIGM AND THE MASS MEDIA

This chapter assessed news coverage of the HD paradigm as promoted by the UN between 1990 and 2022. Mass media coverage of the HDRs demonstrate that the media can be very influential as an intervening variable in the process of diffusing norms and ideology, including norms coming from international organizations to states and the global public. Overwhelmingly, we found news reporters and op-ed columnists treated the HDR and indicators like the HDI as authoritative. Global mass media has regularly re-iterated positive framing of HD, thereby challenging older, more narrow ideas of development referring only to indicators such as GDP or per capita income. Positive reporting of the HD paradigm by journalists makes an impression on countries and encourages them to follow the course of development that the UN promotes. Increasing foreign aid is also a major norm the UN pushes in the HDRs and it is echoed by reporters encouraging wealthier states to increase aid to developing countries, as in this example: "The UN report, the third in an annual series prepared by an independent team of economists, says aid should increase according to a donor country's means. Foreign aid has not done the job, according to the United Nations. Poor countries are worse off now than they were in 1960" (Canadian Press, 1992, A10).

As demonstrated in this chapter, political communication through the mass media is crucial to legitimizing HD ideas, concepts, and theories. In the case of the HD ideology, the reputation that the UN has built up over time as a less coercive and less threatening actor than multi-national corporations, other international organizations, or nation-states has helped it to gain credibility with global mass media. The media, in turn, readily amplify core themes in the HDRs rather than ignoring, attacking, or ridiculing them. The HDRs are primarily treated as credible in mass media, and consistently have a high degree of resonance, not only with journalists but also with writers of editorial and opinion columns. The decentralization of HDRs in the form of locally produced national, regional, and subnational reports also clearly supports UN promotion of the HD ideology in conveying increasing local ownership of HD norms and revealing that regional, national, and subnational decision-makers share priorities promoted by the HDRs.

An important lesson here is that under certain conditions and with effective support from the mass media, international organizations can experience greater success in the diffusion of an ideology and its associated norms and ideas. If a set of ideas is spreading, we would expect to see mass media coverage legitimizing the promoter of the ideas and their messages, and increasing prevalence and articulation of a message vis-à-vis competing ideas. In the case of the HDRs, our analysis found strong evidence of both, suggesting that political communication plays a central role in the international spread of ideas and is therefore deserving of greater attention by international relations and development scholars interested in how ideologies diffuse to global mass publics.

One aspect of media analysis not conducted here, but that also merits discussion and future research, is the role that social media plays in promoting the HD ideology through platforms like Twitter, Facebook, Instagram, TikTok, Snapchat, and so on. Such digital communication

vehicles have garnered an intense amount of followers since the founding of Facebook in 2004. Indeed, many people, especially youth under
thirty years old, report that they get their news primarily from social
media sources and that they trust such sources more than traditional
news sources (Liedke and Gottfried, 2022). To identify the potential
that social media has in spreading a message, a quick search of Twitter
on two of the terms explored in newspapers in this chapter (*human
development* and *world development*) reveals the extent to which social media is a major source of information and opinions. A search
for the term "human development" resulted in 15,900 results for just
one week (July 21–27, 2023) with 49,000 engaged accounts, whereas
"world development" garnered only 719 results with 1,600 accounts
engaging.[17] As one example, the @UNDPSouthAfrica twitter account
was included in the top results with a tweet announcing the publication of the national South Africa HDR.[18] This one example shows the
extraordinary potential of social media to reach a wide audience and
promote the HD ideology and merits further study.

Additionally, while this chapter illustrates that mass media played
a pivotal role in spreading ideas about the HD paradigm as expressed
through the HDRs, further research is still needed to assess the level
of internalization of the HD ideology in specific states, and how the
general public in different countries have absorbed or been impacted
by media messages about human development. What we have demonstrated in this chapter is that newspaper articles citing the HDI and the
HDRs appear in every world region and greatly exceed those mentioning their main ideological rival, the WDR. News reports on the HDRs
have also increased over time and the media has overwhelmingly portrayed them in a way favorable to dissemination of the HD ideology.

NOTES

1. Some sections of this chapter are reproduced from the following sources: Joshi
and O'Dell (2017) and Joshi (2021b). We thank the publishers for giving us permission to reproduce selected portions of those works here.

2. The term *mass media* references the changes that occurred during the industrial revolution in terms of technological advances in printing and communication
that allowed for a greater audience to receive the same messages. It refers not only
to the ways in which political and social messages are shared with or disseminated

to a large audience but also the actors (whether individuals or organizations) who are responsible for such dissemination.

3. Chapter 2 covered the extent of the HD ideology and connected HDCA norms, ideas, and practices. Chapter 3 additionally reviewed specific ideas brought by academics and the power of academia in promoting and globalizing the HD ideology.

4. Source: Julian Beltrame, "We're No. 1—Still: UN Report Finds Canada is Tops for 4th Straight Year," *The Gazette* (Montreal), June 12, 1997.

5. Newspapers also fall into a type of mass media one might call traditional.

6. Our search only includes sources that cite the three words together by using the quotations as a Boolean search term.

7. See, for example, Hovland and Weiss, 1951; McQuail, 2010, 509–510; Rahman, 2014.

8. See, for example, Zimbardo and Leippe, 1991; Petty and Wegener, 1998.

9. We used a binary coding scheme to ascertain whether mass media in fact treated HDRs as credible. See Joshi and O'Dell (2017), for more details.

10. Source: "A Year After the Delhi Gang-Rape, Has Anything Changed?," *Hindustan Times*, December 3, 2012.

11. Growth in the number of articles may partially be a function of the LexisNexis archive expanding over time to include newspaper sources from more countries. Nevertheless, articles covering the HDR are still much more frequent than those covering the WDR.

12. As discussed in Joshi and O'Dell (2017), over its first 25 years the HDRs were covered more frequently than the WDRs in Africa News by a margin of five-to-one, and more than twice as often during the 2010s. Also worth noting in Africa News reporting is the rapid increase of articles discussing the HDI, which by the mid-2010s appeared twice as often as articles discussing the HDRs.

13. Likewise, Murphy (2006) notes how HDRs provide consistent emphasis on the capabilities approach and reporting of the HDI concerning the three main components of health, education, and living standard.

14. Visual symbols are powerful and a key force behind them is the UN's unparalleled capacity for original data collection and analysis framed in ways the UN perceives global problems and solutions (Ward, 2004).

15. UNDP website: http://hdr.undp.org.

16. Author's interview with India UNDP-HDRO director in New Delhi, March 2006.

17. The search of Twitter was conducted using Talkwalker on July 27, 2023.

18. Tweet announcing the South Africa HDR with link to the UNDP press release appeared on July 27, 2023.

CHAPTER 5

THE UNITED NATIONS AND THE GLOBALIZATION OF HUMAN DEVELOPMENT

After one of the hottest summers on the meteorological record in 2019, 16-year-old climate activist Greta Thunberg spoke at the United Nations (UN) Climate Action Summit in New York. The summit was one of many UN international meetings in which delegates representing most of the world's countries gather to discuss how to collaborate on addressing climate change. Thunberg chastised delegates from 70 countries who attended that year with the words, "You have stolen my dreams and my childhood with your empty words. And yet I'm one of the lucky ones. People are suffering. People are dying. Entire ecosystems are collapsing. We are in the beginning of a mass extinction, and all you can talk about is money and fairy tales of eternal economic growth. How dare you!" (Thunberg, 2019).

A year earlier, in August 2018, Thunberg's activism started when she eschewed institutional education norms by skipping school on Fridays to sit alone (although others soon joined her) on a cobblestoned street outside the Swedish Parliament in Stockholm to advocate for better environmental policies. A sign propped against the grey-stoned building at her side read "Skolstrejk För Klimatet" (School Strike for Climate Action). The months preceding her strike were some of the hottest on record for Sweden. The increase in average global temperatures caused by human behavior was already contributing to major climate catastrophes including species extinctions, reductions in biodiversity, increasing ocean acidity, and rising sea levels. Thunberg noted in her speeches how neither the international community, nor her own government, were doing enough to address, ameliorate, and reduce greenhouse gases, or to rectify the causes and effects of pollution. As she wrote in a pamphlet that she shared with passersby, "you adults are shitting on my future" (Crouch, 2018). Thunberg's protests spread worldwide as people learned about her activism and were inspired to engage in the Fridays for Future movement that she started.

Thunberg is one of many young people who have spoken to the UN, calling for action over the years. Similarly, Severn Suzuki, a 12-year-old Canadian girl speaking on behalf of the Environmental Children's Organization at the 1992 Earth Summit, challenged 178 country delegates in the same manner almost 30 years earlier. Suzuki's speech was damning: "In my anger, I'm not blind: and in my fear, I'm not afraid of telling the world how I feel . . . I am only a child yet I know, if all the money spent on war was spent on finding environmental answers, ending poverty, and finding treaties: what a wonderful place this Earth would be . . . I challenge you please, make your actions reflect your words" (Suzuki, 1992).

The concern shown in the speeches, protests, and actions by Thunberg, Suzuki, and other climate activists regarding the environment and the connections between all living things, as well as with nonliving entities, is mirrored in the human development (HD) paradigm and appears regularly in UN discussions, debates, international conferences, and the work of the UN's programs, departments, and projects. Indeed, Thunberg's 2019 speech excerpted above sounds remarkably similar to the UN Development Programme (UNDP) Administrator William H. Draper III's admonition in the first Human Development Report (HDR) in 1990 when he wrote that policymakers must be concerned about more than just economic growth and increases in income.

It is perhaps no coincidence that the UN invited Thunberg and Suzuki to speak to its members since their values—concerning preserving the environment to ensure that humans can continue to thrive for present and future generations—have motivated UN action from its very inception. As the UN Intellectual History Project (UNIHP) has observed, "ideas and concepts have clearly been a driving force in many areas of human progress. They are arguably the most important legacy of the United Nations" (Emmerij et al., 2001, p. 3).

In this chapter we look at how the HD paradigm has been globalizing by and through the UN during the twentieth and early twenty-first centuries. The UN has sometimes been called the Parliament of the World or the Parliament of Man because it brings delegates from every country of the world to meet together to debate, discuss, write, and pass agreements on how to coordinate responses to shared threats and how to achieve shared goals.[1] It does this through the UN General Assembly (UNGA), its Economic and Social Council (ECOSOC), and other permanent bodies as well as through ad-hoc conferences on specific issues. Indeed, massive UN conferences have been held since the 1950s on major issues like the human environment, population control, children and women's rights, racism, least developed countries (LDCs), and other important global topics. Such gatherings reveal how the UN proffers institutional support for marginalized groups of people who collectively constitute a majority of the world's population: people living under environmental stresses, women, and people living in LDCs. The conferences also reveal ways in which the HD paradigm coalesced and globalized as a shared consciousness of how to think about humans in development practice. By analyzing key events and currents of thought in the UN's approach to development thinking and policy, this chapter shows how the HD approach was ineluctably connected with changes to human thought, life, and practice in the current era of globalization.

HUMAN DEVELOPMENT FROM THE LEAGUE OF NATIONS TO THE UNITED NATIONS

HD concerns related to education, health, and general welfare were foundational to the original discussions and arguments involved in setting up international cooperation on economic, social, and political

124 CHAPTER 5

issues following the world wars of the twentieth century. Indeed, some of the main concerns that come up in the debates that occurred in creating the League of Nations (in 1919) and the UN that followed in its footsteps (in 1945) were about human well-being and security, even while couched in language of state-based development and international collective security. Such ideas and concerns existed largely because of the experiences of war, but also due to the influence of persistent individuals who thought that humans should be able to live and thrive in their social, economic, ecological, and political environments. Attention to HD concerns continued to evolve through dialogue, discussion, and policy-making in the 1950s and 60s as the UN and its specialized agencies sought to support state cooperation and coordination in the aftermath of the Second World War (ending in 1945) amid the tensions of the Cold War (1947–1991). What is crucial to note from this history is that the UN's creation and concern with HD rhetoric and theories was tempered by the rumble and tumble of international relations, concerns about state sovereignty, and great power politics.

Of special note for thinking about the expansion of economic freedoms and concern for human well-being and living standards are the Bruce Report (1939) and the creation of the UN ECOSOC (1945). Whereas the League of Nations, created in the aftermath of the First World War, was meant to act as a collective security organization, it was criticized by many as lacking a necessary focus on human living standards and economic concerns. A new direction was envisioned in the Bruce Report, named after Stanley Bruce, emphasizing the necessity of economic cooperation and engaging in reforms focused on humans (see Kennedy, 2007, p. 24; Way, 2013, p. 175). Partially influenced by the Bruce Report, there was a deep recognition of the need for international economic coordination to avoid war, and the report heavily inspired the negotiations conducted to replace the League of Nations after it collapsed in 1939.

Indeed, the work that led to the San Francisco Conference of 1945 that created the UN was extensive, facilitated primarily by and through the United States, a country that was emerging at that time as a probable victor of the Second World War.[2] The discussions included concern with economic coordination, alleviating poverty, raising living standards, and how to structure an international security organization to meet the needs of the new international order of the day

(Schlesinger, 2005; Kennedy, 2007). The result was the creation of three parliamentary organs in the UN through which states could coordinate over the goals of collective security (as had already been available in the League), but could also more efficiently facilitate economic and social cooperation. ECOSOC was therefore set up in part to counter the UN Security Council's power in the economic realm, coordinating countries on social and economic policies (Kennedy, 2007; O'Dell, 2023b).

International development policy-making then went through many iterations from the 1950s onward, guided by ECOSOC and the UNGA and its various departments, but the conversation typically stayed at the state and macroeconomic level rather than focusing on individual human lives and outcomes. Basically, in the 1940s and 50s, core HD concerns regarding human health, education, and well-being were largely eclipsed at the UN by macro-economic growth ideas (e.g., Stokke, 2009). However, many people working in academia and developing country governments noticed that development policy began going awry and that a focus on merely expanding gross domestic product (GDP) or gross national income (GNI) did not necessarily reduce, and in some cases, actually increased poverty and inequality. This was Mahbub ul Haq's main finding from his work as an economist for the Pakistani government. One way that country delegates to the UN responded to such challenges was convening international conferences through the UNGA and ECOSOC where delegates could come together to debate and discuss such issues, create agreements (both binding and non-binding) to coordinate their work, and to call the world's attention—as Thunberg has done through her activism—to the special challenges facing humanity.

CONFERENCE DIPLOMACY AND HUMAN DEVELOPMENT IDEAS, CONCEPTS, AND THEORETICAL FOUNDATIONS

UN-organized international conferences became a crucial space where many ideas now incorporated into the HD paradigm first blossomed and spread (Jolly et al., 2004; Stokke, 2009). Conference diplomacy is a key foundation of multilateral cooperation at the UN because it allows state delegates to find common ground, and to prepare for and arrive at agreements to address an issue, theme, or goal (Kauffman, 1968). International conferences also reveal the opportunities and possibilities of globalization in several ways. First, the recent era of globalization with its expansion of transportation technologies, especially after the Second World War, allows for a much larger number of people to gather easily around the world, as revealed by the number of governments and delegates attending international conferences, sometimes amounting to thousands of people. The number of conferences as well as side conferences with civil society participation have increased over the years. The opportunity for increased travel to conferences by people from different parts of the world also brought about a second possibility of globalization, that is, allowing for greater interaction between people groups, knowledge of others, and the ability to work together to come to agreements on issues related to human well-being. Table 5.1 provides a small sample of such UN conferences, especially those related to HD themes. Globalization is reflected in such conferences in that they included attendees and delegates from almost every country and have taken places in many parts of the world, spanning North America (New York City, Mexico City), South America (Rio de Janeiro), Africa (Nairobi), the Middle East (Istanbul), Asia (Beijing), and Europe (Stockholm, Paris, Vienna, etc.).

While the crucial roles of education and health are well recognized to be at the core of the HD paradigm, it is also worth noting how the UN has long promoted ideas that would become deeply integrated into the HD approach via conferences on three other issue areas: 1) environment and sustainability, 2) women, and 3) least developed countries (LDCs). Overarching themes related to HD that were addressed at these conferences included creating and maintaining the human environment so that all humans can thrive, promoting and respecting the equal rights and participation of women in all aspects of life, and addressing the specific challenges of poverty in LDCs, especially related to education, health, and income or job opportunities. We now review major concerns and challenges that incentivized the planning, discussions, and interactions that occurred in the lead up to and during the conferences, highlighting how the themes included acted as a foundation for the HD paradigm.

Table 5.1. Selected UN-Sponsored International Conferences on HD Themes (1972–2022)

International UN Conference and Location	Year	Attending Governments	% Attending Governments
UN Conference on the Human Environment (Stockholm, Sweden)	1972	113	85%
First UN World Conference of the International Women's Year (Mexico City, Mexico)	1975	133	92%
WHO and UNICEF International Conference on Primary Healthcare (Alma-Ata, Soviet Union)	1978	134	89%
Second UN World Conference of the UN Decade for Women (Copenhagen, Denmark)	1980	145	94%
First UN Conference on the Least Developed Countries (Paris, France)	1981	138	87%
Third World Conference to Review and Appraise the Achievements of the United Nations Decade for Women (Nairobi, Kenya)	1985	157	98%
UNESCO World Conference on Education for All (Jomtien, Thailand)	1990	160	100%
Second Conference on the Least Developed Countries (LDC-II) (Paris, France)	1990	129	81%
World Summit for Children (New York, USA)	1990	159	100%
UN Conference on Environment and Development (Earth Summit) (Rio de Janeiro, Brazil)	1992	178	99%
World Conference on Human Rights (Vienna, Austria)	1993	171	93%
Fourth World Conference on Women (Beijing, China)	1995	189	100%
World Summit for Social Development (Copenhagen, Denmark)	1995	117	63%
UN Millennium Summit (New York, USA)	2000	189	100%

Third Conference on the Least Developed Countries (LDC-III) (Brussels, Belgium)	2001	159	84%
UN Conference on Sustainable Development (Rio+20) (Rio de Janeiro, Brazil)	2011	192	99%
Fourth Conference on the Least Developed Countries (LDC-IV) (Istanbul, Turkey)	2011	156	81%
UN Summit on Sustainable Development (New York, USA)	2015	192	99%
Stockholm+50: A Healthy Planet for the Prosperity of All (Stockholm, Sweden)	2022	122	63%

Sources: Attending government numbers and percentages compiled by authors, taken from final reports to the UNGA or other UN governing organ after each conference.

HUMAN DEVELOPMENT AND UN CONFERENCES TO SUPPORT THE ENVIRONMENT

In order for humans to thrive in their political, economic, and social worlds they need a well-functioning environment—an Earth—that is healthy and can support them. Recognizing this crucial fact, UN conferences have been bringing governments together to discuss ecological and environmental concerns since 1972. The challenge, as Severn Suzuki put it in the speech she delivered at the 1992 Earth Summit, is that of putting words into action. Yet the discussions, debates, and outcome documents of UN conferences on the environment show that much of the reason for why such conferences gained support and notoriety was because they were couched in HD language and ideas. They envisioned protecting the Earth as a means to protect and provide for human thriving and ensure greater access to opportunities.

The Swedish organizers of the 1972 *Only One Earth* conference held in Stockholm led the charge in organizing an international conference on the environment, but it was an uphill battle to gain support for the environment without having humans at the center of the discussion.[3] Most of the warnings came from books written by journalists or scientists who argued that the Earth was being destroyed by human activities.[4] Yet early on in conference planning, the Swedish delegate Sverker Åström was aware that the language of any policy or report needed to focus on saving the environment *for humans* and *for human well-being* (Paglia, 2021, p. 4). Thus, the themes and language surrounding the discussion of environmental degradation focused on human well-being. For instance, the UNGA resolution that called for a UN conference—drafted by the Swedish delegation—references the environment only in relation to humans, using the adjectives "his" referring to mankind or "human," so that the issue is not the environment itself, but the environment that is centered around and experienced by humans and that supports humans: indeed, "human environment" is referenced 11 times (UNGA, 1968). Several paragraphs illuminate the intentions: paragraph 1 emphasizes the "relationship between man and his environment," paragraph four notes delegates were "concerned about the consequent effects on the condition of man, his physical, mental and social well-being, his dignity and his enjoyment of basic human rights, in developing as well as developed countries," and paragraph 11 suggests the need to "limit and, where possible, eliminate the impairment of the human environment in order to protect and improve the natural surroundings *in the interest of man*" (italics added). The UNGA resolution that approved the conference on December 15, 1969, included similar language.

Industrializing countries in the 1960s were initially wary of a conference that might ask them to limit their industrializing and development practices in order to protect the environment, even while much of their populations lived in poverty.[5] The concern may have been well founded considering pronouncements in the Club of Rome Report *Limits to Growth* (Meadows et al., 1972) that seemed to argue for policies protecting the environment over economic growth (Paglia, 2021, p. 7). But the 1971 preparatory meeting in Founex, Switzerland, was groundbreaking in that some argue it saved the Stockholm conference. At the Founex meeting, Mahbub ul Haq played a major role in the negotiations by "marrying the concerns of environment and development into a single concept of an environmentally sound, people-centered development paradigm—a forerunner of the current concept of sustainable human development" (Haq, 1995, p. ix; Haq and Ponzio, 2008, p. 82). The Founex negotiations, and later published Founex Report, became an important foundation for the rhetoric, language, and documents of the Stockholm conference (Manulak, 2017; Paglia, 2021, p. 7). It was clear to the conference planners and organizers that the best way to incentivize country delegates to support the conference was to focus on what the environment has done, is doing, and would or would not do for human well-being and livelihood.

The UNGA unanimously approved the Declaration of the UN Conference on the Human Environment, often called the Stockholm Declaration. The declaration mirrors the HD paradigm and narrative with a "human-centric approach . . . an anthropocentric perspective on respecting nature" (Handl, 2012, p. 3). It highlights how the environment either supports or hinders human well-being, dignity, equality, health, and human needs for education, shelter, and food. Some further argue that the language of the declaration was influenced and supported by the human rights argument and narrative (Ebbesson, 2022), and indeed the language of rights is evident in the document (UN, 1973, paragraph 1), however slim the human rights theory might be that underpinned it (Handl, 2012, p. 3). But more than rights, the document highlights what the HD ideology supports, that of an environment in which humans can thrive.

Words indicating particular concern with what humans can do and be in the world are highlighted throughout the Stockholm Declaration including well-being (para 1, 2, 6, principle 1), equality (principle 1), dignity (principle 1), education (para 4, principle 19), and health (para 3, 4, principle 7) (UN, 1973). Paragraph 3 and principle 1 further highlight the anthropocentric focus of the document and negotiations: "Millions continue to live far below the minimum levels required for a decent human existence, deprived of adequate food and clothing, shelter and education, health and sanitation . . . " and "Man has the fundamental right to freedom, equality and adequate conditions of life, in an environment of a quality that permits a life of dignity and well-being, and he bears a solemn responsibility to protect and improve the environment for present and future generations . . . " (UN, 1973). Even the debates during the conference between delegates reflect the HD focus when discussing the environment: "In the opinion of many speakers, the only criterion of the success of environmental programs was the substantial improvement of the conditions of life of the vast majority of mankind" (UN, 1973,, paragraph 47).

Much discussion and work on environmental issues followed the 1972 Stockholm conference, as seen in UNGA debates. They included the creation and work of the UN Environment Programme (UNEP) and other treaties and agreements that addressed environmental issues of whaling, nuclear waste, and the law of the sea.[6] While the language and rationale for focusing on environment degradation was challenged by those who thought that social and human concerns should be separate from, not integral to, the discussions, the human focus typically won the day, largely because of a report published almost two decades later, the *Report of the World Commission on Environment and Development: Our Common Future* (1987), also known as the Brundtland Report (Handl, 2012, p. 3). The document was named after Gro Harlem Brundtland, former Prime Minister of Norway, as she was the main author and chairperson of the commission that produced the report. What is important about the Brundtland Report, which is still influential today, is that it defined sustainable development as deeply connected to HD and human survival concerns:

> When the terms of reference of our Commission were originally being discussed in 1982, there were those who wanted its considerations to be limited to "environmental issues" only. This would have been a grave mistake. The environment does not exist as a sphere separate from human actions, ambitions, and needs, and attempts to defend it in isolation from human concerns have given the very word "environment" a connotation of naivety in some political circles . . . the "environment" is where we all live; and "development" is what we all do in attempting to improve our lot within that abode. The two are inseparable. (Chairman's Foreword)

Thus, when the report reaches the crucial point of defining sustainable development, its first sentence reads: "Humanity has the ability to make development sustainable to ensure that it meets the needs of the present without compromising the ability of future generations to meet their own needs" (1987, paragraph 27). The phrase has been powerful and has been reproduced worldwide in the imaginations, policy debates, and publications of those who would define national and international environmental policies, global development goals, and grassroots mobilization on issues of climate change, biological diversity, economic growth, and environmental protection since that time.

Documents and discussions like those presented in the Brundtland Report carried through to the Earth Summit in 1992, which produced multiple important agreements that have had an immeasurable impact on international cooperation since then. The main agreements are summed up nicely in what is known as the Rio Declaration on Environment and Development which includes 27 principles. A review of the 27 principles reveals how influential the discussion of the concerns about human well-being were to the Earth Summit. They all connect in some way with core HD ideas, starting out with the clear statement in Principle I that "Human beings are at the center of concerns for sustainable development. They are entitled to a healthy and productive life in harmony with nature." Indeed, the Rio outcome document was produced two years after the influential first HDR of 1990 and may very well have taken some of its ideas and inspiration from those laid out in that and subsequent HDRs. Table 5.2 provides a side-by-side comparison of the 27 principles and the five important freedoms that Amartya Sen argued are necessary for humans "to live the way they would like to live" (Sen, 1999, p. 38). The comparison reveals that the same considerations of HD freedoms, as expressed in the HDCA, were the foundation for principles on sustainability and environment.

The environment has continued to capture the attention and concern of the world and the UN since the 1992 Earth Summit. Several UN conferences followed in its footsteps by continuing the attempt to create more binding treaties and agreements related to protecting forests, biological diversity, and reducing carbon emissions. However, none of them have been as successful in gaining strong commitment from member states (Newell, 2002; Seyfang, 2003; Robinson, 2021). Indeed, several academics have argued that the language and discussion has since become much more focused on the environment than on human well-being (Handl, 2012). However, connecting the arguments about protecting the environment to human well-being may be the best and only way we have to gain political will and commitment to stopping human-induced environmental degradation and climate change. Some argue that bringing back the human-centered, anthropocentric focus—as Mahbub ul Haq understood back in the 1960s—is the best way to get political will and motivation on international environmental policy back on track (Paglia, 2021; Ebbessen, 2022). The challenge of including a focus on humans over the environment has continued through to the Sustainable Development Goals which seeks to marry the two concerns, even though their targets and goals often conflict.

Table 5.2. Comparison of Sen's Five HD Freedoms to the 1992 Earth Summit Principles

Five Freedoms of the Human Development Perspective outlined by Sen (1999, pp. 38–40)	*Similar phrases and concerns about human freedoms found in the "27 Principles" (labeled P1, P2, etc.) of the 1992 Rio Declaration on Environment and Development (Earth Summit Outcome Document)*
Political Freedoms: "refer to the opportunities that people have to determine who should govern and on what principles . . ." (38)	P2: States have . . . the sovereign right to exploit their own resources pursuant to . . . development policies . . . P10: Environmental issues are best handled with the participation of all concerned citizens . . . access to information concerning the environment . . . the opportunity to participate in decision-making processes. P20: Women have a vital role . . . Their full participation is therefore essential to achieve sustainable development. P21: The creativity, ideals and courage of the youth of the world should be mobilized . . . P22: . . . States should recognize and duly support [Indigenous people and their communities] identity, culture and interests, and enable their effective participation . . .
Economic Facilities: "refers to the opportunities that individuals respectively enjoy to utilize economic resources for the purposes of consumption, or production, or exchange" (38–39)	P3: The right to development must be fulfilled so as to equitably meet . . . needs of present and future generations. P4: . . . environmental protection shall constitute an integral part of the development process . . . P5: All states and all people shall cooperation in . . . eradicating poverty . . . to decrease the disparities in the standards of living and better meet the needs of the majority of the people of the world. P8: To achieve sustainable development and a higher quality of life for all people, States should reduce and eliminate unsustainable patterns . . . P12: States should cooperate to promote a supportive and open international economic system that would lead to economic growth and sustainable development in all countries . . . . P16: National authorities should endeavor to promote the internationalization of environmental costs and the use of economic instruments . . . with due regard to the public interest . . .

Social opportunities: "refer to the arrangements that society makes for education, health care, and so on . . . " (39)

Transparency Guarantees: "deal with the need for openness that people can expect: the freedom to deal with one another under guarantees of disclosure and lucidity" (39)

Protective Security: "to provide a social safety net for preventing the affected population from being reduced to abject misery . . . . starvation and death" (40)

P14: States should effectively cooperate to discourage and prevent the relocations and transfer to other States of any activist and substances that . . . are found to be harmful to human health.

P6: The special situation and needs of developing countries . . . shall be given special priority."

P7: States shall cooperate in a spirit of global partnership . . . States have common but differentiated responsibilities.

Principle 10: . . . Effective access to judicial and administrative proceedings, including redress and remedy, shall be provided.

P11: States shall enact effective environmental legislation . . .

P15: In order to protect the environment, the precautionary approach shall be widely applied . . .

P17: Environmental impact assessment . . . shall be undertaken . . .

Principle 18: States shall immediately notify other States of any natural disasters or other emergencies . . .

P19: States shall provide prior and timely notification . . . on activities that may have a significant adverse transboundary environmental effect . . .

P9: States should cooperate to strengthen endogenous capacity-building for sustainable development . . .

P13: States shall develop national law regarding liability and compensation for the victims of pollution and other environmental damage . . .

P23: The environment and natural resources of people under oppression, domination and occupation shall be protected.

P24: Warfare is inherently destructive of sustainable development . . .

P25: Peace, development and environmental protection are interdependent and indivisible.

P26: States shall resolve all their environmental disputes peacefully.

HUMAN DEVELOPMENT AND UN
CONFERENCES TO SUPPORT WOMEN

Before 1990, the UN convened two international conferences on women followed by a third in 1990 and fourth in 1995 (see Table 5.1). One of the most important HD themes expressed in these conferences is the full participation of women in development (1975) and in all aspects of political, social, and economic life (especially discussed at the 1995 conference). Participation is a staple of the HDCA, as articulated by both Sen and Nussbaum, and clearly was crucial in the debates and discussions about women's role in society. Concern about women's issues and feminist activism had been building for decades leading up to the UN declared *Decade for Women* launched at the 1975 Mexico City Conference.[7] The women's movement had lobbied governments to include women and to discuss policies directly addressing challenges women face. They organized and galvanized civil society organizations to promote women's rights, and they challenged the dominant patriarchal perspective (Zinsser, 2002, pp. 143–144). And yet, women were still left out of most official discussions, and women's issues were still subservient to what were considered more important international relations topics (Zinsser, 2002, p. 139; O'Donoghue and Rowe, 2022, p. 88). The extent of women's lobbying efforts, particularly in organizing civil society groups to have an impact on international negotiations (at the UN and even before, at the League of Nations) resulted in—as just one example of their efforts—the 1972 UNGA resolution to convene a conference on women that came at the request of the UN Commission on the Status of Women (CSW).[8]

Even with all of the work done up to that point on challenges faced by women—such as the drafting of legal documents, research, and NGO coordination conducted by the CSW since its formation in 1947—it was still not enough to convene a conference solely for the purpose of focusing on women's issues. What put women on the agenda and overcame UNGA country delegate opposition was connecting economic and development issues with challenges women face (Olcott, 2017, pp. 7–11; O'Donoghue and Rowe, 2022, p. 88). Decolonization had led to more UNGA member states, increasing from 50 in 1945 to 144 in 1975, and new member states meant a rise of *developing* or *Global South* countries in UNGA voting power (as a voting bloc, the Group of 77 formed in 1964). The new group of states were concerned with industrialization and economic progress, with reducing poverty and increasing the well-being of people in their borders, with fairer trade agreements, and with transforming the international economic system to benefit all states rather than (only or primarily) the developed ones. For instance, when the UNGA passed a resolution condemning discrimination against women in the 1960s, it did so by "presenting 'discriminatory customs and traditions' as impediments to the economic transformation," and indeed "to the majority of UN members in the 1960s and 1970s, acting autonomously for the first time in post-war international relations, 'development' was the all-consuming issue" (Zinsser 2002, 145). This marked the 1975 Conference on Women which focused on women's ability to participate in development and the economy—at least that was the focus from the Global South countries.

UN women's conferences were sites of contested ideas over state's rights (rights to sovereignty and to economic development) and human rights (women's rights, deprivations, and women's lived experiences). Ultimately, they presented a challenge to structural economic institutions and patriarchal cultural norms and values (e.g., Ghodsee, 2010; Olcott, 2017). People attending these conferences and NGO parallel conferences (called NGO tribunes) recognized the disagreements and embraced them to show that women's issues were deeply social, economic, and political issues and that not all women everywhere faced the same issues: "disunity was, in fact, an achievement of [the International Women's Year]" (Olcott, 2017, 5). Despite the "strategic use of secondary status of women's issues" (Zinsser, 2002, p. 146), the Mexico City Conference demonstrated that women had just as much to say about international relations as men did, and that women were deeply affected by and deserved to participate in political and economic decisions at all national and international levels.

The HD themes of well-being, dignity, equality, health, and education all surface in the negotiations, documents, agreements, and legacies of the women's conferences, even while other international relations issues or contested ideological debates seemed to get more attention. The 1975 Mexico City Conference was the first to specifically address women's concerns, rights, challenges, and issues, though not the first to call for them. The CSW was influenced by NGO workers with whom it coordinated. In fact, the international women's year was inspired by two women, Florica Andrei from Romania and Helvi Sipila from Finland. The conference was meant to investigate the two themes of equality and development (Chen, 1995, p. 478). The UNGA Resolution 3010 added a third theme of peace (UNGA, 1972; UN, 1996, p. 33). The women's conferences focused on all three concerns, which represented the aims of three major Cold War voting blocs: "(a) To promote equality between men and women; (b) To ensure the full integration of women in the total development effort . . . [and] (c) To recognize the importance of women's increasing contribution to the development of friendly relations and co-operation among States and to the strengthening of world peace" (UNGA, 1972), representing respectively the a) Western ideals led by the United States, b) non-aligned or G-77 countries and ideals, and c) the Soviet Union ideals (Zinsser 2002, 147; Bonfiglioli 2016). The three themes influenced discussions on women's rights, challenges, and issues that ensued in the following conferences and subsequent decades, molding and delimiting progress on women's rights while also expanding the discussion to show that "women's rights are human rights" as US representative Hillary Clinton proclaimed at the 1995 Beijing Women's Conference.

The Mexico City conference outcome documents—*Declaration of Mexico* and the *World Plan of Action for Implementation of the Objectives of the International Women's Year*—outlined the issues and challenges women faced in the areas of equality, development, and peace, and specifically focused on structural problems that led to such challenges (e.g., paragraph 3 of the *Declaration*: "It is the responsibility of the State to create the necessary facilities so that women may be integrated into society . . . ") (UN, 1976). The conference negotiations finally allowed country delegates in the UNGA to begin discussions of how to address discrimination against women, a topic that the UNGA had recognized for years but on which it was stymied by disagreement on how to eliminate discrimination (UN, 1996, p. 23, paragraph 87). The documents highlight HD concerns that "equality between men and women means equality in their dignity and worth as human beings" (paragraph 1), and that women should have education and opportunities for work, participation, health, and other elements that make a human life worth living. Even so, reflecting the previous decades of non-action on women's issues based on lack of consensus on how to achieve equality, the plan of action highlights state sovereignty and national plans for implementation over universal values and objectives.

The two subsequent conferences in Copenhagen and Nairobi, despite being plagued by international and Cold War politics (Ghodsee, 2010), made further progress on women's rights and continued to promote the vision of an integrated discussion of human well-being and women's participation that took on a holistic vision of human life. For instance, Zinsser (2002) notes that the language and the way that women were described in the resolutions and outcome documents changed as the decade proceeded. Starting out with victimization language and a more passive tone in the Mexico City Conference documents, a shift became evident in the Copenhagen and Nairobi Conference documents as women came to be considered as more central and active participants in the process. Women's rights, and women as agents rather than victims, came to the fore in the documents, language, and even the ways the objectives and plans of action were articulated. In this process, women became "central, not peripheral, to the realization of the broader goals of the United Nations" (Zinsser, 2002, p. 158).

What is more, the women's conferences offered civil society organizations insight into lobbying practices and ways to impact and influence the outcome of international negotiations, conference diplomacy, and national actions to address development issues (O'Donoghue and Row, 2022) and this indeed "served to galvanize the international women's movement" (Chen, 1995, p. 477). The conferences allowed women from different cultures, perspectives, societies, and ideologies to listen and argue with one another about their lived experiences and priorities. In this way, the conferences motivated and prompted more discussion and awareness of a holistic view of human life on Earth that later became prominently articulated in the UNDP's HDRs. Despite the work of the international conferences on women, and the agreements arrived at during and after the conferences, gender inequality continues to be a problem in the UN and in international negotiation trainings and practices (Jain, 2005; O'Dell et al., 2023).

HUMAN DEVELOPMENT AND UN CONFERENCES
TO SUPPORT THE LEAST DEVELOPED COUNTRIES

The UN has long focused on trying to identify the countries that are in most need of development assistance. At first, such support was offered in the form of development technical assistance through the Expanded Programme of Technical Assistance (EPTA). Development assistance discussions are now often framed as discussions about financial support to achieve the Millennium Development Goals (MDGs) and the Sustainable Development Goals (SDGs). In the 1970s, a focus and concern with Least Developed Countries (LDCs) came to the fore, inspired by the UN Conference on Trade and Development (UNCTAD) and its innovative leaders. UNCTAD called for an international conference on LDCs, and called for the UNGA to approve a list of LDCs so as to concentrate international aid to support them. The initial list of 24 LDCs, defined based on their low GDP and later according to a more expansive set of indicators, increased over the years to 46 countries as of the most recent triennial review in 2021 (down from 49 in 2001).[9] Leading up to the first 1981 conference, in line with the provocative language of the *New International Economic Order* (NIEO), UNCTAD called on the international community to be concerned about the challenges LDCs face and to create a *Substantial New Program of Action for the 1980s for the LDCs* (SNPA, 1981), championed in large part by UNCTAD Secretary General Gamani Corea from Sri Lanka (Corea, 1981).

Each of the five LDC conferences have produced a Programme of Action (PoA), the first labeled the SNPA (1981) with four follow-up PoAs named for the location of the LDC conference: Paris (PPoA, 1990), Brussels (BPoA, 2001), Istanbul (IPoA, 2011), and Doha (DPoA, 2023). The PoAs describe general conditions of the LDCs at the time, both of the people and their situation in the international economic and political order. They also identified specific interventions necessary for development (agricultural and manufacturing support were initially prominent). The sections in the PoAs on how the international community and LDCs can think about and support humans living within their borders provide an understanding of how HD issues were built into the discussion of LDCs. The sections that are of particular note in each PoA and that we assessed through a qualitative and quantitative content analysis are labeled "Human Resources" (SNPA, 1981), "Mobilizing and

Developing Human Capacities in the LDCs" (PpoA, 1990), "Building Human and Institutional Capacities" (BpoA, 2001), "Human and Social Development" (IpoA, 2011), and finally, in the language of the SDGs, "Investing in People in the Least Developed Countries: Eradicating Poverty and Building Capacity to Leave No One Behind" (DpoA, 2023).

Our analysis of key words and language used in the texts of the five PoAs and the general debate speeches given by delegates at the conferences reveals the influence of the HD ideology on thinking about how to improve the situation of LDCs. It shows that thinking from 1981 to 2023 moved away from a focus on macro-economic structural concerns to greater focus on human well-being, particularly education, health, and environment and sustainable development concerns. The analysis of the five LDC conference PoAs is displayed in Figure 5.1 where a review of the main keywords under eight categories in each document is presented. The categories reveal and compare the general ways in which the documents characterized development, LDC situations, and

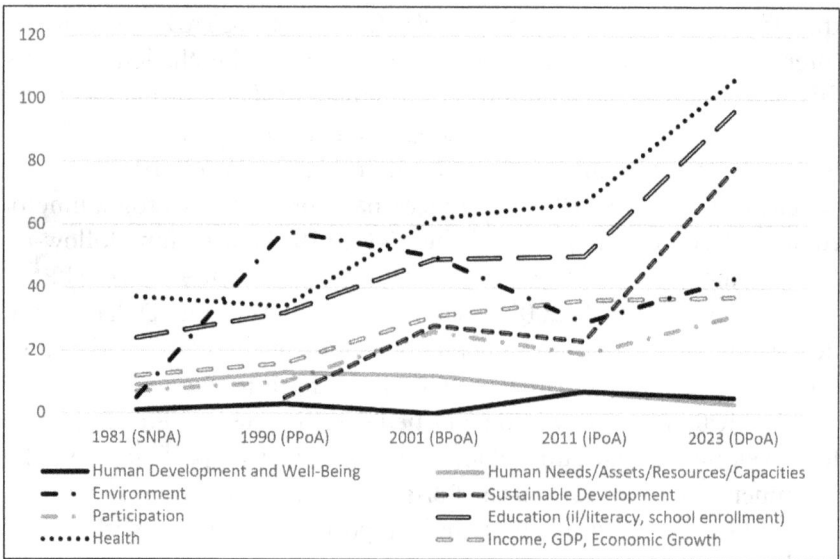

Figure 5.1. Presence of Themes in UN LDC Conference Programmes of Action (1981–2023). *Source: Author created database. The quantitative content analysis was conducted on the five LDC conference Programmes of Action (PoAs) from 1981 to 2023 under six categories. We assessed the presence of, and context of, multiple keywords related to each of the categories, then compiled them in this figure.*

international ideology related to LDCs. Textual analysis illuminates the thinking and ideas behind the key words and language.

What we found, firstly, was that the way humans are described in the PoAs has shifted from a focus on humans as means of development, to a more concerted effort to reveal humans as ends of development in line with HD ideology. The language of the SNPA (1981) was in line with the basic needs approach, the idea that was in vogue at the time, particularly at the World Bank (Streeten, 1979). It encouraged support so that LDCs could "provide at least internationally accepted minimum standards" (SNPA, 1981). But what is noticeable in the SNPA (1981) and PPoA (1990) is how humans are discussed as means to development rather than as ends. Essentially, the text argues that development will not happen without mobilizing human resources and that human resources must be mobilized to ensure development outcomes. For instance, under the heading of education and culture, the problem of illiteracy is not framed as a lack of opportunities for humans, but as posing a problem for the state's development: "illiteracy . . . as well as limited possibilities for basic education, are serious obstacles to improved economic performance and social standards" (SNPA, 1981, para 24). And in a discussion of health and nutrition, the language states that the problem with lack of health care is that it detracts from a state's ability to develop, not that it keeps humans from living well: "health and nutrition standards . . . are a serious impediment to their socio-economic development" (para 35).

The shift to a more complex and human-centered focus, in which humans are discussed as ends in themselves rather than as means, first appears in the 1990 PPoA. For example, Section IV of the PPoA states that: "Men and women are the essential resource and beneficiaries of the development of the LDCs" (para 64) and "Development should be human-centered and broadly based, offering equal opportunities to all people, both women and men, to participate fully and freely in economic, social, cultural, and political activities" (para 65). What is more, there is a heavy emphasis on the participation of all people in development processes, with an emphasis on women (recall the 1975 Conference on Women in which women from less developed countries emphasized including women in development), as well as public-private partnerships, NGOs, etc. The BPoA (2001) also highlights human well-being by including the topic earlier in its report and with more emphasis: Commitment 1 shows a shift in focus: "Fostering a people-centered policy framework." Paragraphs 22–23 under this category use language that reveals a shift in thinking about human beings as the end, rather than means, of development. It discusses creating an "enabling environment" to eradicate poverty, one "that provides opportunities for all, particularly the poorest . . . on the principle that human beings are at the center of the concerns for sustainable development." The paragraphs focus on the ideas of strengthening "human capacities" and "empowering the poor."

The shift to describing humans as ends in themselves is more obvious in the 2001–2023 documents (10 to 30 years after the first HDR, revealing perhaps the influence of the HD paradigm). In the 1981 and 1990 PoAs, the language of human needs, humans as assets, and human resources is emphasized, but such language eventually is rivaled by the language of *human development* and human well-being (especially in the 2011 and 2023 documents). The 2011 PoA specifically references LDC measurement and progress on the HDI, and the term *human development* itself overtakes that of *human resources* and *human capacities*.[10] In 1990, the language of *human development* does not make it into the PoA, but it does appear in delegate speeches during the general debate. For example, the UNDP representative said that, "with the advent of a new decade, a new era inspired by the irresistible wave of human freedom was emerging" referring to the break-up of the Soviet Union. He then goes on to talk about how the UNDP is and has been supporting LDCs. He then proposes a financial assistance plan that would include support for "human development programmes" (para 60). It is perhaps not surprising that the UNDP representative would include a reference to HD, considering that the UNDP was only recently involved in the new HDR publication, but three other mentions of HD are noteworthy from the representatives of Norway, Morocco, and the Netherlands. For instance, the representative of Norway was concerned with marginalization of LDCs and "emphasized the need for a broader approach to human development encompassing political freedom, respect for human rights and the right of the people to participate in the decision-making process."

Language favoring income generation, macro-economic growth, and gross domestic product (GDP) appear in all the PoA documents and steadily increase over time, but these elements do not appear as often as mention of three key elements of the HD paradigm: education, health, and the environment. The SNPA (1981) is perhaps most expressive of the need to focus on economic growth and support macroeconomic projects (e.g., in the agricultural and manufacturing sectors). That focus does not necessarily diminish in the later PoAs and is often taken up with the exact same phrases and sections. An overall focus on structural problems, both internal and external, cannot be missed in any of the documents (especially in the 1990 and 2001 criticisms of structural adjustment programs and in the lack of LDC progress toward most development metrics). All of the PoAs have significant sections on trade, finance, and international cooperation in the form of development assistance to support LDCs.

Yet, by 2001, there is a shift in attention away from macroeconomic growth in favor of an HD focus. BPoA (2001) starts out with similar language as the previous two reports, noting the poverty and structural challenges LDCs face and especially pointing to challenges associated with globalization and lack of access to information and communication technologies (among other technologies). Yet the tone and language are different. BPoA discusses human capacity and sustainable development, terms that did not appear in the previous programs, and it specifically includes goals and issues discussed and passed by the Millennium Declaration only a few months earlier. While economic growth and income are a priority, amounting to two out of the four national policies highlighted, the language is now more concerned with human well-being, as indicated in its first sentence under the heading *Objectives*, that "This Programme of Action aims to significantly improve the human conditions of more than 600 million people in 49 LDCs during the present decade" (BpoA, 2001).

Because the HD paradigm is so closely connected with the HDI (with its indicators of education, health, and living standard), and it highlights the importance of participation in society, comparing PoA documents to see how these concepts appear gives insight into the influence of the HD ideology over time. Attention to education and health found in all the PoAs increases over time along with a less noticeable but still significant rise in discussion of the importance of participation. Education is a major point of focus for the 2001, 2011, and 2023 PoAs and in the education category, support for bolstering school enrollment increases from a mention of four times in 1981 to 19 times in 2023. The overall emphasis on education is high throughout the PoAs, and it is framed first as a way for humans to advance development (1981), but then shifts to being discussed as a right in and of itself (2023). The term *education* itself appears 68 times in 2023 compared to only 14 times in 1981.

Another important point is how discussion of literacy and illiteracy changes over time in the PoAs. In 1981, governments are charged to ensure all citizens are able to read while the DPoA (2023) mentions the importance of all having digital and financial literacy. The latter's section on "Achieving Universal Access to Quality Education, Skills and Lifelong Learning" includes a discussion of the lack of education and specific targets to be achieved (mirroring the SDGs) (paragraphs 43–52). While some of the language still hints at humans as means, as in education used to "harness the demographic dividend," there remains a sustained focus on the importance of all types of education including job training, lifelong learning, and equitable access to education for girls and boys. Indeed, the 2011 and 2023 PoAs mirror the language of the MDGs and SDGs, by emphasizing the importance of ensuring all children and especially girls being able to "have access to and complete, free and compulsory primary education of good quality" (BPoA 2001, para 36).

The health category (i.e., how important it is for a population to have access to affordable health care and to be healthy) is also consistently emphasized in the PoAs, but the language on why health is important and the focus within health changes too. The first few PoAs emphasize health as part of a list of basic needs, or minimum standards necessary for people to contribute (as human resources or human capacities) to development and growth. Then in 2001 we see a shift toward a more nuanced discussion of health including supporting health care systems, training health care personnel, and providing health care as a basic right to the population. By 2011, the language further changes to supporting access to health care as part of "people-centered poverty reduction strategies." Portraying health as a holistic issue, it emphasizes training health professionals, and supporting national health systems and health care financing (BPoA, 2011, para 2, a).

Two interesting changes in language related to reproductive and sexual rights and disease also reflect evolving concerns. In earlier reports, there is a major concern with population growth as a detriment to reducing poverty and development. LDCs are encouraged to promote "family planning and population control" and research on "acceptable techniques of family planning" (SNPA, 1981, para 39). By 2001 and 2011, the language changes from "family planning" to "reproductive and sexual health care and promoting reproductive rights" (PPoA, 2001, para 35) and concerns about population growth as a detriment to development are not as evident. In fact, the term "population growth" occurs four and seven times, respectively in 1981 and 1991, but disappears in 2001, coming back only three times in 2011 and once in 2023. Concerns about communicable diseases also change between the PoAs. For instance, COVID-19 appears 65 times in 2023 whereas no other mention of a specific communicable disease came close, with HIV/AIDS the second highest mention far behind (at 16 times in 2001). Throughout the conferences, as revealed in the PoAs, health concerns became more than just a means to support economic growth but rather an important human right and an element supporting human lives of dignity.

Likewise, language on participation—a key component of HD ideology—shifts between 1981 and 2023 to reflect the importance of human participation in all aspects of political, social, and economic life. In 1981, there were only five instances discussing the importance of participation in the development process. By contrast, 56 mentions of participation appear in 1990 with many of them referring to broader participation in the social, economic, and political dimensions of society. The shift in 1990 is evident in paragraph 11 emphasizing "the importance of adequate participation in the decision-making process at all levels . . . " and in a statement by the representative of the Federal Republic of Germany expressing the need for "broad participation in the political decision-making process" (paragraph 64). Significantly, in 2001 all references to participation (except one) concern people's participation in the economy, in politics, women's participation in all aspects of life, and the participation of LDCs and stakeholders in decision-making. This pattern continues in 2011 and 2023 with language like: "Development strategies and programmes of least developed countries and their partners should strive to enhance the participation and empowerment of the poor and marginalized in their own development and benefit the most vulnerable, ensuring social justice, democracy, gender equality and sustained, inclusive and equitable economic growth and sustainable development . . . " (2011, para 29).

Aside from these changes, there was also a notable increase and change in discussion of the environment and sustainable development. The latter was not mentioned at all in the 1981 document, little surprise since the Brundtland Report had only defined it in 1987, but starting from 1990 there was a huge rise in use of the term and even a special focus in 2023 on helping the LDCs to achieve the SDGs by 2030.

THE UNDP DEFINES HUMAN DEVELOPMENT THROUGH THE HUMAN DEVELOPMENT REPORTS

In our analysis of UN conference documents above, we focused on the specific indicators that comprise the HDI (education, health, and income) plus environmental concerns, women's empowerment, and the political, economic, and social freedoms humans need in order to live decent, dignified lives. But HD covers more than just those topics and the extent of what HD covers has been of significant discussion since the first HDR was published. Attempts at defining and expanding the HD paradigm include creating a more accurate and expansive index or set of indicators that would more reliably measure important capabilities and opportunities that humans need (like participation in society, for instance). Some contributions have redefined and expanded on existing concepts, offering alternative ways of envisioning and practicing policies so as to focus on humans as the center and reason for action (in redefining peacekeeping as human security, for instance). And the major global attempts led by the UN to create specific and measurable development goals with specific deadlines in the MDGs and SDGs can be seen as a way to implement the HD ideology by creating concrete opportunities for humans to have the capabilities they need to thrive.

THE HUMAN DEVELOPMENT REPORTS OFFICE AT THE UNDP

The Human Development Reports Office (HDRO) was established at the UNDP headquarters in New York with Mahbub ul Haq as its first Director after he successfully convinced UNDP Administrator William H. Draper III in 1989 to support the creation of the HDRs and HDI under the UNDP's aegis. Subsequently, the first HDR was published in

1990.[11] Since then hundreds of HDRs have been published and supported by the HDRO including annual global-level HDRs and many national (country-specific) and sub-national (e.g., provincial and sub-provincial level) HDRs. In total, HD-related publications supported by the HDRO including background and occasional papers, number in the thousands.

The HDRO is actually not a large organization—proving that a small group of people really can change the world. It has been run by a director or co-director along with a small staff whose research and work is supplemented by academic and practitioner consultants (each background paper, occasional paper, and HDR includes a list of the people who contributed to the research and writing). These publications are intended to be unbiased, produced outside of the political influence of countries (and their governments), and available to legislators, policymakers and the public at large (often freely downloadable on the internet with global-level HDRs available in multiple languages). While the independence of the HDRs has been challenged by some from the beginning (as discussed by Hirai, 2017, pp. 36–37), HDR influence has nonetheless been widespread and exceptional in directing "attention toward the social and human aspects of development and away from the traditional indicators of economic growth" (Stokke, 2009, p. 344).

The early research, writing, and discussions that created the HDRs centered around how to define human development (Kaul, 2003), how to measure human choices rather than commodities through the new composite indicator of the HDI (Haq, 1995, pp. 46–66), and how to update the HDI (Anand and Sen, 2003). Indeed, long-time HDRO Director Sakiko Fukuda-Parr (who was present for much of the HDRO's early work), and her colleague A. K. Shiva Kumar, indicated that the dialogue, debate, and intellectual discussion was paramount and exciting: "From the beginning the atmosphere in the [HDRO] in New York has been exhilarating. Intense intellectual exchanges and debates between eminent thinkers, development practitioners, and social activists on the one hand, and young and committed professionals . . . have led to the crafting and articulation of many compelling ideas" (Fukuda-Parr and Shiva Kumar, 2003, p. xxiii).

The work of the HDRO team has been extensive to say the least. Between 1990 and 2023, the team produced 29 large global-level reports (there were only a few years in which the HDR combined two years or skipped a year). On top of this, they will soon be producing global HDRs on rapid technological change and digital technologies (2024), and planetary pressures and inequalities (2025).[12] From its inception under Haq's leadership, the HDRO has also supported many governments in creating their own HDRs. As Inge Kaul remembers, Haq would regularly say that "no national minister would act on global analyses, however fascinating" (2003, p. 90). Thus, Haq encouraged the team to expand their work beyond global annual reports to include national and subnational reports even while funding, staff, and consultants were limited. Altogether, over 800 national HDRs produced since the 1990s offer country-level analysis of HD themes and measurements (Hall, 2019). Thus, "on the one hand, the global HDRs can propose universal normative standards of human development; on the other hand, the regional and national HDRs can contextualize [sic] them taking their complex and various circumstances into account" (Hirai, 2017, p. 37). Disaggregated information in the national and subnational reports also points the way for implementing HD in specific national contexts as articulated within local discourses and discussions about capabilities. This move was a practical choice to expand the influence of the HDRs.

DIMENSIONS OF GLOBALIZATION ADDRESSED IN THE HDRS

At the epicenter of disseminating the HD ideology, the HDRs share a common foundation in the human development and capability approach but each annual report also typically ties this to a particular theme or issue area. As shown in Table 5.3, the global level HDRs have covered a large number of topics that can be roughly catalogued according to four different dimensions of globalization: economic, political, ecological, and cultural.

THE ECONOMIC DIMENSION

At the heart of discussions about HD from the beginning has been the complicated issue of its relationship to economic growth, gross national income (GNI), and other macroeconomic indicators, as well as how to measure HD as separate or distinct from income and income poverty. The major contribution of the 1990 HDR to this debate was

Table 5.3. Dimensions of Globalization in Global Human Development Reports (1990–2023)

Year	HDR Shortened Title	Main Dimension of Globalization Covered
1990	Concept and Measurement of HD	Economic
1991	Financing HD	Economic
1992	Global Dimensions of HD	All dimensions
1993	People's Participation	Political
1994	New Dimensions of Human Security	Political
1995	Gender and HD	Cultural
1996	Economic Growth and HD	Economic
1997	HD to Eradicate Poverty	Economic
1998	Consumption for HD	Economic and Ecological
1999	Globalization with a Human Face	Economic
2000	Human Rights and HD	Cultural and Political
2001	Making New Technologies Work for HD	Economic
2002	Deepening Democracy in a Fragmented World	Political
2003	Millennium Development Goals	All dimensions
2004	Cultural Liberty in Today's Diverse World	Cultural
2005	International Cooperation (Aid, Trade, and Security)	Political
2006	Power, Poverty, and the Global Water Crisis	Ecological
2007	Fighting Climate Change: Human Solidarity	Ecological
2009	Human Mobility and Development	Cultural and Political
2010	Pathways to HD	Cultural and Political
2011	Sustainability and Equity	Ecological
2013	The Rise of the South	Cultural and Political
2014	Sustaining Progress: Reducing Vulnerabilities	Cultural and Political
2015	Work for HD	Economic
2016	HD for Everyone	Cultural
2018	HD Indices and Indicators Statistical Update	Economic
2019	Inequalities in HD in the 21st Century	Economic
2020	HD and the Anthropocene	Ecological
2022	Uncertain Times, Unsettled Lives: Shaping our Future	All dimensions
2023	Societal Polarization and Collective Action	Cultural and Political

its launching of the Human Development Index (HDI), an index that combines measurements of education, health, and income to provide a multidimensional analysis of human well-being. Several HDRs have followed up on this discussion as have many academic studies and working papers. One of the first attempts to summarize and combine some of the leading papers was titled *Readings in Human Development* which included nine previously published papers on how to measure HD (Fukuda-Parr and Shiva Kumar, 2003).

Measuring HD is difficult because the HD paradigm attempts to consider everything that is important for humans that make their lives valuable, dignified, and worth living, (i.e., the process of enlarging people's choices). The HDI, however, was meant to be simplistic so that it could counter the simplicity of per capita GNP (or GDP or GNI), but could also encourage thinking about human well-being. The purpose of the measurement was to open up a channel for dialogue to discuss and refocus the way development funds were spent, to analyze which projects would be supported and how those projects would connect with supporting human well-being, and to assess how to make updates to the way that funding is distributed within and between countries.

The HDI measures the level of education in a society by collecting information on average years of schooling (for children) and mean years of schooling (collected on adults aged 25 years or older). Education is a crucial element of a person's quality of life as it supports one's ability to critically think through the implications of one's actions and it supports one in searching for or creating new opportunities. With more education, one has a greater likelihood of finding or taking advantage of new opportunities and a greater possibility of coming up with new ways of addressing challenges in one's life.

The HDI incorporates life expectancy at birth to measure the health of a society and its population. The life expectancy measure indicates how long people live on average in a given society. A lower life expectancy may indicate lower access to health care, lower quality health care, lack of or limited access to nutritional foods, limited access to maternal health care, and so on. The final HDI component included in the index is GNI per capita (i.e., the value of all goods and services produced in a country during a given year divided by its total population). This is perhaps the most problematic of the measures because it does not account for the way that money is distributed in society. Rather, it only accounts for the total value of production, assuming that this total, divided by the population, gives some insight into how much money people have in a society on average.

But the creators of the HDI did not think that their work had finished with that index. They understood that the HDI was a crude measure, and they also knew that important elements of the HD ideology had been left out, especially regarding the ability to participate in one's society. Indeed, more than a decade later, the 2013 HDR noted that using simplistic measurements to assess country or human well-being does not provide us with sufficient information: "We may, for the sake of convenience, use many simple indicators of human development . . . but the quest cannot end there . . . Assessing the quality of life is a much more complex exercise than what can be captured through only one number . . . " (UNDP, 2013, p. 24). Updates to the HDI measurements and new indexes to measure elements missing from the HDI have been featured in the HDRs since 1990. For instance, the 2018 HDR reported on the progress of measuring HD, providing a statistical update to the HDI and other indexes introduced in the HDRs up to that point (Table 5.4). Achim Steiner, the UNDP Administrator, noted in his introduction to the report that "Human development data, analysis and reporting have been at the heart of that paradigm" (p. iii). The 2018 HDR also provides a breakdown of many disaggregated indicators as well, revealing how particular groups might benefit more than others on HD outcomes.

The HDI is calculated by averaging the scores on four basic indicators each of which are scaled so that the final outcome is a number between 0 and 1 whereby the closer a society scores to 1, the higher their HD, meaning that the people are better off (Anand and Sen, 2003). The UNDP has updated this index annually in its HDRs since 1990, including notes at the end of each HDR on updates to measurement techniques. The HDI itself utilizes ideas from previous indexes, like the PQLI (shown in Table 5.4) which was based on the Basic Needs approach to development, but sought to measure some similar outcomes. Created by David Morris at the Overseas Development Institute (1979), the PQLI chose similar indicators to what Haq and his team would later choose for the HDI. The primary difference was the HDI adding income as a measure of living standards and shifting the education indicator to capture a more nuanced understanding of the knowledge people have,

Table 5.4. **Commonly Used Human Development–Related Indexes and Indicators (1990–2023)**

Indexes Used to Measure HD	Indicators upon Which the Index Is Based
Human Development Index (HDI)	• Education (mean years of schooling for adults aged 25 years or older; expected years of schooling for school age children) • Health (life expectancy at birth) • Standard of living (gross national income per capita)
Inequality Adjusted HDI (IHDI)	• Same indicators as the HDI, but takes the averages of those indictors by adjusting them for inequality. If there is no inequality in a country, the IHDI and HDI are the same.
Gender Development Index (GDI)	• Same indicators as the HDI, but measures the difference in female and male achievement on the indicators.
Multidimensional Poverty Index (MPI)	• Health (mal/nutrition rates; child mortality age 18 years or less) • Education (years of schooling for school age children over six years old; school attendance of school age children) • Standard of living (access to and rates of electricity, sanitation, drinking water, housing, cooking fuel, and assets)
Gender Inequality Index (GII)	• Reproductive health (maternal mortality ratio; adolescent birth rate) • Empowerment (female and male share of parliamentary seats and secondary education levels) • Labor market (female and male labor force participation rate)
Physical Quality of Life Index (PQLI)	• Education (literacy rate) • Health (life expectancy; infant mortality)

Source: "Technical Notes" from http://www.undp.org. For more specific information on the composition of these indexes, see https://hdr.undp.org/system/files/documents/technical-notes-calculating-human-development-indices.pdf.

not just their ability to read. Even so, the initial HDI left out quite a lot of what the HD paradigm insists is important for human life, and it also did not distinguish between different groups in society and the opportunities available to them. The Inequality-adjusted Human Development Index (IHDI) then came along using the same indictors as the HDI, but with scores adjusted for inequalities between and within groups in society. The Gender Development Index (GDI) also uses the same measures as the HDI but separates out access to opportunities between males and females, recognizing that disaggregating such information is crucial to understanding the vast difference between the way that males and females are able to function in society.

A heightened concern with female access to opportunities and participation in society is salient in the writings of prominent HDCA authors like Amartya Sen and Martha Nussbaum and also in the international community's engagement through conference diplomacy in creating resolutions and treaties to encourage women's participation (as outlined in previous sections of this chapter). In response to such concerns about gender, two indexes were thus developed to offer even more insight into HD from a gender perspective. The Gender Inequality Index (GII) measures female health outcomes specific to maternal health, and reports on female access to education and the workplace. A more recently proposed index is the Gender Social Norms Index (GSNI), which attempts to measure bias against women through country-level surveys that ask people about their perceptions of male and female roles in political, education, economic, and physical lives. The main finding from surveys conducted in 95 countries since 2005 is that even in economically developed countries there is a significant bias against women (by both men and women) in public life that acts as a barrier to women's full participation (UNDP, 2023).

Beyond issues of measurement, substantive issues of economic globalization have been addressed in various HDRs, including financing for HD (1991), economic growth (1996), eradicating poverty (1997), new technologies and economies of globalization (1999, 2001), productive and creative work (2015), and the challenge of inequality (2019). What stands out in these reports is that they do not always endorse status quo economic frameworks and indeed sometimes reject them. A prime example is HDR 2015 entitled *Work for Human Development,* which is not just about employment in the formal labor market. Rather, "work, not just jobs, contributes to human progress and enhances [HD] . . . the jobs framework fails to capture many kinds of work that have important [HD] implications—as with care work, voluntary work and such creative work as writing and painting" (UNDP, 2015, p. 3). Likewise, earlier reports addressing economic dimensions such as how to finance HD (1991) and how to compare HD with economic growth (1996) challenged existing economic and financial structures and called on them to have a deeper understanding of where financing and economic growth are happening, what is being funded, and how economic growth and reallocation of funding contributes to actual human well-being.

CULTURAL AND POLITICAL DIMENSIONS

Several of the HDRs broach subjects that fall under political and cultural dimensions of globalization including those that address potentially sensitive subjects like gender (1995), or potential conflict between cultures and liberty (2004). Indeed, the ideal of being culturally sensitive has been a thorny issue for the HD paradigm from the beginning. HD has sought to manage tensions between particularity and universalism and connect itself at times with a universal notion of human rights (as addressed in the 2000 HDR). Indeed, Mark Malloch Brown as UNDP Administrator wrote in the 2004 HDR that it was "a time when the notion of a global 'clash of cultures' is resonating so powerfully—and worryingly—around the world . . . finding answers to the old questions of how best to manage and mitigate conflict over language, religion, culture, and ethnicity has taken on renewed importance" (UNDP, 2004, p. vi). The HDRs have had to ride a fine line between calling cultures out for discrimination against women, children, foreigners, and other minority or racial groups, while also attempting to respect the histories and beliefs that people groups hold dear. But the HD also takes a stand, as Nussbaum did in her book on the topic of gender and as the human rights regime has done, by arguing that all people, no matter their gender or other identity, should enjoy equal rights and equal access to capabilities and opportunities. In the case of gender, the HDRs have been unequivocal in their support of female human development, and they have introduced the GII and GDI as important measurements to provide gender-disaggregated information on how males versus females are doing in society (e.g., UNDP, 1995, p. 72).

There are also several HDRs that cover the issue of international cooperation to achieve HD outcomes and development goals in general (2005; 2010; 2016; 2019; 2022) with one specifically dedicated to the Millennium Development Goals (2003). Indeed, international agreement and cooperation is essential if the HD framework is to be realized, as the HDRs point out. Consider the 2005 HDR, which discusses in some depth how the international community can come together to reorient and rethink how development aid is provided. It returns to the issue of financing addressed earlier in the 1991 HDR but also references the important ways in which the MDGs need resources if they are to be achieved. Presciently, the report notes that without changes in aid and support from the international community, many countries will not be able to achieve HD or MDG goals, not necessarily for lack of political will, but for lack of financing and other support (pp. 75–76).

THE ECOLOGICAL DIMENSION

During the early years, HDRs mentioned issues related to the ecological environment in which people need to live and thrive, but it was not until the 1998 HDR that a concerted effort was made by the HDRs to discuss the environment. The 1998 HDR examined the conflict between better living standards for people around the world (which the HD paradigm supports) and the strain that such living standards place on the environment. Other reports specifically addressing ecological issues followed including a report addressing the global water crisis (2006) and concerning problems caused by increases in average global temperatures and the impact this would have on biodiversity (2007). A report discussing sustainable development practices to prevent against environmental destruction came out in 2011, and a 2020 report specifically addressed changes that human activities have wrought on the environment. What ties all these reports to the ecological dimension of globalization is that they identify the conflict between increasing human living standards and environmental destruction. They note that sustainable development is needed, warn of a coming ecological crisis associated with human activities, and impress upon the reader that there are substantial inequities between people groups. On the last point, they discuss how some people are not only benefitting at a greater rate than others in the current era of globalization but that people in poverty are more likely to experience the detrimental effects of environmental degradation (UNDP, 2020, pp. 69–88).

DEVELOPMENT GOALS: MDGs AND SDGs

The advent of HD thinking in the 1990s, as represented in the HDRs, was also at the forefront of international conferences and high-level committees that led to the creation of the 2000–2015 Millennium Development Goals (MDGs) (Fukuda-Parr and Hulme, 2011, p. 18; Fukuda-Parr, 2011). The MDG targets corresponded closely with the HD idea of poverty as multidimensional and related to deprivations concerning human capabilities. The MDGs also served to bring the development community together under a massive global campaign focused on goals that would reduce poverty and increase human freedoms (Jolly et al., 2004; Fukuda-Parr and Hulme, 2011) which "quickly became the development priority of the entire UN system" (Thérien, 2012a, p. 6). The Millennium Declaration that launched the MDGs was approved by the UNGA in September 2000 and set the tone by stating that "we recognize that . . . we have a collective responsibility to uphold the principles of human dignity, equality, and equity at the global level" (UN, 2000, Section I.2). 189 countries unanimously approved the MDGs.

As scholars have noted, not only the UNDP, but many other UN agencies and departments that report to the UNGA and ECOSOC took up ideas related to HD. Reflecting the adoption of the HD paradigm throughout much of the UN system, the HD discourse of putting people first (over capital accumulation, over nation-states, over territorial boundaries, and over other species) became increasingly evident in the UN's terminology of a) *human* rights, b) *human* development and c) *human* security (Jolly et al., 2004; Jolly, Emmerij, and Weiss, 2009; Thérien, 2012a, 2012b). As UN Secretary-General Kofi Annan insisted, "we will not enjoy development without security, we will not enjoy security without development and we will not enjoy either without respect for human rights" (as quoted in Thérien, 2014, p. 380). UN Secretary-General Ban Ki-moon (2010) likewise signaled that HD is a top priority of the UN; "everything we do is tested by one criterion: has it improved peoples' lives?"

The HD paradigm is also highly prevalent in the wording, justifications, and choices of the goals incorporated into the UN's 2015–2030 Sustainable Development Goals (SDGs) campaign. In fact, the first 4 of the 17 SDGs directly mirror the three components of the HDI. SDG 1 is to "end poverty in all its forms everywhere" and SDG 2 is to "end hunger, achieve food security and improved nutrition and promote sustainable agriculture," both of which reflect the living standard component of the HDI and give highest prioritization to improving the well-being of those in poverty. SDG 3 is to "ensure healthy lives and promote well-being for all at all ages," which is related to the health component of the HDI as traditionally measured by life expectancy. SDG 4 is to "ensure inclusive and equitable quality education and promote lifelong learning opportunities for all" which is tied to the education component of the HDI. The SDGs also go beyond the three core dimensions of capabilities (health, education, and income well-being) in the same way that the broader HD approach transcends the more limited indicators incorporated into the HDI (Alkire, 2002). This is evident in SDG 5 on "gender equality" which is another core theme of the HD paradigm that has been emphasized in gender-related HD indexes including the GDI and GII. On top of this are the other 12 SDGs, many of which are related to how humans interact with the natural environment and sustainability given that ecological health is likewise essential for human development in the present and in the future.[13]

NEXT STEPS FOR HUMAN DEVELOPMENT AND INTERNATIONAL COOPERATION

In this chapter we examined the role of the UN in globalizing HD. As demonstrated here, the UN has been at the forefront of promoting HD ideas and practices, accelerated through conference diplomacy whereby the UN, through its main UNGA and ECOSOC organs, sponsored and organized large international conferences that dealt with many HD related themes (e.g., environment, women, health, education, children, and food). Just as Greta Thunberg's activism was built upon decades of work by scientists, researchers, and activists calling for much greater attention to the environment, the HD paradigm had likewise been long in the making. Many women and men played an important role in building its foundations, re-framing the issues, and mobilizing discussions and debate that would coalesce into the prominence of the UNDP's HDRs that began with William H. Draper III's support under Mahbub ul Haq's leadership. The HD ideology has also been immensely influential in the formulation of global development goals during the twenty-first century, specifically the 2000–2015 Millennium Development Goals (MDGs) and 2015–2030 Sustainable Development Goals (SDGs) forged in the light of an expanding and increasingly globalizing HD paradigm.

Yet while we see much discussion and promotion of HD concepts, ideas, and theories in UN documents, debate, and rhetoric from 1945 to the present, we also see some limitations on the promotion of the HD ideology. When examining the role of the UN, it is arguably more a story of globalization *with* human development than globalization *of* (or *for*) human development. For example, there has been very little by way of global disarmament, ending warfare, freedom of migration, or shifting away from nation-state centered employment, education, and health delivery models in favor of a more global approach. State government officials still hold on dearly to the notion of state sovereignty in many parts of the world. Further, there are still many people who appear to be indifferent to the HD of those they see as the *other,* such as people of a different race, ethnicity, country, socio-economic class, religion, age group, gender, or even family. Environmental degradation is still a major worldwide problem with many people tragically ignoring it, as Thunberg continues to passionately inveigh as of 2023 (indeed, she was arrested in June as she peacefully demonstrated in Malmö, Sweden). And despite the attempt to rethink and reinvigorate the concept of collective security as human security, for instance, the debate in UN organs like the UNSC still primarily concerns state power and realist politics. Anti-human development ideas and practices are still present among many people and places in the world, even if they are also becoming more antiquated.

Nevertheless, there has been some progress over the past 75 years. As discussed above, the HD paradigm was embraced by the UN in its main organs, particularly through ECOSOC, and by the departments and programs created in the 1960s and '70s (especially UNCTAD and UNDP). Indeed, it is the UNDP that promoted the HD paradigm to the rest of the UN through the HDRs, and HD is now widely accepted by many worldwide development organizations as a guiding paradigm for development thinking and practice. The HD approach has also become a powerful ideological contender to the neoliberal vision of development. Lastly, the globalization *with* human development focus, which has emerged as the dominant model, is arguably more advantageous for most people than a kind of globalization that goes *against* human development, even if it may be significantly less preferable for most of the world's people than a true globalization *of* human development.

NOTES

1. Kennedy's book on this topic is thusly named *The Parliament of Man* (2007).

2. Much of the work for the initial reports that laid out the structures of the proposed new UN came from years of committee work in the US State Department, notably organized by an economist and US State Department official, Leo Pasvolsky (1893–1953), but also deeply influenced by US Secretary of State, Cordell Hull (1871–1955), and Under-Secretary of State, Benjamin Sumner Welles (1892–1961), and US President, Franklin D. Roosevelt (1882–1945).

3. See Engfeldt, 1973; Handl, 2012; Paglia, 2021; Robinson, 2021.

4. Prominent examples include Osborn, 1948; Carson, 1962; Palmstierna, 1967; Ehrlich, 1968; Falk, 1971.

5. See UN, 1973, chapter VIII, paragraphs 44–50; Handl, 2012, p. 2; Marklund, 2020, p. 387; Najam, 2005; Rajamani, 2003.

6. See Handl, 2012; Robinson, 2021, 365; Manulak, 2017; Haas, 2022.

7. See Chen, 1995, p. 477; Olcott, 2017, p. 19; O'Donoghue and Rowe, 2022, pp. 88–91.

8. See Chen, 1995, p. 498; Zinsser, 2002, p. 144; Donoghue and Rowe, 2022, pp. 88–91.

9. Data Source: UN. 2023. "Creation of the LDC Category and Timeline of Changes to LDC Membership and Criteria" (https://www.un.org/development /desa) and "The LDC Category After the 2021 Triennial Review" (https://www .un.org/development/desa/dpad/wp-content/uploads/sites/45/LDC-category-2021 .pdf).

10. In 2011 and 2023, the terms "human well-being" and "human development" are used seven and five times, respectively, whereas "human resource/s" and "human capacity/ies" are used six and three times, respectively.

11. The Directors, Co-Directors, and Deputy Directors overseeing the work since 1990 as mentioned in the acknowledgments pages of HDRs include the following list but also include many others who served as special advisors or principal consultants whom we cannot list fully: Mahbub ul Haq, Project Director (1990–1991) and Principle Coordinator (1992–1996); Inge Kaul, Director (1991–1995); Sakiko Fukuda-Parr, Director (1995–2004); Richard Jolly, Principle Coordinator (1996–2000); Selim Jahan, Deputy Director (1996–2001); Omar Noman, Deputy Director (2002–2003); Sarah Burd-Sharps, Deputy Director (2005–2007); Kevin Watkins, Director (2005–2007); Jeni Klugman, Director (2009–2011); Khalid Malik, Director (2013–2014); Eva Jesperson, Deputy Directory (2009–2016); Selim Jahan, Director (2015–2018); Thangavel Palanivel, Deputy Director (2018); and Pedro Conceição, Director (2019–2022). The authors thank Sarah Minghini for help in compiling this list.

12. Source: UNDP website: https://hdr.undp.org.

13. For more on the SDGs, see https://sdgs.un.org/goals.

CHAPTER 6

THE ROLE OF THE GLOBAL SOUTH IN GLOBALIZING HUMAN DEVELOPMENT

Sometime in 1999, Omololu Falobi, a Nigerian journalist and activist, bought a personal laptop computer that would support his engagement in the burgeoning new communications technology of the internet and facilitate the work he would conduct over the subsequent years in raising awareness about the HIV/AIDS health crisis (The Nation, 2021). Indeed, by the early 2000s, the health crisis caused by the infectious disease of HIV/AIDS was catastrophic, and at the time it appeared that the trend was getting worse, not better. Falobi attended and presented at the Fourteenth International AIDS Conference in Barcelona in July 2002 where he and many other speakers (including South African president Nelson Mandela and US president Bill Clinton) intoned on the major health crisis. The statistics at that time were dismal: 40 million people infected, 20 million dead, and predictions of a total death count of 60 million by 2020 in the absence of further commitments to combatting HIV/AIDS. Such statistics were presented in reports and by speakers, such as in a speech by a World Health Organization (WHO) epidemiologist who was described as using language that "almost appeared desperate" (Berger, 2002). A follow-up television news interview asked US epidemiologist Anthony Fauci about the conference and he responded that "the prevailing theme was the absolute enormity of the problem."[1] Like so many others who attended the conference, Omololu Falobi was dedicated to raising awareness about HIV/AIDS and pressuring governments and health providers to make available better education and more affordable medicine to reduce ill-health and death.

"All of us have to choose to respond to the challenges of our own times; for me, the challenge is HIV/AIDS," Falobi was quoted saying.[2] And indeed, Falobi's contribution to the fight against HIV/AIDS in Nigeria had a worldwide impact. He made use of globalizing technologies, especially internet communication technologies that were emerging during the 1990s and early 2000s. One person recounted their first meeting with Falobi when an internet search on HIV/AIDS in Nigeria introduced them to the organization he founded, Journalists against AIDS (JAAIDS) where: "There were researchers seeking collaborators, students seeking information, field workers sharing examples of best practice, epidemiologists exchanging updates on knowledge, people with HIV sharing their unique perspectives, everyone debating Nigerian HIV policy or the absence of it—in short, if it related to HIV in Nigeria then you could find it there" (Anya, 2006). Twenty years later, JAAIDS continues to provide "innovative communication interventions that will facilitate positive behavior change to reduce the spread of HIV/AIDS" (JAAIDS, 2023).

Unfortunately, Falobi was a victim of random violence when he was shot and killed near his home on October 5, 2006. But his legacy and worldwide impact in educating people about health challenges of HIV/AIDS through new communications technologies continues. In fact, Falobi was named an Ashoka Fellow in 2001 for his work in creating "a customized, low cost HIV/AIDS prevention and education model, targeting civil society organizations, care providers, and foundations in Nigeria" (Ashoka, 2001). Several other websites still have tributes posted that praise his work; they include dozens of replies and responses from people and organizations with whom he connected, like this one from a representative of Internews Nigeria: "Omololu's death came as a shock to all of us . . . this young man proved himself as a committed advocate to the cause . . . [he] crossed boundaries beyond his beloved Nigeria to advocate for the rights of People Living with HIV and AIDS, and to ensure Africans (not just Nigerians) are well informed about the virus. He [knew] the power of the media and he used it to pass on the message."[3] Falobi wrote for the popular Nigerian weekly paper *The Punch*, and when he left to commit himself full-time to JAAIDS, he edited and produced many reports and book-length volumes that raised awareness about HIV/AIDS, like *Beyond the Shadows: Unmasking HIV/AIDS-Related Stigma and Discrimination in Nigeria* (2004).

Falobi's journalism and activism related to education and health on HIV/AIDS is an example of the impact and influence that Global South voices can and do have in international development. Education and health are two major themes in the human development (HD) ideology, and Falobi's work in raising awareness through the use of twenty-first century globalization technologies provides insight into the power of Global South voices. As one tribute noted: "He caught the vision of the digital age far back as 1999 when . . . access to computers was still very limited and not many knew how to use it. He was one of the earliest users of the internet. He shared resources and opportunities about making the best of media skills" (The Nation, 2021). While not all progress on HIV/AIDS education and provision of health care access in Nigeria (and worldwide) may be directly connected to Falobi's work, it is clear that his impact was deep.[4] In 2023, HIV/AIDS presents less of a health crisis worldwide than when Falobi was fighting against it in the early 2000s. In fact, UNAIDS released a report that promisingly predicts the end of the crisis (2023). But the disease continues to be a major problem in countries that have limited education, health care, and where the cost of life-saving medications is beyond the means of people in poverty (UNAIDS, 2023).

As this chapter will discuss, concerns with human well-being—and the message that international development projects should focus on both the economic and social concerns of human beings—have frequently been voiced by people in the Global South demanding justice and better living standards. This was the case during the shift from the League of Nations to the UN, which allowed for a structural change in international organization and negotiation that would call on delegates to challenge IR realist and collective security ideas. The pressure from

Global South countries at the creation of the UN resulted in, as one example, the Economic and Social Council (ECOSOC) as a new organ of the UN that would allow for a dedicated and concerted body of delegates to debate on education and health outcomes, for instance, and not just on inter-state warfare which was the purview of the UN Security Council (UNSC). The Global South also played a key role in international development thinking and practices from the 1950s onward, as shown in the dueling between UN development projects and programs on the one hand and the World Bank on the other, to variously control or define international development. As UN membership expanded during decolonization, Global South countries amplified their voices in the UN General Assembly (UNGA) to challenge the status quo in efforts such as the New International Economic Order (NIEO) resolution and in many non-UN-settings. Many of the various concerns raised by Global South voices in the UN and other international forums came to the fore when Mahbub ul Haq, a Pakistani economist, led a group of diverse academics and development practitioners to produce the first 1990 Human Development Report (HDR) through the UN Development Programme (UNDP).

In this chapter, we review ways of thinking about what constitutes the "Global South" before assessing how Global South countries and individuals have claimed and revealed their political independence in contrast to Global North countries. We then look at what Global South voices and perspectives have contributed to the formation and spread of the HD paradigm.

THE GLOBAL SOUTH AND HUMAN DEVELOPMENT

The polysemous (i.e., a word that has more than one meaning) term Global South acts as a less demeaning synonym for so-called "developing," "third world," "backward," "less-developed," or "industrializing" countries (Dados and Connell, 2012; Haug et al., 2021). Such terms for categorizing countries made their way into international development practices of Western countries beginning in the 1940s. The labels of developing, backward, and less developed countries were utilized by the UN, World Bank, and in international relations (IR) more generally to describe transfers of technological and financial assistance. After having transferred large amounts of resource wealth out of the so-called developing countries for decades, Western countries sought to give a portion of it back in "aid" as a means of having influence over political, economic, and social developments in territories in Africa, Asia, Latin America, and small island countries which (in some cases) they no longer directly controlled. As Haug et al. note, the category of Global South aimed to represent "poor and/or socio-economically marginalized parts of the world, usually from a country-based perspective" (Haug et al., 2021, p. 1928). In other words, belonging to the "Global South" signified that a country was on the lower end of economic prosperity, usually identified by measuring some form of income or macroeconomic growth indicator, such as gross national product (GNP) or gross national income (GNI). Some also use the term Global South to represent areas of the world that do not have the same access to technological capabilities in producing goods and services, that have less travel or communications infrastructure, or less job and educational opportunities, and so on, in comparison to the more economically developed countries.

The term Global South is associated with various international institutions (Braveboy-Wagner, 2009) and has also been used to describe a UN voting bloc of countries uniting behind shared experiences and interests of de-colonization and anti-imperialism.[5] As dominant international development practices (involving sharing technology and supporting countries through financial loans or grants for infrastructure development) were fleshed out in the aftermath of the Second World War, animosity arose between two major hegemonic and nuclear powers in the Global North: the United States (US) and United Soviet Socialist Republic (USSR). By the end of the 1940s, the United States motivated by the ideology of capitalism and the USSR as an adherent of the ideology of communism began using bilateral and multilateral development assistance to counter each other's power and influence in selected countries around the world.[6] Seeing through such Cold War antics, Latin American country leaders began uniting with newly decolonizing countries and attempted to counter the influence of both the United States and USSR. These countries met to form allegiances and discuss shared interests at meetings like the 1955 Bandung Conference, in the Non-Aligned Movement (NAM) and through the Group of 77 (or G-77) voting bloc at the UNGA (Haug et al., 2021, p. 1929). Seeking to avoid being dominated or controlled by either the

United States or the USSR, these countries were labeled as belonging to the *third world*—with the *first world* referring to the United States and its allies, and the *second world* to the USSR and its allies. The terms first, second, and third world started as terms to signify the alliances during the Cold War.[7] As for the *third world* category, this group of heterogeneous countries pooled interests to try to counter the brutal violence of Western hegemony and dominance as witnessed in the nuclear bombs the United States dropped on innocent civilians in Japan and also on various Pacific Islands later followed by other atrocities including the killing of millions of Vietnamese people during the US–Vietnam War (1964–1975).[8]

The Global South stands in as a term for resistance against oppression and subjugation by more powerful countries (Acharya, 2016; Golub, 2013; Haug et al., 2021). But the idea of a Global South also references a group of countries arguing for equity, fairness, and a challenge to the international relations status quo. They stand against those who would benefit from the pain intentionally inflicted on others in the pursuit of profit and ideology. Instead, they call for a change in the structure of the international system wherein currently a small proportion of the world's population enjoys a preponderance of the Earth's wealth, resources, and opportunities. Thus, Global South more broadly references spaces, theories, and a vocabulary of resistance against the negative outcomes of our current and past economic and political systems. This latter meaning of Global South implies not so much particular states around the world but especially actions and sentiments that form within any country as "a space of resistance against not only 'Northern' dominance in multilateral settings but also neoliberal capitalism and other forms of global hegemonic power more generally" (Haug et al., 2021, p. 1929). Indeed, some argue that the term may have even originated from the philosopher and political activist Antonio Gramsci's analysis of northern Italy's colonization and subjugation of southern Italy (Haug et al., 2021).

INTERNATIONAL DEVELOPMENT AND THE GLOBAL SOUTH

A number of Global South countries and individual leaders from the Global South have worked through international organizations (IOs) since the founding of the United Nations (UN) to promote human development (HD) in practice and as an idea. First of all, at international meetings, Global South countries and representatives were concerned with and wanted to ameliorate the poverty of individuals by improving living conditions of the underrepresented and marginalized populations of the world. In IOs, these countries were represented at first mostly by Latin American countries at the San Francisco Conference (that founded the UN) and in the Economic Commission for Latin America (ECLA) in the 1940s and 50s (which became the Economic Commission for Latin America and the Caribbean [ECLAC] in 1984). The number of such countries expanded with burgeoning new UN membership in the 1960s and '70s (as more states became decolonized). They also formed an anti-imperialist voting bloc in the Non-Aligned Movement (NAM), Group of 77 (G-77), and the UN Conference on Trade and Development (UNCTAD) as mentioned earlier. Representatives from the Global South also engaged in discussions in North-South Dialogues in the 1980s (like the North-South Round Table meetings) and in the leadership and growing capacity of the UNDP in the 1980s and 90s. In short, people from Global South countries—and their official representatives—were involved in creating and developing HD ideas and concepts which would become promoted by the UN and widely disseminated via the HDRs starting in the 1990s.

Some histories of international development activities after the Second World War focus on how the US government promoted and supported the idea of reconstructing Europe through the creation of the International Bank for Reconstruction and Development (IBRD, which later became known as the World Bank). US President Harry Truman also expounded on the importance of sharing technical knowledge and ending poverty in his 1949 inaugural address. But others provide a different narrative of the nascence, impetus, and influence of development and anti-poverty ideas (Helleiner, 2014). Indeed, African, Asian, and Latin American individuals and countries were influential. Thus, while the major powers that emerged victorious from the wars ended up gaining attention, taking credit, and writing some of the most well-known histories, deeper investigations reveal a better understanding of influence.

During the early twentieth century, people from less-wealthy countries came together to lobby for measures to facilitate economic growth and economic freedoms through transferring resources and wealth back from the richer to the less-wealthy countries. One major example was Chinese revolutionary politician Sun Yat-sen (1886–1925) who sought to reform and advance Chinese society. He sought to gain economic support from countries like the United States and Russia (pre-USSR) (both of which turned him down) for Chinese industrialization and infrastructure building. Having written a book about the *International Development of China* (1922), Sun encouraged the delegates of the Paris Peace Conference to include international development funding as part of the treaty. At the time "these arguments fell on deaf ears," but later on "with the creation of the IBRD [25 years later], Sun's ideas were finally realized" (Helleiner, 2014, p. 377, p. 378). Moreover, the ideology that Sun adopted for his nationalist (KMT) party was known as the "three principles of the people" (nationalism, democracy, and people's livelihood), a people-centered approach to nation-building and major forerunner to the HD ideology as it emphasized both people's economic well-being as well as their political participation in a democracy (Sun, 1938; Lorenzo, 2013).

During the first half of the twentieth century, Latin American countries were also deeply involved in and concerned with supporting economic growth. They sought out development lending that would be beneficial to developing countries for building infrastructure and diversifying their economies while also seeking to protect their political freedoms and sovereignty. In the years between WWI and WWII, the United States worked closely with Latin American countries, and Latin American countries collaborated together on international ventures that influenced the major powers' deliberations to end WWII and set up the post-WWII international order. Two examples provide special insight into Latin American influence: the creation of the IBRD (i.e., World Bank) and the Universal Declaration of Human Rights (UDHR), both of which had precursors in Latin American international cooperation and collaboration. First, Latin American countries called for an Inter-American Bank (IAB) at the 1933 Inter-American Montevideo Conference during which the famous Convention of Montevideo was signed that proffers the four requirements of a state (Helleiner, 2014, pp. 380–384). As Helleiner (2014, p. 382) observed, the IAB "design clearly inspired the early US proposals for the Bretton Woods Institutions" out of which the World Bank evolved.

Second, Latin American countries were heavily involved in negotiations that ended the Second World War and in participating in the San Francisco Conference among the fifty countries that signed the UN Charter in 1945.[9] The conference attendees, particularly from the United States, were quite aware of the coordinated voting bloc of 26 Latin American countries (out of the 50 that attended the conference and eventually signed the Charter). The Latin American countries themselves were afraid that the newly formed UN might be strong enough to challenge their own state self-determination (including political freedoms) and sovereignty (Schlessinger, 2005, pp. 175–192), hence they exerted pressure on how the UN would be configured. Their biggest influence on the UN Charter was its guarantee of state sovereignty and recognition of the right of self-defense (through recognition of regional agreements or individual country self-defense) as well as placing limits on the UNSC Permanent Five (P5) countries' veto power (this referred to the United States, United Kingdom (UK), USSR, France, and the Republic of China). Such discussions laid a foundation for human development thinking in the programs and policies of the UN as the UN Charter included references to specific individual human freedoms—seven references to human rights, four to health, nine to education, and one to standard of living—largely thanks to the indefatigable lobbying of Latin American and other civil society organizations involved in the negotiations and private discussions outside of the formal state representative meetings at the 1945 San Francisco Conference (Eichelberger, 1977, pp. 261–298; Schlessinger, 2005, pp. 121–126).

THE GLOBAL SOUTH AND THE UNITED NATIONS

During the 1945 UN conference negotiations, Latin American country delegates representing the Global South supported creation of the UN's Economic and Social Council (ECOSOC) to counter the influence of the UN Security Council (Kennedy, 2007, p. 43, pp. 116–117). Not only would ECOSOC focus on worldwide economic well-being and social exchanges of knowledge and culture, it was a UN organ where Global South countries would have more power than in either the UNGA or the UNSC and a space where they could air their grievances (Kennedy, 2007, p. 123). The UNSC was heavily skewed and undemocratic because it allowed only five permanent members (China, France, USSR [later Russia], the UK, and the United States) to have the ability to guide international responses to security through binding resolutions because they were entitled to veto power over resolutions supported by the majority of countries. The UNGA allowed all countries an equal vote and the passage of non-binding resolutions on any other topic not related to security issues covered by the UNSC. ECOSOC was set up like the UNSC so that a limited number of members can pass resolutions related to social and economic issues, thus giving them a similar power to the UNSC, even while there are no veto powers in ECOSOC.

Yet ECOSOC did not end up having the power and influence that the Global South countries envisioned and the challenges of maintaining sovereignty, supporting self-determination, and connecting that to social and economic well-being surfaced immediately as the BWIs and UN began their work. Indeed, in the early years the United States dominated the discussions, being the most powerful and wealthy member country of the fledgling UN, and the country that would be able to financially support economic and social well-being projects. The idea of international development via these institutions as a way to transfer technical and scientific knowledge and expertise was promoted by mainstream Keynesian economists proliferating under US presidents Franklin D. Roosevelt and Harry Truman. Truman's 1949 inaugural address is widely cited as the culmination of the idea of development support and the impetus for further US funding and thinking in this direction, particularly in the way that Truman emphasized the need to transfer technical knowledge from those who have it to those without it in point four of his speech. But more than that, the United States had been planning and working on such efforts since the early 1940s and was instrumental in the negotiations, which led to the founding of ECOSOC as the main branch dealing with non-security issues in the UN. Out of ECOSOC, the Extended Programme for Technical Assistance (EPTA) was created in 1949, backed by a US contingent of delegates in the UN pushing for technical support for developing countries.

The idea of supporting governments in developing countries only through technical assistance and with minimal financial support was seen to be not enough by many countries, particularly those in Latin America. Through such organizations as the Economic Commission for Latin America (ECLA), eminent leaders like Raúl Prebisch argued that what they needed were loans provided at low concessional rates rather than at higher market rates. This pressure led to a large debate in the UN that culminated in affluent countries providing more financial assistance and greater access to capital to governments in former colonies and less affluent nations. As a result, the Special Fund of the UN was created under ECOSOC, and the World Bank began to offer concessional loans through the creation of its International Development Association (IDA) branch. Later in the 1960s, the UN Special Fund and the Expanded Programme for Technical Assistance (EPTA) were combined to create the United Nations Development Programme (UNDP).

The challenge to economic development thinking, which came from the Global South countries, was clearly visible in the discussions, language, and practices of the ECOSOC and the UNDP reporting to it. ECOSOC would act to address economic issues, ensure economic prosperity for all, and identify ways in which countries could coordinate and benefit from each other. In the beginning, there was emphasis on sharing technical knowledge and skills and supporting countries in making plans for expanding their industrial sectors. The rhetoric and project development led by developing countries that came out of those early years—particularly through technical projects supported through the EPTA—promoted economic growth in a capitalistic, industrialized, modernized worldview.

As UN membership expanded in the 1960s and '70s with more countries from the Global South decolonizing and gaining independence, there were increasing challenges to Western hegemonic ideas about economic growth, capital accumulation, industrialization and the dominant paradigm of modernization. Within the UN secretariat, the UNDP (founded in 1965) challenged prevailing ideas about how to achieve economic growth and its priority compared to other development imperatives (Hirai, 2017, p. 34; Kennedy, 2007, p. 126). So too, did the United Nations Conference on Trade and Development (UNCTAD, founded 1964) as exemplified by calls for a New International Economic Order (NIEO) that came from UNCTAD. Outside of the UN system, the Bandung Conference of 1955—in which Global South countries deliberated on how best to become truly free (i.e., liberated from colonialism and imperialism)—led to the formation of the Non-Aligned Movement (NAM) and the Group of 77 (or G-77) voting blocs exerting pressure through UNGA against the world's most militarily powerful (i.e., in terms of the means of destruction) countries by calling for changes in the international economic order to shift away from a set of rules that they perceived as systematically benefitting the Global North at the expense of the Global South.

THE GLOBAL SOUTH AND THE NON-ALIGNED MOVEMENT

Indian Prime Minister Jawaharlal Nehru's (1947–1964) call to maintain a non-aligned status was especially important during the Cold War period. The impetus for the non-aligned movement (NAM) was a meeting of Global South leaders that took place at the Bandung conference held in Indonesia in 1955. During this conference, leaders from newly sovereign states gathered to discuss their particular concerns and issues. Of main concern was the growing realization that the men controlling political and economic power in the United States and USSR made the choice to face off against each other in a fight for global control and hegemony and they would use their *allies* to fight their wars. To avoid becoming entangled in this superpower battle of egos, the leaders at the Bandung conference began the NAM to encourage states in the Global South (i.e., Asia, Africa, and Latin America) and their governments to not get caught up in the violence. The conference created a few stipulations for NAM membership including that members had to declare their sovereignty and avoid engaging in an alliance in support of either superpower, as well as to declare their non-nuclear status. Perhaps one of the most misrepresented or misunderstood organizations to emerge during this time, NAM was created by leaders of newly decolonized countries who had concerns about the international order that their fledgling countries were entering. Whereas 46 countries joined NAM during the 1960s, its membership would eventually double so that by the 1980s there were nearly a hundred members with 98 countries declaring their non-aligned status during the Cold War. An additional 22 countries joined NAM after the end of the Cold War, some of them formerly belonging to the USSR, bringing the total membership to 120 states plus 17 observer states in 2022.

The NAM movement also brought together states whose interests were similar in refusing to become entangled in the superpower Cold War, rejecting nuclear proliferation, and demanding to be treated as sovereign equals in international relations. NAM was a method of building alliances in multilateral organizations—most notably in the UNGA and ECOSOC—so as to call Global North states to account, to call out their hypocrisy, and to demand restitution for the unacceptable brutality of colonization, racism, inequality, and subjugation in the global economic system. NAM summits are held roughly every three years. A new host country runs the meeting each time and the most recent is scheduled (19th summit) to be held in January 2024 in Kamapala, Uganda. One might say the movement is ad-hoc as it lacks a permanent meeting place, constitution, or articles of agreement. Even so, the movement helps countries in the Global South work together to discuss specific issues and policies they might want to pursue related to development, international cooperation, and confronting shared threats.

In addition to the NAM, countries in the Global South meet in other international forums to coordinate efforts in opposition to or in relation to their former colonizers and other Global North states. One of the most well-known is the Group of 77 (or G-77) which was created for the purpose of supporting "South-South" cooperation. Although originally starting out with 77 member states, the G-77 now has 134 member countries and it is "the largest intergovernmental organization of developing countries in the United Nations (UN)" serving to "articulate and promote their collective economic interests and enhance their joint negotiating capacity on all major international economic issues within the UN system" (G-77, n.d.).

When looking back to the period before the HD ideology first emerged, the two UN Development Decades (1960s and '70s) featured an increase in Global South countries through decolonization, concomitant UN enlargement, ongoing Cold War political conflicts over international development funding, and demands from the Global South to rethink and reconfigure international economic relations and structures. At face value, the overarching message of the two Development Decades was to promote economic growth by encouraging more development spending on the part of wealthy and imperialist countries. It was the United States, through President John F. Kennedy, and the UN Secretary General U. Thant, who came up with the idea of the development decades (creating focused goals and work toward promoting development). The Global North countries set goals by calling for an agreed upon standard of development funding in the first and second development decades of committing a certain amount of a country's GDP to development funding, but sadly few countries met that level.

Because the development decades laid the issue of development funding so bare and revealed hypocrisy inherent in the way the affluent countries approached development, they helped guide the UN toward a more nuanced and multidimensional concern for the Global South. As Brian Urquhart noted, the UN agenda widened to include many other issues thought inconceivable at the beginning, issues like "development, population, food, environment, water, and other global problems" (quoted in Meisler, 1995, p. 168). Indeed, the initial emergence at the UN of the term *human development* may well have come from the Second Development Decade document (UN, 1970, Section 8), although the term was used in a different manner than Sen and ul Haq's later iterations, as noted by Hirai (2017, p. 8). But the language of the document does challenge the primacy of the nation-state in development practice: "The ultimate objective of development must be to bring sustained improvement in the well-being of the individual and bestow benefits on all. If undue privileges, extremes of wealth and social injustices persist, then development fails in its essential purpose" (UN, 1970, Preamble). Times were changing and even the World Bank was shifting its focus in response to international discussions, largely promoted by countries in the Global South (Kapur et al., 1997, p. 16; Marshall, 2008; Engel, 2010; Hirai, 2017, p. 9).

Finally, amid the Third Development Decade in the 1980s and major shifts in international negotiation occurring at the UNGA and other UN organs, the tide of development thinking turned toward the HD approach. UNCTAD had been pressuring the UN and Global North countries to make greater commitments to the Global South, and debates around the NIEO had further challenged legacies of colonialism and imperialism at the UN, as did rising intellectual currents like World Systems Theory (e.g., Wallerstein, 1979) in academia. Thinking about development during this decade shifted away from a simple notion of providing governments of Global South countries with development funding toward a focus on empowering people living in the Global South to participate and engage in decisions and discussions shaping their lives (Hirai, 2017, pp. 10–11). Another spatial shift was in the location of North-South Roundtables set up by the UNDP which occurred in locations like Istanbul, Santiago, Salzburg, Budapest, and

Amman. Although four of these five meetings took place in either Europe or the Middle East, with the exception of Salzburg, the other locations were not in particularly affluent countries at that time (Hirai, 2017, p. 8).[10] The Roundtables were a space for Global South countries to voice their views as they were not limited to any single agenda (Haq, 1997). Many people active in the Roundtables also became involved in creating HDRs at the UNDP including Giovanni Andrea Cornia, Mahbub ul Haq, Richard Jolly, Gustav Ranis, and Frances Stewart (Hirai, 2017, p. 34). Through forums like the UNDP, its North-South Roundtables and in places like the Brundtland and Founex Reports, the UN became a sort of incubator (by incorporating Global South voices) for re-visioning how and what global development should look like— though such limited measures to combat global inequalities and deprivation were also challenged by emerging intellectual currents including the rise of postcolonialism.

POSTCOLONIALISM AND THE HUMAN DEVELOPMENT IDEOLOGY

In the latter part of the twentieth century, postcolonialism offered an important and powerful critique of dominant trends in global development. Its viewpoint was at odds with the dominant ideology of globalization (neoliberalism) and it leveled many pertinent criticisms toward prevailing and dehumanizing practices of international relations and international development over the past several centuries. At a general level, postcolonialism can be defined as a "perspective or worldview of those who believe that it is possible to understand today's world only by foregrounding the history of colonialism—defined in a very preliminary way as the domination of certain societies and peoples by others— over the past five centuries" (Krishna, 2009, p. 3). Most importantly, postcolonial authors argued that neoliberal globalization is a powerful force working *against* human development.

Whereas most promoters of neoliberalism have been men from the Global North, postcolonial writers have mostly hailed from the Global South and many have come from Asia (a world region with a much larger population than Europe and North America combined).[11] Having grown up in the Global South, there has been a tendency for such authors to feel that they have a better understanding (as compared to men and women who have never even lived in the Global South aside from perhaps short visits) of what exactly at least one Global South society is like, what it wants, why it is the way it is, and how to change it.

Most importantly, the postcolonial perspective attributes low living standards and high poverty (found in many parts of Africa, Asia, and Latin America) primarily to underdevelopment created by European colonizers. It has exposed how Western countries (including but not limited to the UK, France, Netherlands, Spain, Portugal, and the United States) were able to amass great wealth by controlling the territories and lives of many people in the Global South under colonialism, land expropriation, labor exploitation, language impositions, corporal punishments, placing restrictions on people's movements and livelihoods through slavery, and so on. Hence, including the term *post* in postcolonialism is meant to emphasize the continued relevance of colonialism and "its impact on the state, politics, class formation, military, bureaucracy, economy, and other crucial parts of a third-world country's development after decolonization" (Krishna, 2009, p. 66).

Opposing the racism of Eurocentrism, postcolonialism stresses the importance of cultural decolonization, confronting the psychological aspects of domination, and addressing the problem of global inequalities. As Krishna notes in his book on *Globalization and Postcolonialism*:

> When one looks at the world today, an inescapable fact is the vastly unequal distribution of assets, wealth, affluence, and life prospects. We live in a world where a relatively small number of people, about one-sixth the world's total population of approximately 6 billion people, have a preponderant share of the planet's wealth and resources, while a significant majority of the remaining 5 billion people lead lives marked by insecurity, poverty, and misery . . . at an everyday level the different life prospects between first and third worlds is indicated by the large numbers of people in the latter desirous of emigrating—legally or illegally—to the former, and the marked absence of a movement of people in the opposite direction, except for tourism. (Krishna, 2009, p. 7, p. 9)

To correct this gross imbalance, the postcolonial perspective argues that "human development must, of necessity, also be an act of profound decolonization that tries to reverse the political, social, economic, and cultural domination of the rest by the West . . . postcolonialism, unlike [neo-liberal] globalization, is motivated by a desire not for mimesis but rather for a form of human development that is decolonized and beyond Eurocentrism" (Krishna, 2009, p. 28, p. 30).

Despite obvious differences, there are, however, some commonalities between a postcolonial perspective (emanating from the Global South) and the HD ideology (which incorporates both Global South and Global North viewpoints). First of all, both are dismayed by over-emphasis on consumerism in the modern world, the breakdown of communities and loss of human connection. Unlike postcolonialism, however, the HD approach does not emphasize transformative restructuring of state boundaries (which are the main obstacle to human migration and freedom of movement globally) or repayments and apologies for past wrongs (thereby letting the perpetrators of killings, thefts, and other abuses to go free despite the harm they have caused). Nor does the HD paradigm view capitalism as inherently problematic in contrast to many of the first wave of postcolonial authors. In this sense, the HD ideology can be considered as less opposed to dominant structures of global power. Rather, the HD ideology's relative silence on these pertinent issues suggests that the intense trauma experienced by darker skinned non-Caucasian people around the world on account of past and present injustices can be simply swept under the rug by calls for countries to unite and strengthen current structures with the hope that they can somehow be sufficiently reformed to ensure that all people's needs are met. Indeed, the HD paradigm may in this respect be akin to the welfare state, it is more about taming capitalism and redirecting some of the negative outcomes of modernity, as opposed to rejecting either or finding a better alternative.

While offering "an endless and yet ethical critique" (Krishna, 2009, p. 172), another difference is that postcolonialism has been interpreted by some as providing less in the way of concrete, workable solutions to policy-makers enjoying the comforts of modernity in the Global North. Relatively speaking, one might say the HD ideology offers a more pragmatic vision to move forward in terms of communicating specific guideposts, benchmarks, and measures of progress (or regress) toward its ideals as in the MDGs and SDGs.[12]

PROGRESS, SETBACKS, POSSIBILITIES ON ACHIEVING HUMAN DEVELOPMENT IN THE GLOBAL SOUTH

So far we have identified some important points of interaction between the Global South and North through international organizations and debates concerning international development theory and practice. We now look at some of the ways Global South countries are currently promoting HD and their progress on composite HD indicators.

As evident from the discussion above, there is no easy or fixed answer as to which states belong in the category of Global South, and in fact, many argue that the category is misleading, problematic, and detrimental. As Weiss (2012, p. 72) contends, "the artificial division of the world into a global North and a global South is a simplification; and, like all simplifications, it overlooks substantial parts of reality." Thus, which countries are categorized as belonging to the Global South (as a more ideological than geographical concept) depends on the meaning assigned to the term, how it is measured, as well as the date and time the list is made and who is making the categorization. That said, it often has racial connotations and is frequently used as a term to denote those countries (or a subset of them) where the majority of the population is of a race or ethnicity that is non-Western or non-European origin.

Four different ways that international development practice has conceptualized and demarcated the Global South include: 1) countries with low-levels of per capita income (from World Bank data), 2) "least developed countries" according to the UN Commission on Population and Development, 3) low scores on the human development index (from UNDP data), or 4) membership in non-Western voting blocs such as the G-77 or NAM. Category one is based on income and presupposes a dichotomous separation of states (e.g., rich/poor or developed/developing) based on GNI per capita as reported by the World Bank.[13] Based on this approach, one might say that the 82 countries with a GNI per capita of less than $4,095 constitute the Global South. According to category two, as defined by the UN, there are currently 46 "least developed countries."[14] Based on category three, which examines health, education, and income attainments, there are 70 countries with a "low" or "medium" level HDI score (<0.699).[15] Based on category four, there are currently 120 NAM member states joined by 17 observer states.

Notably, most of the NAM states do not score highly on the HDI, but there are some exceptions.[16]

EDUCATION

The HD paradigm highly stresses the importance of education. The story at the beginning of this chapter about Imololu Faboli working to educate and inform people about how not to spread and how to get treatments for HIV/AIDS speaks to just how much education matters for good health. A good quality education is also important for gaining better jobs, reasoning and thinking critically, and participating fully in economic, political, and social life. Merely having laws stipulating compulsory education is not enough to ensure that all people are getting the kind and quality of education that will truly enhance their capabilities and well-being. Although the 2021–2022 Human Development Report does not measure the quality of education, it does indicate that there are regional discrepancies in both expected and average years of schooling. Among world regions, higher levels of average schooling were found in Europe and Central Asia (10.5 years), Latin America (8.9 years), and Arab States (8 years). In some countries, like Sudan which is currently in the midst of a war, educational attainments are much lower as many schools have had to close down. Hence, a key lesson is that if international organizations are serious about supporting human development, they need to ensure that peace is maintained and they need to regulate or reduce the production, sale, and circulation of arms and weapons of all types which are being used by states and rebel groups to enact violence.

One of the global trends in support of education, as declared at the UN organized 2000 World Education Forum meeting in Dakar, Senegal, is the slogan of "education for all" enshrined in MDG #4 (universal primary education) and SDG #7 (quality education for all). Support for this trend is shown in the adoption of compulsory education legislation by almost every government in the world (Cohen, Bloom, and Malin, 2006). However, countries differ in how seriously they enforce compulsory education requirements and the number of years that children are required to attend school. There are also countries like Afghanistan where the dominant ideology of its rulers at various points has exhibited disdain for educating girls and women. This again reinforces a key point of this book, namely how important ideology is for human development. Formal support for education is also a function of institutional choices. For instance, the duration of compulsory schooling time is much lower in Haiti (6 years) than it is in Bolivia (14 years).[17] In some countries, the average number of schooling years in the population exceeds compulsory education requirements by several years as in Tajikistan and Kyrgyzstan. Those countries were formerly incorporated in the USSR (a former state whose national ideology emphasized educational equality) and since gaining independence they have maintained relatively high levels of education in spite of economic difficulties caused by the dissolution of the USSR. By contrast, according to World Bank data, there are countries where actual school attendance fails to meet national targets such as in Pakistan (4.5 mean years versus 12 compulsory years) or Ethiopia (3.2 mean years versus 8 compulsory years). In some of the larger Global South countries, the average years of schooling is estimated to lie between six and ten years as in India, Nigeria, Algeria, and the Philippines.

Among these countries, India stands out as the most populous in the world with a population of 1.4 billion in 2023. Since the HD paradigm was first launched in 1990, average years of schooling in India have increased from 2.7 to 6.6 years in 2021. Although it has not increased educational attainments as quickly as neighboring China, growth in Indian education has been facilitated by various policies of India's central and state-level governments (Smith and Joshi, 2016). Increases in overall education levels in the population contribute to schooling eventually becoming a norm for all sections of the population (not just for the elite) which has been precisely the goal of the HD ideology as championed by authors like Amartya Sen who went to school as a young boy in India himself. These changing norms and aspirations for further advance in education are expressed in the opening phrase of India's 2020 National Education Policy which states: "Education is fundamental for achieving full human potential, developing an equitable and just society, and promoting national development. Providing universal access to quality education is the key to India's continued ascent . . . " (NEP, 2020, p. 3). One factor that has also helped to make a significant difference has been increased public spending on education.[18]

LIFE EXPECTANCY

The HDI incorporates life expectancy at birth as a crude measure of health and well-being in a society. While no single indicator can capture something as complex as physical (not to mention emotional and mental) health, how long a person lives on average gives some indication of health prospects and opportunities in a society. It helps to inform us at a general level about the state of health care access, prevalence of sickness and disease, and whether people receive adequate nutrition. Health is a core capability in the HD paradigm because of its role in enabling humans to do other things they value. As Nussbaum explains when locating *Life* as the first capability on her list of ten, it is important to be: "able to live to the end of a human life of normal length, not dying prematurely or before one's life is so reduced as to be not worth living" (Nussbaum, 1999, p. 41). Returning to Omololu Faboli and other activists promoting HIV/AIDS education, a population should not only have the educational and medical means to avoid infectious disease but also be able to live decent and long lives even if infected.

As with average years of schooling, the UN has documented life expectancy increases in many countries of the Global South between 1990 and 2021. In some countries like Timor-Leste the increase was dramatic (from 44.9 years in 1990 to 67.7 years in 2021). That said, as of 2021 people live much longer on average in Algeria (76.3 years) than in Africa's most populated country, Nigeria (52.6 years).[19] With mortality stemming from a combination of communicable diseases (e.g., malaria and tuberculosis) and non-communicable diseases (high incidents of hypertension and diabetes) plus traffic accidents, the World Health Organization reports that "Nigeria's health outcome indicators are still unacceptably high, in spite of modest improvements."[20] Nigeria has been passing a number of national laws to address these issues, but it remains to be seen as to how effective they will be in curbing premature mortality.

INCOME AND INEQUALITY

The UN not only compiles an HDI score for each country but also tabulates an "inequality-adjusted HDI" (IHDI) score to incorporate inequalities in health, education, and income. Using Nigeria—a former British colony that became an independent country in 1960—as an example, we can investigate income and inequality. High inequality contributes to immigration and Nigerians seeking to immigrate to other countries. Inequalities in Nigeria, a highly ethnically diverse multi-lingual and multi-religious country, are not only related to education, health, and income but also to gender and region. One very positive development is that Nigeria's poverty headcount ratio declined from 1996 (58.4%) to 2018 (30.9%) as measured by the share of its population living on less than US $2.15 per day on the basis of purchasing power parity.[21] Less positive is the fact that there are still a great many people living in poverty. Although Nigeria is an oil-exporting country earning revenue for its government from high world demand for that fossil fuel resource, it has not been sufficient and not been sufficiently allocated toward public goods and social services in key HD priority areas. Coupled with problems of corruption both by its own leading government officials and that of other players (including multi-national corporations, other governments, and local businesses) in the oil and related industries, Nigeria has faced major difficulties in reducing stark inequalities.

MULTIDIMENSIONAL POVERTY

Beyond income poverty, the HD paradigm has been attentive to multiple dimensions of poverty (or capability deprivation) and one attempt to measure this has been the Multidimensional Poverty Index (MPI) (Alkire and Jahan, 2018). The MPI relies on survey data from countries. It includes the three dimensions of health, education, and standard of living included in the HDI but uses different indicators. For instance, health is measured by nutrition access and child mortality outcomes (rather than by life expectancy), and standard of living is measured by assessing access to a combination of several goods and services that are necessary for a decent standard of living: electricity, sanitation, drinking water, housing, cooking fuel, and assets. Country rankings on the HDI and MPI do not vary a lot but there are certain discrepancies. For instance, countries like Haiti, Pakistan, and Kyrgyzstan fared somewhat better on the MPI than the HDI. Conversely, countries like Bolivia, Nigeria, and the Philippines scored lower on MPI than on HDI. Scores of selected Global South countries and world regions on multidimensional poverty (MP) are displayed in Table 6.1.

Table 6.1. Multidimensional Poverty (MP) in the Global South (2010–2021)

Territories (sorted by highest MPI (1= total deprivation) to lowest MPI (0= non-deprivation)	MPI Value	Population (in thousands) living in MP (2020)	Population living in Severe MP (%)	Population living below National Poverty Line (%)	Population living on less than PPP $1.90/ day (%)
Selected Countries					
Ethiopia	0.367	80,553	41.9	23.5	30.8
Sudan	0.279	23,255	30.9	46.5	12.2
Nigeria	0.254	96,699	26.8	40.1	39.1
Timor-Leste	0.222	627	17.4	41.8	22
Haiti	0.200	4,666	18.5	58.5	24.5
Pakistan	0.198	87,089	21.5	21.9	3.6
India	0.069	228,907	4.2	21.9	22.5
Bolivia	0.038	1,081	1.9	39	4.4
Tajikistan	0.029	710	0.7	26.3	4.1
Philippines	0.024	6,503	1.3	16.7	2.7
Algeria	0.005	600	0.2	5.5	0.4
Kyrgyzstan	0.001	25	0.0	25.3	1.1
World Regions					
Sub-Saharan Africa	0.286	578,765	30.9	41.1	41.1
South Asia	0.091	385,103	6.9	22.6	19.0
Arab States	0.074	51,444	6.8	26.4	5.0
Latin America and Caribbean	0.027	37,374	1.6	40.8	4.0
East Asia/Pacific	0.022	108,651	1.0	3.8	0.9
Europe and Central Asia	0.004	1,109	0.1	10.9	0.9

Source: UN "2022 MPI Statistical Data Table." https://hdr.undp.org/content/2022-global-multidimensional-poverty -index-mpi#/indicies/MPI accessed July 18, 2023. All data in charts was gathered from surveys from 2010–2021.

The MPI is an important innovation of the HD approach that aims to provide deeper insight into the actual lived experience of the people in a country, and it offers greater depth for thinking about policy interventions. A country can look worse on the HDI, but better on the MPI if it is providing its population with the necessary social services that the MPI measures (like electricity and sanitation). For instance, Kyrgyzstan has a relatively high HDI (only behind Algeria and the Philippines) among the 12 countries displayed in Table 6.1, but ranks first on the list when looking at its MPI (0.001) which is close to zero, meaning it has the least deprived population. This indicates that despite relatively low average incomes, Kyrgyzstan's population has access to the main goods and services that are important to lead a non-deprived life. Although it has almost no people living in multidimensional poverty, Kyrgyzstan does still have people living on less than $1.90 per day PPP (1.1% of the population) and a fairly sizable share of people live under its national poverty line (25.3%). Comparing these measurements reveals more clearly why measuring development on the basis of income (via GNI per capita) alone does not give a clear picture of the actual life outcomes experienced by people.

GENDER EQUALITY

Gender equality is an essential *means to an end* of development from the human development perspective. For this reason, the UN created gender-related development indexes to account for the fact that access or outcomes for females may lag (in some cases significantly) behind males on key indicators of development like health, education, and income (as discussed in chapter 5). For instance, the Gender Development Index (GDI) scores countries between 1 (closest to gender parity) and 5 (furthest from gender parity). Some of the countries falling into category 5 include Pakistan, India, Nigeria, Sudan, Algeria, and Haiti. But other Global South countries score much higher. Bolivia and Kyrgyzstan are in category 2, and the Philippines falls in category 1.[22] Generally, countries with low HDI scores are also low on GDI.

As the HDR 2018 identifies, the main problem of inequality in achieving gender parity in the HDI is "due to women's lower income and educational attainment in many countries" (UNDP, 2018, p. 5). Pakistan and India are clear examples of this. In these countries, respectively, females attend school an average of 1.1 and 0.9 fewer years than males, and female estimated GNI per capita is only $2,277 per year for India and $1,569 for Pakistan, which is respectively $8,356 and $6,050 less than the males.

Comparing the GDI to other gender equality measures is interesting as well since they use different indicators that are more specific to measuring women's participation in society or measuring bias against women. Indeed, a major dimension of HD is women's participation in all aspects of social, political, and economic life. The UN's Gender Inequality Index (GII) therefore measures health and education specific to women plus women's share of seats in parliament and women's labor force participation rate. Many, but not all, Global South countries fare poorly on the GII. Among the sample of countries listed in Table 6.1, Kyrgyzstan and Timor-Leste came out best on the GII while Haiti and Nigeria scored worst. Timor-Leste (38.5%), had the third highest female share of seats in parliament (after Ethiopia and Bolivia), while Haiti had a low of 2.7% female share of seats, followed by Nigeria at 4.5 %. As for female labor force participation, Algeria (15.7%) and India (19.2%) were both rather low whereas women's participation in paid work was rather high in Ethiopia (72.3%), Bolivia (68.3%), and Timor-Leste (61%).

One reason that women are below gender parity in parliamentary representation and labor force participation is due to biases against them which are captured in the Gender Social Norms Index (GSNI). The GSNI, which is based on survey data, measures the biases of people regarding women's physical integrity and women's participation in politics, education, and the economy. Among countries listed in Table 6.1 with available data, those featuring at least one bias against women (and thereby scoring 99% or higher) were Tajikistan, Pakistan, Nigeria, the Philippines, and India followed by Haiti, Ethiopia, and Kyrgyzstan (at 98–99%). The best scoring was Bolivia with only 91% of its population reporting at least one bias and even fewer (57.11%) reporting at least two biases. Bolivia also scored the highest among this sample when biases are disaggregated (less than 40% of the Bolivian population exhibited a political, education, or economic bias against women, though there was a high physical integrity bias at 82%). Such survey data can tell development practitioners and politicians a great deal about the best ways to assess why and how much a country deviates from gender parity and in identifying ways to work toward better gender outcomes.

GLOBAL SOUTH PROGRESS ON MDGs AND SDGs

The UN has placed much effort on creating indicators to measure each of the SDG targets and goals and the discussion above provided a snapshot of progress among certain Global South countries on attaining several SDGs. Gathering the vast amount of data necessary to measure 17 goals and 169 targets is no small task, and it takes an intense amount of negotiating and bargaining effort. There are currently 222 official indicators used to measure progress toward the SDGs, and the UN reports on how countries are doing by providing an SDG index score and country ranking.[23] While some might view such an intense obsession with indicators and numbers as a meaningless fetishism of big data and perverse effort to infantilize the Global South in the way that Western countries have been doing to the non-West and their own non-Caucasian populations via Orientalism for centuries (see Said, 1993 and 2003, for an extended discussion of Orientalism). Yet the goals do contribute toward diffusing global norms for better or worse. At times, the indexes themselves might present a violation of the broader human development approach (as discussed in chapter 2) by oversimplifying a complex reality and ignoring the contexts in which individual human capabilities matter, but they do incentivize countries to change their policies and to gather statistical data on the indicators which may eventually result in developing stronger national statistics offices, resources, and statisticians over time, especially if supported by additional funds and assistance from affluent countries, foundations, and international organizations. Another challenge to data collection concerns issues of reputation and sovereignty, and willingness to report or share indicators with the UN and world (this is difficult for some countries to do who, for instance, may not wish to be called out for gender inequality in education or job outcomes).[24]

THE FUTURE OF THE GLOBAL SOUTH
AND HUMAN DEVELOPMENT

The opening vignette to this chapter revealed the power and possibilities of activists in the current age of globalization. Omololu Falobi, the late Nigerian journalist and HIV/AIDS activist, utilized the burgeoning power of internet communication technologies to create an organization and internet planform that educated many people about HIV/AIDS infections and medications. Falobi zeroed in on something that the HD paradigm also prioritizes: that education and health are important aspects of a decent human life and that governments must prioritize such social services in order to support thriving populations. Indeed, one of the main arguments of the HD paradigm is that humans should be considered first and foremost in government spending and practices, as the end and main reason for policy, not as a means to some other end.

Unfortunately, one of the biggest challenges to advancing HD in the Global South has been in addressing cultural barriers (for instance, this chapter reviewed the measurements on women's participation in the Global South as connected with biases against women). On the issue of cultural barriers, it is also important to acknowledge that another major challenge to improving HD in the Global South has been the stinginess of many individuals and countries in the Global North who, while regularly benefitting from unequal trade, lopsided economic policies, and historical extraction from the Global South (including exploitation of its low wage labor force), are often still unwilling to give even a small portion (of what they have taken away) back in the form of foreign aid or adopting more just economic policies and political arrangements. Other cultural problems in the Global North that harm people living in the Global South include ignorance about what people in the South truly value and discriminatory immigration policies that prevent people in the Global South from escaping violence.

A major problem in countries like Nigeria, as illustrated in the introductory vignette, is the absence of public safety, for it was gun violence by an active shooter in an armed robbery that cut short Falobi's life at the young age of 35 years old, nearly 18 years younger than average Nigerian life expectancy today. This is not to deny that there are also some countries in the Global North like the United States where frequent gun violence is a major source of insecurity, anxiety, and lives cut prematurely short. For instance, in the first seven months of 2023 alone, over 25,000 people died in the United States from gun violence.[25] Fortunately some countries are much safer, but the problem of violence as an obstacle to HD is truly global and not limited to only a few countries.

As this chapter has demonstrated, a number of key individuals and governments from the Global South have significantly impacted the way that international development is conceived and implemented. Examples include Latin American countries influencing the formation of the UN and calling for concessional loans in development spending, newly decolonized countries at the UNGA pushing for transitioning to a New International Economic Order that would be more fair and just, the North-South Roundtable discussions of the UNDP, and the Human Development Reports Office set up by the UNDP which were initially led by Mahbub ul Haq. Through such efforts, individuals from the Global South challenged the racist status quo and hegemonic paradigms of development, particularly those of modernization theory and neoliberalism. Their crucial role in identifying flaws and limitations to how the Global North approached international development during the twentieth century was a major impetus to the emergence of the HD paradigm.

As this chapter also discussed, postcolonialism is another way of looking at development that is grounded in experiences of the Global South, and unlike the HD paradigm, it has been challenging the Global North to consider how practices of colonialism continue today to keep many non-Western countries less developed and with many people in poverty. Although sharing certain commonalities with postcolonialism, the HD ideology is less attentive to historical explanations for why some people and societies have diminished capabilities, but it has been successful in gaining the backing of the UN and serving as a major competitor to other ideologies of globalization during the post–Cold War period from 1990 to the present. From the HD perspective, a positive and desirable globalization would be one that enlarges the choices of all people, especially those who currently have few choices. By contrast, a negative and dysfunctional globalization is one that fails to enlarge, or actually shrinks, people's meaningful choices. Thus, the HD approach aims to create a more humane world than what people have been experiencing under neoliberal globalization (i.e., *market globalism*) and many of the key articulators of the HD vision like Amartya Sen and Mahbub ul Haq are people living in or originating from the Global South.

NOTES

1. As quoted in CSPAN, 2022.

2. As quoted in an article from DEVCOMS Newsroom "Falobi: Journalist, advocate extraordinaire!" by Lekan Otufodunrin. https://devcomsradio.com/falobi-journalist-advocate-extraordinaire-by-lekan-otufodunrin/.

3. Blogspot. 2006. "Omololu Tributes." http://omololu-falobi.blogspot.com/.

4. For more details, see Waisbord, 2009; D'Angelo et al., 2013; Moyo and Moqasa, 2017.

5. See Freeman, 2017; Golub, 2013; Gray and Gillis, 2016; Helleiner, 2014; Horner and Carmody, 2019.

6. The US Marshall Plan to rebuild Western European economies is an early example of foreign aid.

7. The *three worlds* terminology was also used as development terminology and is still used today to indicate a very different meaning than originally, but it is still tied to the way in which development funding was funneled to support allies rather than purely for development projects, technical assistance, and poverty reduction.

8. For more details on longer term impacts of the US–Vietnam War on Vietnamese politics and society, see Joshi and Thimothy (2019).

9. Five countries planned and sponsored the San Francisco Conference: China, France, the United States, the United Kingdom, and the Union of Soviet Socialist Republics. Also invited were all the countries who had signed the Declaration of the United Nations as allied powers during the war and a few more were added to the invitation list during the conference. In all, 50 countries participated and signed the UN Charter in 1945. For more about the conference, see O'Dell, Breger Bush (2021), chapters 4–5; https://www.un.org/en/about-us/history-of-the-un/san-francisco-conference.

10. This notably contrasted with UN conferences on the Least Developed Countries (as discussed in chapter 5) which were held in the Global North.

11. Some prominent examples of postcolonialists of South Asian origin are the Subaltern Studies Collective, Homi Bhabha, and Gayatri Spivak.

12. As noted in chapter 5, the HD paradigm adopted by the UN is heavily concerned with gathering actual and detailed data about conditions around the world and changes over time, especially through the HDI and other indexes.

13. The World Bank income-based classification of GNI per capita Atlas Method creates four categories: Low-Income ($1,045 or less), Lower-Middle-Income ($1,046–$4,095), Upper-Middle Income ($4,096–$12,695), and High-Income ($12,696 or more). Breaking this up into two categories means that the Global South would include Low-Income to Lower-Middle-Income states (GNI per capita of $1,045–$4,095). The West Bank and Gaza are not included in this list because they are not included in other lists, thus making comparison difficult.

14. "The LDC Category After the 2021 Triennial Review" (https://www.un.org/development/desa/dpad/wp-).

15. According to the 2020 Human Development Report (HDR), countries fall into four categories: Low Human Development (HD) (less than 0.550), Medium HD (0.550–0.699), High HD (0.700–0.799), and Very High HD (0.800 or greater).

16. NAM membership overlaps with Low-Income to Lower-Middle Income and Low to Medium HD lists but adds quite a few members who have either or

both an Upper-Middle-Income or High-Income status and a High or Very High HD level.

17. Source for data in this section comes from the World Bank: "Compulsory Education, Duration (Years) in 2021," https://data.worldbank.org/indicator/SE .COM.DURS?locations=DZ-BO-ET-HT-IN-KG-NG-PK-PH-SD-TJ-TL&most_re-cent_value_desc=true. Accessed July 20, 2023.

18. An OECD review of India's education system noted its higher than OECD average spending on education: "Public spending on primary to tertiary education was 14.5% of total government expenditure in India . . . higher than the OECD average (10.6%). Also, relative to GDP, public spending on primary to tertiary education (4.5%) is higher than the OECD average (4.4%)" (OECD, 2022, p. 2).

19. Nigeria was also four years below the mean for Sub-Saharan Africa (56.6 years).

20. World Health Organization. 2018. "Country Cooperation Strategy at a Glance: Nigeria." Accessed July 20, 2023. https://apps.who.int/iris/bitstream/handle/10665/136785/ccsbrief_nga_en.pdf;sequence=1.

21. World Bank Data. "Poverty Headcount Ration at $2.15 a Day (2017PPP) (% of Population)," accessed July 20, 2023.

22. On this measure, the Philippines is in the same group as the United States.

23. SDG Rankings and Scores are available in UN Sustainable Development Report 2023 and on the SDG website. https://dashboards.sdgindex.org/rankings. Accessed July 20, 2023.

24. Given immense global disparities, the SDGs also present countries in the Global South with the opportunity to potentially get more foreign aid by reporting low scores or underreporting their achievements as it is not only countries in the Global North that play the game of deception and manipulation.

25. Data Source: https://abcnews.go.com/US/116-people-died-gun-violence -day-us-year/story?id=97382759.

CHAPTER 7

GLOBALIZING HUMAN DEVELOPMENT

A SUCCESS STORY OR A WORK IN PROGRESS?

On September 9, 2021, the President of the United Nations Security Council (UNSC) introduced Malala Yousafzai, the co-founder and board chair of the Malala Fund, who was there to speak on the situation in Afghanistan (UNSC, 2021).[1] Just one month earlier on August 15, 2021, the Taliban consolidated its control of that country after a twenty-year hiatus and years-long campaign against a civilian government backed by the US and Afghan militaries (Reinhard and Zucchino, 2021). The Taliban, made up of many disparate groups, rely on a fundamentalist interpretation of Islam and implement harsh punishments for those who do not obey their laws. "Under [the Taliban's] harsh rule, they have cracked down on women's rights and neglected basic services" (Maizland, 2023). At the UNSC briefing, Yousafzai related her experience living under Taliban rule in neighboring Pakistan where the Taliban would not allow and even banned girls and women from attending schools, implementing a strict version of Sharia law. She called on the UNSC to protect girls' rights to education. She argued that education is a human right, that women's education can secure peace and reduce conflict, and she reminded the UNSC that they had the responsibility to protect the "dignity and worth of the human person" (UNSC, 2021).

Yousafzai has been well known for her activism in support of girls' and women's rights to education, even going back to when she was a young girl of 10 years old. Her experience with the Taliban is crucial to understanding her activism, influence, and world renown. She lived with her father, brothers, and mother in the Swat Valley of Pakistan until 2012. Her father owned a girls' school and the family's livelihood relied on paying customers, which was interrupted when the Taliban took control of the area in 2007 and decreed that girls should not be educated. At that time, the Taliban leaders boarded up and bombed hundreds of girls' schools and told everyone who sought access to education that they would be severely punished. Not to be deterred, even in exile in other Pakistani towns, Yousafzai's father engaged with local leaders and activists to challenge the Taliban and promote educational opportunities. His activism was built on a life of asking questions and challenging social norms, as he relates in his memoir (Yousafzai and Carpenter, 2018). The family, Malala in particular, gained a following when a *New York Times* reporter published two short documentaries in 2009 about their struggles to maintain access to education (Ellick, 2009a, 2009b).

What followed after the 2007 Taliban take-over was a time of great difficulty for Yousafzai, her father, and her family: "I saw my home transformed from a place of peace to a place of fear in just three years. I saw thousands of displaced people. I saw homes and schools destroyed. I was 12 years old," she told the UNSC in 2021. Likewise, in Ellick's 2009 documentary film, Yousafzai discusses her desires to be a doctor or a politician, and mourns the lack of opportunities given that such dreams would be out of her reach without access to an education. But lack of education was not the biggest challenge she would face. As has been related in many venues, including her book, *I Am Malala: The Girl Who Stood up for Education and was Shot by the Taliban*, Yousafzai's life almost came to a premature end when a Taliban gunman boarded a bus to find her on October 9, 2012. After identifying her, he shot her in the head, and shot several of her peers who were on the bus with her. She fortunately survived after being rushed to an army hospital and then to a hospital in Birmingham, England, where she recovered, much to the chagrin of the Taliban, for Yousafzai was not easily silenced. She went on to speak in many venues at the UN and around the world, receiving the Nobel Peace Prize in 2014, and later obtaining a degree from Oxford University.

Yousafzai's life experience and activism shines as an example of the claims of the human development (HD) paradigm. The HD approach, as articulated by Amartya Sen, puts forth the idea that all humans should have instrumental freedoms like education that will allow them to "live the way they would like to live" (Sen, 1999, p. 38). In Martha Nussbaum's words, a society must ensure that people have the capability to practice "senses, imagination, thought" and "practical reason" (1999, p. 41). In an essay specifically reviewing impediments to women, she writes that "Nothing is more important to a woman's life chances than education" (Nussbaum, 1999, p. 100). Indeed, education is so central to HD that it is a core component (along with health and living standards) in the human development index (HDI). As Malala Yousafzai has repeatedly stated, it is essential to ensure all girls and women have access to free primary education so that they can enjoy opportunities in life. While Yousafzai is willing to share her own story, she also makes an enormous effort to show that millions of girls and women face similar challenges. As she said in her UNSC speech: "I do not speak on behalf of Afghan girls and women today . . . women and girls in Afghanistan are speaking out for themselves." Yousafzai works to amplify their voices in her writings as seen in her speeches, her work with the Malala Fund, and her book *We Are Displaced: My Journey and Stories from Refugee Girls around the World* (2021).

Unfortunately, the reality for many girls and women around the world continues to mirror that of Yousafzai's early years, except that many never even get much of an education and their lives are limited and short, including those living in Afghanistan since the Taliban seized control in 2021 (Al Jazeera, 2022). Goal 4 of the Sustainable Development Goals (SDGs), agreed upon by nations around the world, is to ensure education for all people by the year 2030. But achieving this goal for all is in danger (as all SDGs are), even if progress has been occurring globally at a macro-level. As a recent *Global Sustainable Development Report* indicates concerning in school enrollments "the gender gap is less than one percentage point" across the board, yet access to and "achieving quality education" continues to be limited: "Some 64 million children of primary school age were out of school, as were 63 million adolescents of lower-secondary age, and 132 million youth of upper-secondary age" (UN, June 2023, p. 32). But the UN remains committed to promoting the norm of globalizing basic education as exemplified at the beginning of 2023 when UNESCO Director-General Audrey Azoulay made the statement that "no country in the world should bar women and girls from receiving an education" as the International Day of Education (January 24) was dedicated to the women and girls of Afghanistan (UNESCO, 2023).

REVIEWING HUMAN DEVELOPMENT WORLDWIDE: GROWTH AND GAPS

The experience of Malala Yousafzai dramatically illustrates the power of HD, and education in particular, as a force that can (potentially) change people's lives for the better. It shows that there are young people in the Global South who want better education and HD for themselves and their communities, and that some are willing to risk everything, including their lives, to obtain a better life. Her story also demonstrates that considerable efforts to improve HD are still needed because there continue to be opponents in powerful positions who are against supporting and investing in the HD of major population groups such as women and girls, or those of a foreign nationality or of a different ethnicity, race, or religion than themselves. Lastly, and arguably most importantly, Yousafzai's experience reveals that one of the easiest ways to improve HD outcomes for those born in the Global South is migration away from countries that lack opportunities for quality education, that do not have decent job opportunities and where healthcare facilities are of poor quality. Emigrating to high HDI countries, with better opportunities for women's education, better paying jobs, and good quality national health care systems offers a way to improve one's life outcomes. Even though Yousafzai and her family loved their hometown, and show a deep connection to the Swat Valley of Pakistan, they emigrated to the United Kingdom when she was attacked and have not been able to return because of safety concerns. Unfortunately, as mentioned in chapter 6, many families living in unsafe conditions and war-torn countries are denied the opportunity to immigrate to more secure, higher income countries rendering them essentially trapped. What is more, people lose citizenship protections and often face human rights abuses when they migrate (O'Dell, 2023a).

In the early twenty-first century, the gender gap in schooling, and on major HD indicators between countries like Afghanistan or Pakistan and the United Kingdom (for instance) may still be relatively large. But one should also note that the HD paradigm is relatively young, as it was only officially launched in 1990 when the UN issued its first Human Development Report (HDR) and the HDI. Since 1990, the UN has supported the large-scale 2000–2015 Millennium Development Goals (MDGs) and 2015–2030 Sustainable Development Goals (SDGs) to advance the human development and capability approach (HDCA) globally. In fact, the number of countries and regions for which the UN was able to calculate the HDI in 1990 was 152. In 2021, the number of countries and regions was 202. This, in itself, reflects a globalization of the HD paradigm.

How much progress has been made on the various indicators that comprise the HDI? Most countries have experienced gains over the past three decades, indicating that war-torn countries like Afghanistan are an exception to the general trend and that war is a major impediment to achieving HD. Improvements between 1990 and 2021 on the HDI occurred in every region of the world (Figure 7.1). According to UN data, the highest scoring region in 2021 was Europe and Central Asia followed respectively by Latin America and the Caribbean, East Asia and the Pacific, Arab States, South Asia, and Sub-Saharan Africa.[2] The rank order among regions remained the same between 1990 and 2021 with the exception of East Asia and the Pacific which moved from fourth place to third and seems likely to move into second place in the near future.

The good news is that overall, HDI scores have been trending upward and they increased across the world by 0.131 points between 1990 and 2021, but there is also considerable diversity in rates of progress. As can be seen among the sample of countries listed in Table 7.1, very large gains in HDI scores occurred in places like China (+0.284), Bangladesh (+0.264), Thailand (+0.224), Ireland (+0.208), and Saudi

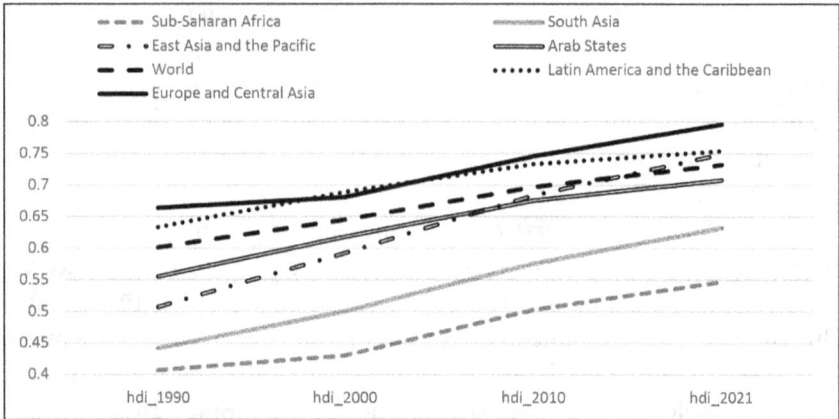

Figure 7.1. HDI Scores by World Regions (1990–2021). *Source: UNDP. 2023. Human Development Index Dataset "All composite indices and components time series (1990-2021)." Downloaded on July 10, 2023, from https://hdr.undp.org/data-center/documentation-and-downloads.*

Arabia (+0.197).[3] Contrastingly, much smaller gains took place in the United States (+0.049), Jamaica (+0.050), Kyrgyzstan (+0.054), Haiti (+0.106), and Italy (+0.117). Accordingly, there have been changes in the rank order of these countries over time. For instance, in 1990 the United States ranked highest among this sample of countries on the HDI, but by 2021 it had been surpassed by South Korea, Finland, and Ireland.

As for the components of the HDI, there is considerable variation across countries but the general trend is positive. Between 1990 and 2021, life expectancy at birth increased in most countries though not all. Increases in life expectancy have been dramatic in countries like Niger (from 42 to 62 years), Sudan (from 50 to 65 years), and South Korea (from 72 to 84 years) over the past three decades. In a number of African countries, there have been improvements in primary health-care, reductions in infant mortality, and gains made in access to safe drinking water, sanitation, and food security that have helped to raise life expectancy. In South Korea, the expansion of a national health insurance system in 1989 to cover the whole nation has also helped to dramatically improve life expectancy.[4] On the other hand, some countries experienced smaller increases or even decreases. Life expectancy gains were relatively smaller in countries like the United States (from 75 to 77 years), Kyrgyzstan (from 64 to 70 years), and Poland (from

Table 7.1.   HDI Scores of Selected Countries (1990–2021)

Country	Region	1990 HDI Score	2021 HDI Score	Improvement
Niger	West Africa	0.216	0.400	+0.184
Sudan	North Africa	0.336	0.508	+0.172
Bangladesh	South Asia	0.397	0.661	+0.264
Haiti	Caribbean	0.429	0.535	+0.106
China	East Asia	0.484	0.768	+0.284
El Salvador	Central America	0.525	0.675	+0.150
Thailand	Southeast Asia	0.576	0.800	+0.224
Brazil	South America	0.610	0.754	+0.144
Kyrgyzstan	Central Asia	0.638	0.692	+0.054
Jamaica	Caribbean	0.659	0.709	+0.050
Saudi Arabia	Middle East	0.678	0.875	+0.197
Poland	Eastern Europe	0.716	0.876	+0.160
Ireland	Western Europe	0.737	0.945	+0.208
South Korea	East Asia	0.737	0.925	+0.188
Italy	Southern Europe	0.778	0.895	+0.117
Finland	Northern Europe	0.814	0.940	+0.126
USA	North America	0.872	0.921	+0.049
World	**Global**	**0.601**	**0.732**	**+0.131**

Source: UNDP. 2023. Human Development Index Dataset (same as Figure 7.1).

71 to 77 years) while ten countries witnessed human lives actually getting shorter (Table 7.2). For instance, between 1990 and 2021 life expectancy in Jamaica declined by almost two years from 72.3 to 70.5 years. Life expectancy also declined in countries like Venezuela (from 71.5 to 70.6 years), Namibia (from 62.5 to 59.3 years), and Lesotho (from 59.4 to 53.1 years).

The number of mean and expected years of schooling for males and females also increased in most countries between 1990 and 2021. For females, it went up in all of our sample countries (Table 7.3). For countries on the lower end, like Niger (from 0.3 to 1.7 years) and Sudan (from 0.9 to 3.4 years), the increases were relatively minimal. The increase in the United States from 12.9 to 13.7 years was also numerically small but still substantively impressive considering its already very high starting point in 1990. For many countries in the

Table 7.2.   Life Expectancy at Birth in Selected Countries (1990–2021).

Country	Region	1990 Life Expectancy (years)	2021 Life Expectancy (years)	Change (years)
Niger	West Africa	41.9	61.6	+19.7
Sudan	North Africa	49.7	65.3	+15.6
Bangladesh	South Asia	56.0	72.4	+16.4
Haiti	Caribbean	53.0	63.2	+10.2
China	East Asia	68.0	78.2	+10.2
El Salvador	Central America	62.6	70.7	+8.1
Thailand	Southeast Asia	70.4	78.7	+8.3
Brazil	South America	66.0	72.8	+6.8
Kyrgyzstan	Central Asia	64.3	70.0	+5.7
Jamaica	Caribbean	72.3	70.5	-1.8
Saudi Arabia	Middle East	68.9	76.9	+8.0
Poland	Eastern Europe	70.7	76.5	+5.8
Ireland	Western Europe	74.8	82.0	+7.2
South Korea	East Asia	71.9	83.7	+11.8
Italy	Southern Europe	77.0	82.9	+5.9
Finland	Northern Europe	75.0	82.0	+7.0
USA	North America	75.4	77.2	+1.8
World average	**Global**	**65.1**	**71.4**	**+6.2**

Source: UNDP. 2023. Human Development Index Dataset (Same as figure 7.1).

sample shown in Table 7.3, the increase over this 31-year period was between 3 to 5 years more for female schooling as seen in Bangladesh, China, El Salvador, Thailand, Brazil, Poland, Ireland, South Korea, Italy, and Finland. An even more dramatic change occurred in Saudi Arabia where women's average years in school increased from 3.5 to 10.7 years between 1990 and 2021.

As for Gross National Income per capita (GNIPC), there have been gains worldwide over the past three decades, but they have been

Table 7.3. Mean Years of Schooling for Females in Selected Countries (1990–2021)

Country	Region	1990 Years of Female Schooling	2021 Years of Female Schooling	Change (years)
Niger	West Africa	0.3	1.7	+1.4
Sudan	North Africa	0.9	3.4	+2.5
Bangladesh	South Asia	2.2	6.8	+4.6
Haiti	Caribbean	1.8	4.6	+2.8
China	East Asia	3.4	7.3	+3.9
El Salvador	Central America	3.6	6.8	+3.2
Thailand	Southeast Asia	4.1	8.6	+4.5
Brazil	South America	3.8	8.3	+4.5
Kyrgyzstan	Central Asia	8.8	11.6	+2.8
Jamaica	Caribbean	6.8	9.7	+2.9
Saudi Arabia	Middle East	3.5	10.7	+7.2
Poland	Eastern Europe	8.9	13.3	+4.4
Ireland	Western Europe	7.1	11.8	+4.7
South Korea	East Asia	8.1	11.9	+3.8
Italy	Southern Europe	7.0	10.6	+3.6
Finland	Northern Europe	9.0	13.0	+4.0
USA	North America	12.9	13.7	+0.8
World Average	**Global**	**5.3**	**8.4**	**+3.1**

Source: UNDP. 2023. Human Development Index Dataset (same as Figure 7.1).

extremely unequal (Figure 7.2). Between 1990 and 2021, GNIPC levels increased in South Asia (from 19% to 33%) and East Asia and the Pacific (from 19 % to 81%), while falling in Sub-Saharan Africa (from 24% to 19%), the Arab States (from 82% to 70%), and Latin America and the Caribbean (from 87% to 75%) when compared with Europe and Central Asia (the wealthiest region). Between 1990 and 2021, GNIPC increases by region were also highly uneven. The low level of gains in Sub-Saharan Africa of USD $820 during this timeframe were

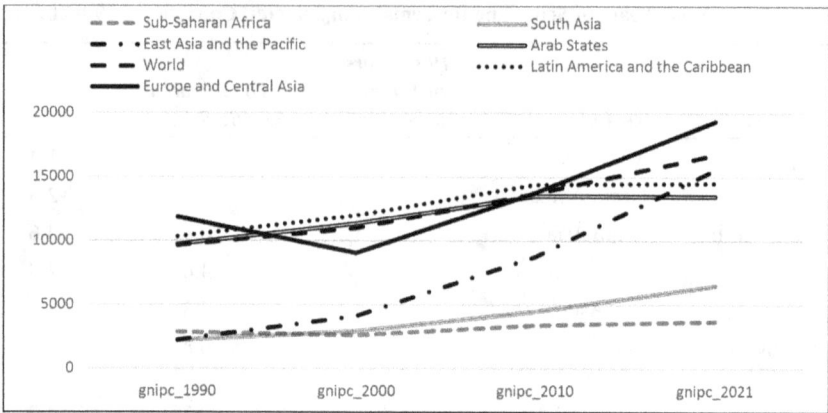

Figure 7.2. Gross National Income per Capita (GNIPC) by World Regions (1990–2021). *Source: UNDP. 2023. Human Development Index Dataset (same as Figure 7.1).*

roughly quadrupled by the medium-level gains made in Arab States ($3,793), Latin America and the Caribbean ($4,208), and South Asia ($4,256). These gains in turn were nearly doubled by the high increases in the world average ($7,123) and Europe and Central Asia ($7,495) and more than tripled by the very high gains made in East Asia and the Pacific ($13,348). Thus, the world's poorest region in terms of purchasing power (Sub-Saharan Africa) had a 2021 GNIPC of $3,699. This was $13,053 lower than the world average of $16,752 in 2021. By contrast, in 1990, Sub-Saharan Africa's GNIPC of $2,878 was only $6,750 lower than the world average of $9,628. Thus, in relative terms Africa has less income per person compared to the rest of the world now than it did three decades ago.

As tables 7.1–7.3 and figures 7.1 and 7.2 demonstrate, most countries improved in total number of schooling years, life expectancy, per capita income, and the composite HDI. Some countries have done better than others but most have experienced growth. As to the meaning of these indicators, however, we still have to be cautious in our interpretations. Quantity of life in years lived may not be equivalent to quality of life which (for some or even many people) might be quite miserable. The number of years a pupil is in school does not guarantee the quality (or relevance) of instruction they receive is high. And higher GNI per capita does not guarantee that the average person has better purchasing power, working conditions, relationships, leisure time, and happiness than before. Higher GNI may simply reflect the rich getting richer which would make the average GNI per capita go up even if the low- and middle-income majority of the population are at more or less the same level as before. Moreover, per capita income increases in some countries and regions, of say 10–30% over three decades, may not feel like much of a gain at all when other countries and regions are experiencing doubling or tripling of their per capita incomes. Keeping these caveats in mind, a clear trend is nevertheless discernible in the data. Most countries have been improving their scores on the HDI and its various component indicators since the index was inaugurated in 1990. We consider this to be an indication of qualified success for the HD paradigm.

HUMAN DEVELOPMENT COMPARED TO ALTERNATIVE APPROACHES

To assess whether the HD paradigm has been successful in terms of becoming a normalized, mainstream, or even dominant way of approaching global development today we now look to the frequency of its appearances in (written) public discourse. Awareness of the HDI and the HD paradigm has changed dramatically over time, as documented in the first six chapters of this book. But it is also important to assess how the HD paradigm compares to alternative international development approaches. Thus, we examined whether the HD approach has made inroads as a broader paradigm of development compared to Marxism, neoliberalism, development economics, modernization theory, dependency theory, and the developmental state, (i.e., the six major development approaches identified by Desai, 2009).

To start, we conducted a bibliometric analysis of publications that focus on a keyword reflecting the main thrust of these six paradigms. As Figure 7.3 reveals, "human development" related publications are now much more frequent than academic publications on neoliberalism, Marxism, and development economics as measured by Google Scholar. Since "human development" is also a term sometimes used in the fields of developmental psychology and biology, we examined the first 100 publication results for 2021 to see whether this might explain the prevalence of the term. What we found in our search of this keyword is that 79% of the results were specifically related to socio-economic issues involving the human development and capability approach

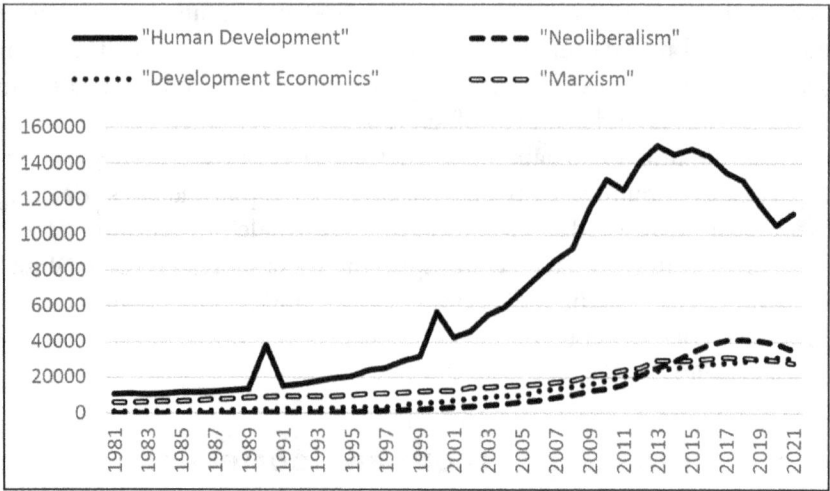

Figure 7.3. Publications on Human Development versus Alternative Paradigms. *Source: Author searches by publication year on Google Scholar. Data search updated on July 7, 2023.*

(HDCA) or the human development index (HDI) while only about one fifth were related to biological or psychological studies. This suggests the HD paradigm has indeed been influential among development paradigms in the new millennium.

As for the other prominent development paradigms, we conducted keyword searches on the "capability approach," which first emerged in the 1990s and found it to appear in more scholarly publications nowadays than either "modernization theory" (originating in the 1950s and 1960s) or "dependency theory" (which became prominent in the 1970s). In fact, only the "developmental state" (popularized in the 1980s) associated mostly with East Asia consistently outnumbered the "capability approach" in academic publications until being eclipsed in 2022 as shown in Figure 7.4.[5]

As these results illustrate, compared to long-standing paradigms of development, the capability approach has emerged as a serious contender in academic scholarship over a relatively short period of time already eclipsing two widely influential development paradigms associated with (or promoted by) the Global North (modernization theory) and Global South (dependency theory). The HD's prominence compared to the other development paradigms might also be due, in part, to older paradigms naturally fading away with the passage of time

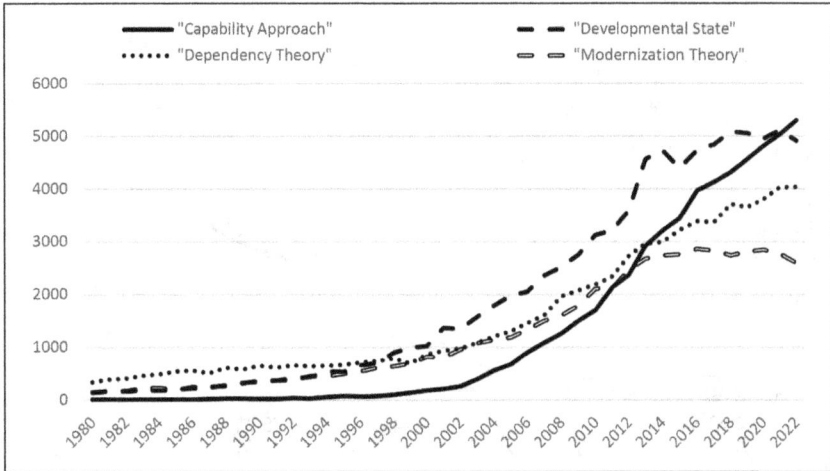

Figure 7.4. Publications on the Capability Approach versus Alternative Approaches. *Source: Author searches by publication year on Google Scholar. Data search updated on July 7, 2023.*

while newer paradigms are more prone to capture public attention. But back in the early 1990s, the rise of the capability approach vis-à-vis competing conceptualizations of development was by no means a foregone conclusion. Comparing new approaches to development that have emerged over the past three decades, "post-development" (see Escobar, 1995; Pieterse, 2010) was actually in the lead by the late 1990s. By the early 2000s, "pro-poor growth" then took the lead only to be followed by "aid effectiveness" in the late 2000s and early 2010s. In fact, it was only after 2015 that the "capability approach" came into the lead as shown in Figure 7.5. At that point it had surpassed "aid effectiveness" as well as "post-development," "pro-poor growth," and "ICT4D" (information and communication technologies for development).

Lastly, comparing overarching paradigms for understanding societies, the *capability approach* may seem like a minor player, but the concept of *human development* has closely rivaled that of *happiness* as a major focal point. In academic writings as captured by Google Scholar, the HD concept has even outpaced many alternative interpretive frameworks promoted in the human sciences over the last three decades including "positive psychology," "rational choice," "postmodernism," "intersectionality," "dialogic" approaches, and the "rule of law" (Figure 7.6). As noted earlier, the HD paradigm's prominence

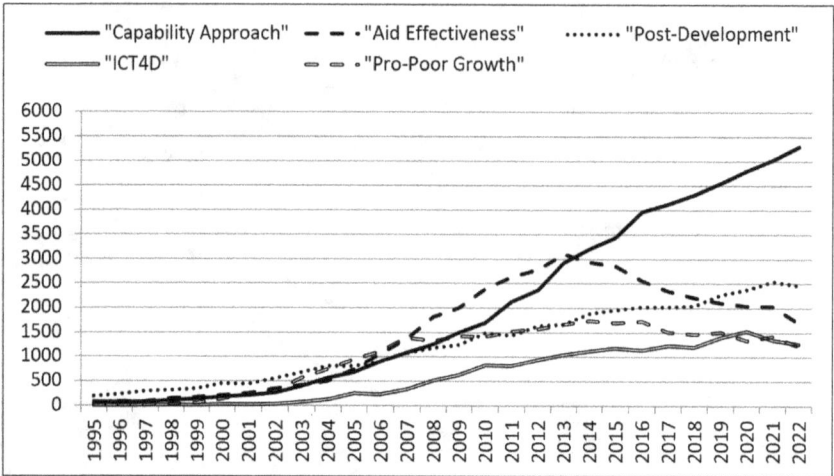

Figure 7.5. Publications on Competing Approaches to International Development. *Source: Author searches by publication year on Google Scholar. Data search updated on July 7, 2023.*

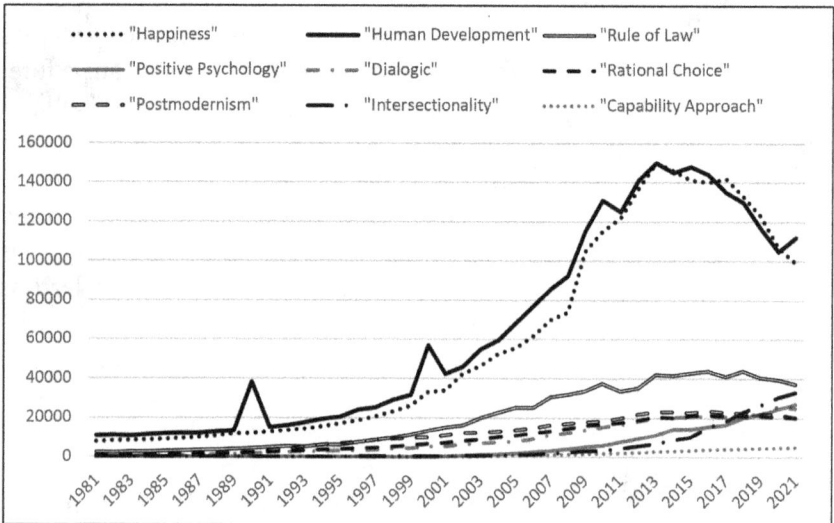

Figure 7.6. Publications on Human Development and other Intellectual Paradigms. *Source: Author searches by publication year on Google Scholar. Data search updated on July 7, 2023.*

would still be evident even if one were to discount the fact that roughly one-quarter to one-fifth of publications using the term "human development" focus on biology or psychology rather than socio-economic issues.

To conclude, although the prominence of a development approach can be difficult to measure, the frequency of scholarly books, journal articles, and reports published on given development topics and approaches can give us a practical sense of which development ideas and concepts are more salient than others at a given point in time. Our comparative bibliometric analyses as shown above have found considerable evidence supporting the assertion that the human development paradigm has indeed been very successful in capturing global attention through its increasing presence in published writings vis-à-vis other development paradigms. While we do not know yet whether this will continue to be the case over the coming decades, the growth trajectory of publications about human development, the capability approach, and related concepts such as human security and (global) development goals as mentioned in chapter 3 has been substantial from the 1990s to the present.

LOCATING THE HUMAN DEVELOPMENT APPROACH ON THE LEFT-RIGHT SPECTRUM

A common means to compare approaches to international development and political ideologies in general is via the *left-right* political spectrum. In what follows we will review some of the political ideologies, regimes, and ideas of the left-right spectrum, and estimate the relative placement of the HD ideology, with qualifications. As discussed below, in our analysis, the HD ideology is not a radical ideology as it does not push too hard or demand too much from political or social actors. Rather, HD ideology leans towards the political center.

While the concepts of "left" and "right" hold different meanings in different societies, a general consensus among political scientists holds that equality serves as the core value of contention between the political left and right (see e.g., Joshi, 2021c). Most scholars concur with the definition of Lipset et al. (1954, p. 1135) that "by left we shall mean advocating social change in the direction of greater equality—political, economic or social; by right we shall mean supporting a traditional more or less hierarchical social order, and opposing change toward greater equality."

When it comes to reducing gaps between people who are wealthy and people in poverty, programmatic political movements further to the left prioritize interventions to reduce inequalities (for example, through regimes or movements labeled as communism which hold equality to be an important idea). Such political movements or parties profess a clear egalitarian ideological agenda for transforming existing structures of power that disadvantage people with no or low incomes or assets. Social movements, political parties, and activists of the center-left (e.g., socialism, social democracy, feminism, or green movements that focus on environmentalism and ecologism) also generally aim to reduce socio-economic inequalities but are not as radical as the far-left and do not seek to eliminate all inequalities. By contrast, we often see lower prioritization of social equalization from populist, non-programmatic, patronage-based, and clientelistic political parties and movements. Such movements sometimes claim to be on the left or to support the poor, but are often actually right-leaning as they are not driven by an agenda to systematically transform political and economic structures in favor of people in poverty (Kohli, 1987; Sandbrook et al., 2007).

As for ideologies that lean toward the center-right (e.g., conservativism, protective liberalism, or Christian democracy) or the far-right (e.g., fascism, imperialism, or libertarianism) of the political spectrum, they are generally less favorable to (or oppose) narrowing the gap between the rich and poor. Such political movements cater to different agendas, and they do not prioritize equalizing economic and social outcomes or opportunities across class, race, and gender (Steger, 2009). As one moves further to the political right, there tends to be more of a competitive, social-Darwinist view that certain social classes, castes, or ethnic/racial group(s) deserve to be at the top and others at the bottom leading to policies that seek to maintain or increase inequality (Ball et al., 2004). For example, far-right regimes often seek to maintain rigid stratification along racial, ethnic, linguistic, religious, or regional lines. Accordingly, these ideologies justify withholding or denying education and healthcare to lower status people or groups. They are also prone to accord low public investment or minimal attention to actual enforcement and implementation of public schooling or health standards. Likewise, in countries influenced by the right-wing ideology of neoliberalism, funding for government schools and public health may at times be cut drastically as privileged classes aim to make education and health (care) a private rather than a public good (Joshi and Smith, 2012).

On the political right, elitist ideologies are more likely to justify rejecting the pursuit of equality in the short-term because such policies are interpreted as potentially retarding material incentives and technological innovations that could otherwise improve human capacities and social achievements in the long run. Purveyors of such ideologies reject the idea that it is necessary to immediately support social services for all, or even most, of a population that is in need. The practices and policies of colonialism offer an insightful example: imperial powers like the United Kingdom (UK) and France emphasized some degree of shared development in the home country but not in the colonies (Meredith, 2005). Such policies are likewise evident in ethnically, regionally, gender, or caste-stratified societies—like South Africa under *apartheid*—where the ethnic, racial, regional, or caste group(s) in power promoted only their own group's modernization (e.g., Gebremedhin and Joshi, 2016). In such cases, the goal was to modernize the elite or privileged in-group to give them an advantage over other groups in the population.

Last but not least, centrist ideologies have a different character than either the left or the right. They are less concerned about achieving social equality than the left, but may still be favorable to supporting policies that provide basic human development for all, or at least basic services that allow for basic needs to be met. Among centrist ideologies, those on the center-right typically aim for less equality than left-of-center ideologies. Center-right ideologies might still be in favor of improving living conditions for both the rich and poor (though often aiming for the rich to benefit more than the poor) and are therefore willing to invest in some degree of public goods (Joshi and O'Dell, 2013). Although they may oppose, for example, equalizing a child's chances to attend upper secondary or tertiary education or they might oppose national health insurance, they may still be willing to invest in universal primary education and maternal and child health services in order to reap its economic (i.e., *human capital*) benefits.

In our view, the HD ideology can more or less be located in the political center and we find that the HD approach is flexible and ambiguous enough that it can be adapted into either center-left or center-right variants (for a more detailed analysis, see Joshi and O'Dell, 2013). Clearly, the HD paradigm does not challenge the status quo as much as compared to some other ideologies of globalization or development. The HD paradigm is also definitely not on the far-left of the left-right political spectrum. It has almost nothing to say about labor unions and it does not embrace socialism. But the writings of Amartya Sen and his co-authors do emphasize justice and public action which suggests perhaps a center-left positioning of the capability approach as "a 'people-centered' approach, which puts human agency (rather than organizations such as markets or governments) at the center of the stage" (Drèze and Sen, 2002, p. 6). Amartya Sen, who was born in the Global South, also points to championing *freedom* as the desirable means and ends of development: "If our concern is with equality of freedom, it is no more adequate to ask for equality of its *means* than it is to seek equality of its *results*. Freedom relates to both, but does not coincide with either" (1995, p. 87).

In some articulations, however, the HD ideology appears to lean a bit more to the center-right when it places more emphasis on aspirations and ideals than concrete measures to enable change and remedy injustices. Some authors writing within the HD paradigm have also expressed opposition to promoting complete equality among humans on the global level by instead arguing for retaining the diversity and richness found in different cultures and people groups. In such cases, support for pluralism is prioritized over a universalistic version of equal rights to enable discussion of different viewpoints through reasoned debate and for people to decide their own fates. For instance, while Martha Nussbaum, who hails from the Global North, takes a progressive stand on certain feminist issues, she has argued that "we need, then, an institutional solution to global problems . . . A world state, however, is probably a bad idea . . . a world state would probably flatten differences too much" (Nussbaum, 2011, p. 120). Whereas equality of social and economic opportunities and outcomes across peoples and nations has long been a goal of leftist (and especially far-left) politics, the HD approach articulated by Sen and Nussbaum emphasizes *freedoms*, *liberties*, and the *individual*. Their vision differs from the left's strong emphasis on substantive equality, labor rights, social justice, solidarity, and collective action. As Nussbaum asserts, "the major liberties that protect pluralism are central items on the capabilities list. The freedom of speech, the freedom of association, the freedom of conscience, political access and opportunity—all these are crucial elements of a society that protects cultural and religious pluralism. By placing them on the list we give them a central and non-negotiable place" (Nussbaum, 2011, p. 110).

Moreover, Nussbaum's version of the HD approach even incorporates conservative political ideas and elements, such as the importance of nationalism and citizenship. Such emphasis suggests a center-right leaning on the political spectrum, which stands in contrast to the more center-left ideology of justice globalism and the transnational solidarity championed by the global justice movement (GJM) as discussed in chapter 1 (see also Della Porta, 2007; Steger et al., 2012). As Nussbaum argues, "the nation is not just a convenient starting place: it has moral importance" and she argues that her version of the capability approach incorporates "a strong defense of national sovereignty" (2011, p. 113). In practice, however, prioritizing nationalism would mean largely reifying and reinforcing the existing unjust international order, even if "the governments of richer nations ought to give a minimum of 2 percent of GDP to poorer nations" (2011, p. 117). While this discussion reveals some divergence among HD authors on the left-right spectrum, overall we find the HD paradigm at its core to be an essentially middle-of-the-road, non-threatening centrist rival to traditional Western development paradigms such as conservatism, communism, and capitalism.

EVALUATING THE HUMAN DEVELOPMENT APPROACH AS AN IDEOLOGY

The HD approach like all development paradigms and globalization ideologies has both strengths and shortcomings or what we might think of as opportunities for improvement. Here we attempt to be critical in our analysis of the HD approach by applying "a discerning mode of thought capable of judging the quality of a thing or a person by separating its constitutive form from mere attributes" (Steger and James, 2019, p. 132). As discussed in chapters 5 and 6, HD ideas and foundational concepts have a long history within the United Nations system, in development practice, and in challenges from the Global South toward some of the dominant ideologies held by the Global North during the Cold War. The HD ideology had strong proponents in academia and among practitioners who have been globalizing the message in intellectual circles and in the mass media which has been favorably reporting on the HDRs and HD indexes which positively contributes to them being known and seen worldwide as credible and reliable as discussed in chapters 3 and 4. The HD ideology contains ideas and foundational concepts that are easily accepted and palatable to most governments or other leaders, (i.e., it does not radically challenge the status quo as covered in chapters 1 and 2).

Yet, all ideologies have their limitations and opportunities for improvement that could potentially make them more impactful. For example, the HD ideology does not appear to offer an adequate response to pressing global crises that require more immediate policy changes and social shifts (on issues of global climate change, outbreaks of war, or refugee and migrant rights, for instance). HD emphasizes deliberation and democracy but the procedures required for adequate decision-making are slow-moving in the face of quick-moving global disasters. Another opportunity for improvement is in the lack of a definitive stance on how to use specific tactics and mobilize power to achieve HD outcomes since such responsibilities are primarily left to individuals or states to decide. Despite its reliance on deliberative democracy, HD does not provide a framework that would adequately unite people groups, whether that be a cohesive framework (like that offered by religion), or a framework that unites a group against others (like that formed against a common enemy). Finally, the jargon and terminology (as reviewed in chapters 1 and 2) used in HD (that of capabilities, functioning, etc.) at times can be somewhat technical and specific, difficult to understand, and potentially alienating to non-intellectuals.

STRENGTHS OF THE HUMAN DEVELOPMENT IDEOLOGY

Our study finds that "human development" (HD) as an ideology, paradigm, and approach, has been widely influential since 1990 in part because it conceptualizes global development from a multidimensional perspective. As seen in chapters 5 and 6 of this volume, the HD focus on putting people first and being concerned about individual human beings in development practice has been on the agenda for decades.

Such ideas were present in the way the UN was created (its function and structure) and during the first decades of development practice (especially in discussions of the UN's Economic and Social Council and the creation of the UN Development Programme and the International Development Agency at the World Bank). These ideas influenced how the Global South challenged the dominant international development ideologies and practices of the Global North during the Cold War (through proposing the New International Economic Order, for example). By the end of the 1980s, the failures of neoliberal ideology (especially visible in disappointing outcomes of structural adjustment programs) and the end of the Cold War offered a momentous occasion for a new ideology of development and globalization to arise. The UNDP stepped in by issuing the Human Development Reports (HDRs) which have since been promoting the HD approach and ideology to the global public. This approach is multidimensional, multidisciplinary, and departs from approaches that treat globalization or development as merely being driven by one phenomenon (such as economics, technology, public policy, or religion). Instead, the HD paradigm recognizes the holistic nature of human experience and that different dimensions of people's lives are integrated and interdependent (for example, one needs nourishment and health in order to participate in political decision-making or to gain a good education).

As this book has examined, the relationship between globalization and human development can be negative as well as positive. If globalization is approached in a way that puts human capabilities, functionings, and opportunities ahead of other objectives, it can be a force for good in people's lives. Chapter 1 posited three possibilities: a) HD as impacting globalization or vice versa, b) HD as being equivalent to globalization with all its positive and negative outcomes, and c) HD globalizing worldwide as an ideology that puts people first. Arguably, the HD ideology has had the biggest impact in this third category. As discussed in this book, through the work of intellectuals (chapter 3), mass media (chapter 4), international organizations like the UN (chapter 5), and representatives of national governments in the Global South (chapter 6), the idea and priorites of human development have been globalizing not only to the general public but also to people in leadership positions who have been thinking and acting in ways that prioritize human freedom and choice in their policies and practices. The HD ideology has also been powerful and has international appeal because it offers a more inclusive alternative to racism, sexism, ageism, ethnocentrism, and exclusive nationalisms. It views all humans as deserving of a life that is meaningful and it opposes prioritizing or providing special advantage to one group or individual identity category over others. Resembling the ideal of human rights, the discourse of human development is supportive of equal access and opportunities to all genders, ethnicities, races, age groups, or other thus far un-identified people groups or individuals globally. In contrast to nationalisms and other national-level ideologies, the HD ideology is inclusive of all of humanity, whereas many ideologies are exclusive and only pertain to the well-being of particular groups or individuals.

The human development approach is accepting of all individuals and people groups and does not seek to alienate or blame certain social groups or individuals. This has presumably facilitated its growth and popularity as it does not abrasively challenge the status quo or demand redress from groups or perpetrators in society. Rather it takes the present as a starting point for success while not really assigning much in the way of blame in contrast to ideologies which explicitly blame various people groups like the rich, foreigners, or ethnic minorities as putative sources of socio-economic problems. As a more centrist ideology, HD does not aim to alienate those who lean toward either the political right or left, as it shares common ground with ideologies on both the political left and right. HD's centrism and overall non-combative stance therefore positions it well to gather a potentially large coalition of supporters. One might say that the HD paradigm has also successfully taken on a rational, technocratic, and depoliticized character as evoked by the HDRs' syntheses and reports on statistical data (see chapter 5). Such reports are widely perceived and interpreted as being relatively neutral, objective, unbiased, accurate, and credible by mass media and the international community (see chapter 4).

The HD paradigm also attempts to set a particular agenda for globalization. It is steeped in a global imaginary as its goal is to maximize the capabilities of all human beings around the world not just those residing in a single country. The HD ideology does not prioritize access to opportunities like education based on citizenship of those residing in a single country, or any other group or individual identity. Additionally, HD recognizes globalization as multi-faceted, involving issues ranging from climate change and migration to trade and aid as seen in the annual HDRs which address topics in the various political, economic, social, and ecological dimensions of globalization (as reviewed in chapter 5).

WEAKNESSES OF THE HUMAN DEVELOPMENT IDEOLOGY

There are also shortcomings to the HD paradigm that limit its power and influence. For instance, its emphasis on open-ended public deliberation has great potential to improve the quality of ideas examined and implemented by governments and international organizations.[6] But we must also take caution that deliberation alone may be insufficient to stop large-scale catastrophes. Indeed, the vignette at the beginning of chapter 5 introduces climate activists Greta Thunberg and Severn Suzuki who pointedly shamed UN delegates in their speeches at UN meetings, calling them out for their failure to act. Despite much discussion and debate in international conferences, and deliberative bodies such as the UNGA, UNSC, and ECOSOC, we still do not see an adequate international response on major problems like global climate change, genocide, ecocide, civil wars, abject poverty, or the ongoing migrant and refugee crises in various areas of the world. Such atrocities are still occurring in the twenty-first century, and problems like global ecological devastation will be most damaging to the youth, non-human species, and those not yet born. Such global problems demand shared agreement and large-scale direct action to prevent further inhibiting the development of humans and their capabilities, but the HD approach has arguably not done enough to demand immediate action and to respond quickly and adequately to such crises.

Further, experience suggests that large-scale action to address global crises is heavily contingent upon the influence and response of *intergovernmental bodies*. Yet another weak point in HD ideology is its relative inattention to the essential role played by intergovernmental actors like the UN. While in practice HD promoters and UN agencies have often cooperated in agenda setting and policy prescriptions, the theoretical importance of intergovernmental bodies is not heavily emphasized in the HD discourse of theorists like Amartya Sen and Martha Nussbaum. In previous generations the importance of intergovernmental organizations for global cooperation was seen as a *sine qua non* for effective globalization (e.g., Claude, 1965). As Steger and James (2019, p. 39, p. 42) note, earlier scholars like Inis Claude "considered the UN as a whole as the most appropriate model for a rationally planned globalization of international cooperation," but "ultimately, the neoliberal revolution of the Thatcher-Reagan era helped turn the globalization-as-market narrative into the dominant meaning cluster."

Another problem is that the HD ideology largely takes the role of the state and especially *state capacity* for granted. The HD ideology, like all globalisms maintains an "ideological orientation towards the world as a single, interdependent place that commanded more attention than the nation-state" (Steger and James, 2019, p. 86). But the HD approach arguably misses something essential by underemphasizing the fundamental importance of state capacity since states still have to deliver (or otherwise make widely available) public goods like education, healthcare, and jobs that are so fundamental to human development. While some authors like Nussbaum (2011) emphasize the importance of government in implementing HD objectives, what also needs to be stressed is states developing the requisite administrative, supervisory, and revenue collecting capacities to meet basic thresholds on all 10 central capabilities. Without proper attention to this, the HD ideology's seeming ambivalence toward the state partially resembles the anti-statism of neo-liberal ideology although for the HD approach it is the captured, corrupted, or dysfunctional state that is problematic not the state itself.[7] Hence, while globalizing HD makes it imperative for us to de-nationalize our consciousness, we must not forget the importance of state capacity in our consciousness and pragmatic action plans.

Another limitation of the HD paradigm, as with neoliberalism, is that both largely fail to meet the *spiritual* or non-material side of human life whereas nationalist populisms and religious globalisms are comparatively stronger in addressing these needs.[8] That is, HD ideology does not offer a uniting framework, either to bind humans together behind an inspiring and cohesive ideology, or against a shared enemy. Thus far, patterns of global integration have contributed to "an identity crisis born of an aversion to the global" making people "take refuge in their nation, locality, and god" (Steger and James, 2019, p. 2). In response, a more compelling ideology of globalization would presumably need to incorporate a spiritual component involving some form of divine (or at least moral) validation for its prescriptions.[9] By contrast, the HD ideology does not incorporate anything like this and more generally underemphasizes the consciousness and psychological aspects of motivating and sustaining collective action. Rather, its pronounced individualism, strong emphasis on diversity, insistence on taking a "thin" approach, and conspicuous lack of an enemy may actually inhibit the forging of a global solidarity among peoples from vastly different backgrounds which is so badly needed to achieve and sustain global collective action. Regrettably, such under-emphasis on building trans-local and trans-national solidarity may even contribute to scapegoating or hate-mongering against racial minorities, women, immigrants, or other marginalized groups. Thus, by emphasizing capabilities over consciousness, the HD ideology's relative inattention to the spiritual dimension of human life and the need to collectively develop—not just unilaterally stipulate—a globally shared sense of values regrettably denudes the ideology of much of its potential moral force.[10]

Significantly, as a narrative for making sense of the world, the HD paradigm is limited as mentioned above by having no clearly specified *enemy* or scapegoat for people to blame for their problems and to direct their energies toward attacking or eliminating. By contrast, most forms of nationalism, and especially nationalist populist movements in recent years, have attracted many supporters by framing *outsiders* (e.g., foreigners, immigrants, ethno-racial minorities, international economic elites, etc.) as being enemies of the *true* people (Wodak, 2015; see also chapter 1 of this volume). Such a xenophobic framing may seem perverse from many ethical and practical standpoints (including the HD perspective), but there is no denying that such nationalist ideologies have attracted many supporters in various countries and probably more ardent supporters worldwide than those willing to dedicate significant amounts of their own time and energy to the HD cause. Similarly, neoliberalism has galvanized supporters (especially among the rich) by positing the *state* or *government* as an enemy to defeat, especially those governments that stand in the way of profit-seeking business entities.

Thus, one lesson HD supporters could potentially learn is the power of using emotionally charged colloquial language and simple, easily memorable *slogans* that are regularly repeated to attract and sustain followers. In this respect, supporters of neoliberalism and various nationalist populisms have actively used mass marketing techniques to connect with the popular psychology of ordinary people and non-intellectuals.

By contrast, HD texts seem to be more often in denial of how and what ordinary people think, and writings on the capability approach are often couched in heavily intellectual (technical, philosophical, and academic) language. Many HD promoters also appear to prefer ivory-tower confines and appear to be less conscious of what makes ideologies (and reformist political movements more broadly) successful and resonate with mass publics.[11] In fact, unlike the approach taken in this text, most HD contributors and adherents do not appear to view their approach as an ideology, and they thereby inhibit their ability to more effectively strategize on fine-tuning and amplifying their appeals, developing clever catchphrases, and gaining more converts. By neglecting such practical measures, they actually open themselves up to criticisms of being comfortable middle-class professionals more interested in making money for their own families—by endlessly talking about and reframing the problems of under-development—than seriously trying to permanently remove the underlying sources of such problems.

Another concern is the HD paradigm's relatively high level of abstraction, reliance on intellectual terminology, and demands for people to apply *reason* to justify their choices and preferences. While the latter criterion has its merits, it may inadvertently create an excessive barrier against many people's participation, given that reasoning well is actually quite difficult and may depend on advanced academic training (or high-quality education). This is problematic because most people rely on short cuts known as *heuristics* or *schemas* in their thinking, but as is evident in the HD indicators discussed in this book, most people have limited access to a good and quality education. Thus, seen from an ideological perspective, the HD's intellectually sophisticated and technocratic approach may help it to gain audiences among certain circles of intellectual and policy elites, while simultaneously constraining it from having a broader mass appeal if perceived to be incomprehensible or irrelevant to people's everyday struggles. As discussed above, the relatively centrist orientation of the HD ideology makes it more appealing (than a radical ideology) to many, but the trade-off is that it lacks certain potentially compelling characteristics found in other ideologies of globalization and development, whether on the political right (such as emphasis on hierarchy), or the left (such as emphasis on equality).

The HD approach also suffers from a number of ambiguities (like most ideologies) stemming from the fact that it elaborates no hierarchy of priorities. For instance, Nussbaum speaks of HD enablers and 10 central human capabilities that are essentially universal, but she intentionally gives no guidance as to which capability or capabilities should take precedence under conditions of scarcity, or in the case of possible conflicts (2011, pp. 33–34). Such distance from pertinent practical concerns in a world undergoing massive stresses potentially makes it very difficult to translate the HD agenda into meaningful policies.

Relatedly, seemingly all individuals' capabilities equally matter, but the HD approach allows for people to have different levels of income, which in practice results in differential purchasing power, and hence differing capabilities. Life expectancy is also a component of the HDI, with the HD paradigm taking no explicit stance on the value of a given person's life compared to another person. Yet critical analysis reveals that preference is given to those who are already born over the unborn in the HDI, a measure that de-contests the concept of *life* by using life expectancy at birth instead of total life expectancy also known as life expectancy at conception.[12]

Finally, and related to problems of ambiguity, is the absence of a meaningful discussion about *power* in the HD ideology. HD is ostensibly about people becoming empowered and having more power over their own lives in the form of capabilities to do and be what they want in life. Thus, in its core pronouncements, some might interpret the HD paradigm as advocating a tremendous shift in power away from the currently powerful to the presently powerless. Indeed, seen from this perspective, the HD paradigm has a deeply radical potential, much like the idea of human rights, which guarantees a long list of entitlements (and thus power) to all humans. Yet, the HD's potential on this matter is muted because it lacks an explicit focus on what power is, who has and wields power, who does not have power, and who should have power and why.[13] At the same time, it is also worth noting that the deeply radical potential of many ideologies is often muted when it comes to putting them into practice because it is difficult for those who are comfortable to muster the courage to challenge those who are powerful and the status quo when doing so might invite backlash.

HUMAN DEVELOPMENT IN THE PRESENT AND FUTURE

The HD ideology, or what we have called *capabilities globalism* as promoted by the UN, has been rather successful in spite of some of the limitations and flaws reviewed in the previous section. On the one hand, HD measurements have been widely influential in promoting a novel understanding of international development and in orienting development theory and practice to focus on the human experience.[14] Countries around the world have been improving on their HD index scores, and overall trends in HD achievement have been positive. On the other hand, HD ideology would likely be more impactful were it to incorporate and stress the pivotal roles of state capacity, spirituality, solidarity, and intergovernmental organizations in solving global collective action problems to advance HD outcomes.

As a centrist approach to globalization, the HD paradigm is simultaneously progressive and compromising. It challenges humans to think of how much better our lives could be if we lived in societies where we could do and be whatever we wanted. The language and framework of HD aims to be palatable to development policy elites and development practitioners by not asking for too much novel or too radical change; it is measured and tepid. Even something as obviously beneficial for global human development, like a universal basic income for all people, has thus far largely escaped the HD approach.

In the HD paradigm, the language and concepts used presumably do not excite, incite, enrage, or inspire emotion the way that other ideologies do; consider how Marxism sought to unite the masses in a "forcible overthrow of all existing social conditions" (Marx and Engels, 1848), or how the Universal Declaration of Human Rights proclaimed that "All human beings are born free and equal in dignity and rights" while demanding that "Everyone is entitled to all the rights and freedoms . . . " (UDHR, 1948). By contrast, it is difficult to become fired up by the HD approach because most of its concepts and theories come across as dry, technocratic, and are expressed in emotion-less language (typical of the bureaucratic discourse and agreements forged by international organizations). By not strongly challenging or taking on global inequalities resulting from the billionaire families and tyrants controlling the majority of the world's wealth and power, and by ignoring mass indebtedness and elite social control of the global propaganda and war machines, the HD ideology is placatory and avoids confrontation.

Despite (or perhaps because of) HD's centrism and ambiguities, the HDRs, HDI, and development goals (the Millennium Development Goals and the Sustainable Development Goals) have fared impressively well in their public reception vis-à-vis other more narrow conceptions of development that rely primarily on economic growth or per capita income to measure human well-being. In other words, the HD ideology may only be slightly more cohesive and acceptable as a globalization paradigm than neoliberalism, but it does appear to have been sufficiently compelling with global audiences to increasingly become a dominant approach to conceptualizing international development and an influential way of thinking about globalization in the twenty-first century. As other scholars, have similarly argued, "the ideology of human development has now become the driving normative force behind the global policies supported by the UN in the area of development" (Thérien, 2012a, p. 1). Within ideological space, it is likewise evident that the HD approach has actively taken the form of a global *counter-ideology* by challenging many conservative prescriptions of neoliberal capitalism. In this respect, HD ideology, with its ultimate stated goal of maximizing individual agency and capabilities, distinguishes itself from ideologies aiming to maximize incomes, commodities, production, happiness, or utility (Alkire, 2005, p. 1).

To those who are not from the West or the Global North, the HD ideology of the UN may seem like yet another drab project of Western cultural imperialism. But as this book has demonstrated, the HD ideology has roots in Western liberalism as well as in challenges to development thinking and practice emanating from the Global South.[15] Further, the HD ideology has shed much of the racist, nationalist, and sexist baggage often associated with earlier variants of liberalism. The HD ideology also stands in contrast to the much stronger focus on global solidarity, substantive equality, human rights, and distributive justice found on the political left. But as a centrist ideology the HD approach aims for broader appeal by compromising and balancing in various areas, presumably with the aim of enhancing its acceptance and usage by political and academic elites vis-à-vis its ideological rivals and competitors.

To conclude, the HD ideology admirably represents a *critical* and *engaged* approach to globalization as advocated by Steger and James (2019).[16] As a theory and practice of international development, the HD paradigm has inspired changes to the way that humans think and act worldwide, and to the way that humans think of their place on the Earth. It has challenged how governments produce and implement policies by calling for social, economic, political, and ecological systems that support human thriving above all else. Substantial global change will ultimately require a shift in human consciousness in the current and future eras of globalization, expanding human knowledge of the Earth and of the entire Universe. There is always the grave danger that "If the structures of the human mind remain unchanged, we will always end up re-creating fundamentally the same world, the same evils, the same dysfunction" as before (Tolle, 2005, p. 22). As explored in this book, the HD ideology, as promoted by the UN, has contributed to consciousness and knowledge expansion in ways that are obvious and subtle, visible and unseen, local and global. It has called upon us to expand our minds concerning how human beings live and thrive on Earth. Dedication to human development and the expansion of global human consciousness is, and will be, vital if we are to adequately address the serious problems humanity faces, both now and in the decades ahead. The spectre that now haunts all humankind is whether humans will make the choices necessary to re-think, re-imagine, and re-create a world in which every human being—and perhaps every non-human living being—has the capability and possibility to live a long, healthy, educated, and happy life.

NOTES

1. Parts of this chapter are taken from Joshi, 2021a. We thank the journal for granting us permission to reprint those portions.

2. Perhaps because it only includes three countries, the UN does not include North America as a world region in its HDI data.

3. While the rise of China is well known, the HD gains in Bangladesh (starting from a lower initial-level of development) have been almost equally impressive.

4. For more on South Korea's national health insurance system, see https://www.nl.go.kr/EN/contents/EN34501000000.do (accessed July 17, 2023).

5. On the "developmental state," we also observed that certain publications emanated from the fields of biology and ecology and were not germane to international development.

6. This was seen in chapters 5 and 6 through the creation of the UN and its various organs and programs, and in the deliberation at international conferences about shared goals and threats.

7. In this respect, the HD paradigm seems at times almost like a kind of soft neo-liberalism. As Jolly (2003) points out, the HD approach and neo-liberalism diverge in certain respects but also share certain commonalities.

8. Relatedly, HD ideology's concomitant rejection of nationalism(s) might limit its diffusion given the continuing appeal of the national imaginary and various sub-national imaginaries in much of the world.

9. The human rights regime, for example, has tried to do this by offering a framework of justice to replace that which formerly was offered by religion in Western societies of the latter twentieth century (Hopgood, 2006).

10. For instance, the work of Nussbaum (1999, 2011) might be seen as stipulating rather than collectively deciding upon global development priorities.

11. An interesting working paper by Alkire and Ritchie (2007) on what makes ideas spread is an exception.

12. Decontesting (as discussed in chapter 2) refers to the ideological maneuver of interpreting or defining a concept in a particular way so as to exclude other possible interpretations of that concept. Through the act of decontesting key terms, ideologies shape people's views on an issue by building in assumptions and presumptions that are then treated as constant or immutable when in fact they are variable and could be understood in other ways (see Freeden, 1996).

13. In this respect, HD ideology is very much unlike Marxist ideology, for example, which clearly rails against class inequality and power differentials.

14. Chapters 5 and 6 provided more details about HD indexes and country progress on them.

15. Chapter 6 especially discussed contributions of the Global South in the evolution of the HD paradigm.

16. See Joshi (2021a) for further discussion on this point.

REFERENCES

Acharya, Amitav. 2004. "How Ideas Spread: Whose Norms Matter? Norm Localization and Institutional Change in Asian Regionalism." *International Organization* 58 (2): 239–275.

Acharya, Amitav. 2016. "Studying the Bandung Conference from a Global IR Perspective." *Australian Journal of International Affairs* 70 (4): 342–357.

Ahmad, Naved. 2005. "Governance, Globalisation, and Human Development in Pakistan [with Comments by Ejaz Ghani]." *The Pakistan Development Review* 44 (4): 585–594.

Akhter, Syed H. 2004. "Is Globalization What It's Cracked Up to Be? Economic Freedom, Corruption, and Human Development." *Journal of World Business* 39 (3): 283–295.

Al Jazeera. 2022. "The Taliban Closes Afghan Girls' Schools Hours After Reopening." *Al Jazeera,* March 23. https://www.aljazeera.com/news/2022/3/23/taliban-orders-girls-schools-shut-hours-after-reopening.

Alkire, Sabina. 2002. "Dimensions of Human Development." *World Development* 30 (2): 181–205.

Alkire, Sabina. 2005. "Capability and Functionings: Definition and Justification." Human Development and Capabilities Association Briefing Note.

Alkire, Sabina. 2010. "Human Development: Definitions, Critiques, and Related Concepts." OPHI Working Papers 36, University of Oxford.

Alkire, Sabina and Selim Jahan. 2018. "The New Global MPI 2018: Aligning with the Sustainable Development Goals." OPHI Working Papers 121, Queen Elizabeth House, University of Oxford.

Alkire, Sabina and Angus Ritchie. 2007. "Winning Ideas: Lessons from Free Market Economics." Oxford Poverty & Human Development Initiative, Working Paper No. 6. http://www.ophi.org.uk/wp-content/uploads/OPHI-wp06.pdf.

Al-Mughrabi, Nidal. 2020. "Gaza Rapper, 11, Strikes Chord with Rhymes about War and Hardship." *Reuters*, August 17. https://www.reuters.com/article/us -palestinians-gaza-rap-idCAKCN25D1WX.

Anand, Sudhir and Amartya Sen. 2000. "The Income Component of the Human Development Index." *Journal of Human Development* 1 (1): 83–106.

Anand, Sudhir and Amartya Sen. 2003. "Human Development Index: Methodology and Measurement" In *Readings in Human Development*, edited by Sakiko Fukuda-Parr and A.K. Shiva Kumar, 138–151. New York: Oxford University Press.

Anya, Ike. 2006. "Omololu Falobi—A Hero Departs." *iNigerian.com*, November 13. https://www.inigerian.com/omololu-falobi-a-hero-departs/.

Arguedas, Amy Ross, Sayan Banerjee, Camila Mont'Alverne, Benjamin Toff, Richard Fletcher, and Rasmus Kleis Nielsen. 2023. *News for the Powerful and Privileged: How Misrepresentation and Underrepresentation of Disadvantaged Communities Undermine Their Trust in News*. Reuters Institute for the Study of Journalism and the University of Oxford.

Asghar, Nabila, Tanveer Ahmed Naveed, and Shaista Saleem. 2017. "Impact of Social, Political and Economic Globalization on Gender Inequality Index in Pakistan: A Time Series Analysis." *South Asian Studies* 32 (2): 419–434.

Ashoka (Foundation). 2001. "Omololu Falobi: Journalists Against AIDS (JAAIDS)." https://www.ashoka.org/en-us/fellow/omololu-falobi.

Asongu, Simplice. 2013. "Globalization and Africa: Implications for Human Development." *International Journal of Development Issues* 12 (3): 213–238.

Asongu, Simplice. 2014. "Globalization (Fighting), Corruption and Development How Are These Phenomena Linearly and Nonlinearly Related in Wealth Effects?" *Journal of Economic Studies* 41 (3): 346–369.

Atif, Syed Muhammad, Mudit Srivastav, Moldir Sauytbekova, and Udeni Kathri Arachchige. 2012. "Globalization and Income Inequality: A Panel Data Analysis of 68 Countries." Kiel und Hamburg: ZBW - Deutsche Zentralbibliothek für Wirtschaftswissenschaften, Leibniz-Informationszentrum Wirtschaft. https:// www.econstor.eu/bitstream/10419 /65664/3/Atif_Globalization_Inequality.pdf.

Atkinson, Anthony B. 1999. "The Contributions of Amartya Sen to Welfare Economics." *The Scandinavian Journal of Economics* 101 (2): 173–190.

Backer, Larry Cata. 2006. "Ideologies of Globalization and Sovereign Debt: Cuba and the IMF." *Penn State International Law Review* 24 (3): 497–561.

Ball, Terence, Richard Dagger, and Daniel I. O'Neill. 2004. *Political Ideologies and the Democratic Ideal, 5th Edition*. New York: Pearson Longman.

Balls, Andrew. 1997. "UN Sets US $80B as Price of Ending World Poverty: The Agency Urges a New Global Political Commitment to Break the Spiral of Decline." *Financial Post* (Toronto) June 18: 54.

Bambas, Alexandra, Juan Antonio Casas, Harold A. Drayto, and América Valdés. 2000. *Health and Human Development in the New Global Economy.* Washington, DC: Pan American Health Organization.

Ban, Ki-moon. 2010. "Remarks at Concluding Session on the 18th Session of the Commission on Sustainable Development." *United Nations,* May 14. http://www .un.org/apps/news/infocus/sgspeeches/statments.

BBC (British Broadcasting Company). 2012. BBC Monitoring Europe. May 16.

Beltrame, Julian. 1997. "We're No. 1—Still: UN Report Finds Canada Is Tops for 4th Straight Year." *Gazette* (Montreal), June 12: A1.

Berger, Peter. 2002. "The XIV International AIDS Conference: A Call for Action . . . Now." *Canadian Medical Association Journal* 167, no. 5 (September 3): 483–484.

Bhagwati, Jagdish N. 2007. *In Defense of Globalization.* Oxford: Oxford University Press.

Biebricher, Thomas. 2018. *The Political Theory of Neoliberalism.* Stanford, CA: Stanford University Press.

Bonfiglioli, Chiara. 2016. "The First UN World Conference on Women (1975) as a Cold War Encounter: Recovering Anti-Imperialist, Non-Aligned, and Socialist Genealogies." *Filozofija i društvo* (Translation) *Philosophy and Society* 27 (3): 521–541.

Boynton, Robert S. 1999. "Who Needs Philosophy? (Interview with Martha Nussbaum)." *New York Times Magazine,* November 21.

Braveboy-Wagner, Jacqueline. 2009. *Institutions of the Global South.* London: Routledge.

Brenan, Mega. 2022. "Americans' Trust in Media Remains Near Record Low." *Gallup,* October 18. https://news.gallup.com/poll/403166/americans-trust-media -remains-near-record-low.aspx.

Brussels Programme of Action for the Least Developed Countries (BPoA). 2001. A/ RES/76/258. *United Nations General Assembly.* https://digitallibrary.un.org/record /444981?ln=en.

Brysk, Alison, (ed.). 2002. *Globalization and Human Rights.* Berkeley: University of California Press.

Buchanan, James. 1969. *Cost and Choice: An Inquiry in Economic Theory.* Chicago: University of Chicago Press.

Bwiire, Isabella. 2012. "Poverty a Result of Denial of Human Rights." *New Vision* (Kampala). http://www.newvision.co.ug/.

Canadian Press. 1992. "Poor Countries Worse Off Despite Aid in the Billions." *Hamilton Spectator,* April 5: A10.

Carson, Rachel. 1962. *Silent Spring.* Boston: Houghton Mifflin Company.

Chanda, Nayan. 2007. *Bound Together: How Traders, Preachers, Adventurers, and Warriors Shaped Globalization.* New Haven: Yale University Press.

Chant, Sylvia. 2006. "Re-thinking the 'Feminization of Poverty' in Relation to Aggregate Gender Indices." *Journal of Human Development* 7 (2): 201–220.

Checkel, Jeffrey T. 2001. "Why Comply? Social Learning and European Identity Change." *International Organization* 55 (3): 553–588.

Cheema, G. Shabbir, and Dennis A. Rondinelli, eds. 2007. *Decentralizing Governance: Concepts and Practices*. Washington, DC: Brookings Institution Press.

Chen, Martha Alter. 1995. "Engendering World Conferences: The International Women's Movement and the United Nations." *Third World Quarterly* 16 (3): 477–494.

Chong, Dennis, and James N. Druckman. 2007. "Framing Theory." *Annual Review of Political Science* 10: 103–126.

Cieślik, A. 2014. "Globalization and Human Development in Post-Transition Countries: Empirical Evidence from Panel Data." *Oeconomia Copernicana* 5 (3): 7–27.

Classens, Juliana. 2016. "The Woman of Substance and Human Flourishing: Proverbs 31:10–31 and Martha Nussbaum's Capabilities Approach." *Journal of Feminist Studies in Religion* 32 (1): 5–19.

Claude, Inis L. 1965. "Implications and Questions for the Future." *International Organization* 19 (3): 835–846.

Cleaver, Frances. 2007. "Understanding Agency in Collective Action." *Journal of Human Development* 8 (2): 223–244.

Cohen, Bernard C. 1963. *The Press and Foreign Policy*. Princeton: Princeton University Press.

Cohen, Joel E., David E. Bloom, Martin B. Malin, and American Academy of Arts and Sciences. 2006. *Educating All Children: A Global Agenda*. Cambridge, MA: MIT Press.

Coleman, James Samuel. 1990. *Foundations of Social Theory*. Cambridge, MA: Belknap Press.

Cooper, Richard N. 2000. "The Road from Serfdom: Amartya Sen Argues That Growth Is Not Enough." *Foreign Affairs* 79 (1): 163–167.

Corea, Gamani. 1981. "North-South Dialogue: Gamani Corea: Secretary-General of UNCTAD." *Third World Quarterly* 3 (4): 603–614.

Cox, Robert. 1981. "Social Forces, States, and World Orders: Beyond International Relations Theory." *Millennium* 10 (2): 126–155.

Crescenzo, Daniel L. 2013. "Loose Integrity and Ecosystem Justice on Nussbaum's Capabilities Approach." *Environmental Philosophy* 10 (2): 53–73.

Crocker, David A. 1995. "Functioning and Capability: The Foundations of Sen's and Nussbaum's Development Ethic, Part 2." In *Women, Culture, and Development: A Study of Human Capabilities*, edited by Martha C. Nussbaum and Jonathan Glober, 153–198. Oxford: Oxford University Press.

Crouch, David. 2018. "The Swedish 15-Year-Old Who's Cutting Class to Fight the Climate Crisis." *The Guardian*, September 1.

CSPAN. 2002. Interview of Dr. Anthony Fauci on International AIDS Conference. *CSPAN,* July 14, 2022. https://www.c-span.org/video/?171182-2/international -aids-conference.

Dados, Nour, and Raewyn Connell. 2012. "The Global South." *Contexts* 11 (1): 12–13.

Damrah, Sadeq, Elma Satrovic, Mohamad Atyeh, and Fekri Ali Shawtari. 2022. "Employing the Panel Quantile Regression Approach to Examine the Role of Natural Resources in Achieving Environmental Sustainability: Does Globalization Create Some Difference?" *Mathematics* 10 (4795): 1–19.

D'Angelo, Paul, John C. Pollock, Kristen Kiernicki, and Donna Shaw. 2013. "Framing of AIDS in Africa: Press-State Relations, HIV/AIDS News, and Journalistic Advocacy in Four Sub-Saharan Anglophone Newspapers." *Politics and the Life Sciences* 32 (2): 100–125.

Daniller, Andrew, Douglas Allen, Ashley Tallevi, and Diana C Mutz. 2017. "Measuring Trust in the Press in a Changing Media Environment." *Communication Methods and Measures* 11 (1): 76–85.

De Wilde, Pieter. 2019. "The Making of Four Ideologies of Globalization." *European Political Science Review* 11 (1): 1–18.

Deen, Thalif. 2011. "Cuba: Bumped from Human Development Index over Missing Data." *Inter Press Service* (Montevideo), January 20, 2011. http:// www.ipsnews.net/2011/01/cuba-bumped-from-human-development-index-over -missing-data/.

Della Porta, Donatella, eds. 2007. *Global Justice Movement: Cross-national and Transnational Perspectives.* New York: Routledge.

Deneulin, Séverine. 2005. "Development as Freedom and the Costa Rican Human Development Story." *Oxford Development Studies* 33 (3–4): 493–510.

Deneulin, Séverine and David Crocker. 2006. Capability and Democracy. HDCA Briefing Note.

Deneulin, Séverine with Lila Shahani, eds. 2009. *An Introduction to the Human Development and Capability Approach.* New York: Earthscan.

Desai, Radhika. 2009. "Theories of Development." In *Introduction to International Development: Approaches, Actors, and Issues,* edited by Paul A. Haslam, Jessica Schafer, and Pierre Beaudet, 45–65. New York: Oxford University Press.

Destutt de Tracy, Antoine Louis Claude, comte. 1970. *Elements d'ideologie.* J. Vrin Paris.

Doha Programme of Action for Least Developed Countries (Draft) (DPoA). 2023. A/ CONF.219/2022/3. *United Nations General Assembly.* https://digitallibrary.un.org /record/3959499?ln=en.

Draper, William. 1990. "Foreword." In UNDP. *Human Development Report 1990: Concept and Measurement of Human Development.* New York: Oxford University Press.

Dreher, Axel. 2006. "Does Globalization affect Growth? Evidence from a New Index of Globalization." *Applied Economics* 38: 1091–1110.

Drèze, Jean and Amartya Sen. 1989. *Hunger and Public Action*. New York: Oxford University Press.

Drèze, Jean and Amartya Sen. 2002. *India: Development and Participation*. New Delhi: Oxford University Press.

Durkin, Sarah, Emily Brennan, and Melanie Wakefield. 2012. "Mass Media Campaigns to Promote Smoking Cessation among Adults: An Integrative Review." *Tobacco Control* 21 (2): 127–138.

Eagleton, Terry. 2007. *Ideology: An Introduction*. New York: Verso.

Easterlin, Richard. 2000. "The Globalization of Human Development." *AAPSS Annals* 570: 32–48.

Ebbesson, Jonas. 2022. "Getting It Right: Advances of Human Rights and the Environment from Stockholm 1972 to Stockholm 2022." *Environmental Policy and Law* 52 (2): 79–92.

Egghe, Leo. 2006. "Theory and Practice of the G-index." *Scientometrics* 69: 131–152.

Ehrlich, Paul. 1968. *The Population Bomb*. New York: Sierra Club Books.

Eichelberger, Clark. 1977. *Organizing for Peace: A Personal History of the Founding of the United Nations*. New York: Harper & Row.

El Khayat, Ranya S. 2018. "The Capabilities Approach: 'A Future Alternative to Neoliberal Higher Education in the MENA Region.'" *International Journal of Higher Education* 7 (3): 36–44.

Ellick, Adam. 2009a. "Class Dismissed in Swat Valley: Documentary." *New York Times*, February 22. https://www.nytimes.com/video/world/asia/1194838044017/class-dismissed-in-swat-valley.html.

Ellick, Adam. 2009b. "A Schoolgirl's Odyssey: Documentary." *New York Times*, October 10. https://www.nytimes.com/video/world/1247465107008/a-schoolgirls-odyssey.html.

Elster, John. 1985. *Making Sense of Marx*. Cambridge: Cambridge University Press.

Emmerij, Louis, Richard Jolly, and Thomas G. Weiss. 2001. *Ahead of the Curve? UN Ideas and Global Challenges*. Bloomington, IN: Indiana University Press.

Engel, Susan. 2010. *The World Bank and the Post-Washington Consensus in Vietnam and Indonesia: Inheritance of Loss*. New York: Routledge.

Engfeldt, Lars-Goran. 1973. "The United Nations and the Human Environment: Some Experiences." *International Organization* 27 (3): 393–412.

Entman, Robert M. 2004. *Projections of Power: Framing News, Public Opinion, and U.S. Foreign Policy*. Chicago: University of Chicago Press.

Epstein, Rachel. 2006. "Cultivating Consensus and Creating Conflict: International Institutions and the (De)Politicization of Economic Policy in Post-communist Europe." *Comparative Political Studies* 39 (8): 1019–1042.

Escobar, Arturo. 1995. *Encountering Development: The Making and Unmaking of the Third World*. Princeton: Princeton University Press.

Fair, Gardner. 1999. "Review: Sex and Social Justice by Martha Nussbaum." *Social Theory and Practice* 25 (2): 344–352.

Falk, Richard A. 1971. *This Endangered Planet: Prospects and Proposals for Human Survival*. New York: Random House.

Flaurbaey, Marc. 2002. "Development, Capabilities, and Freedom." *Studies in Comparative International Development* 37 (2): 71–77.

Folbre, Nancy. 2006. "Measuring Care: Gender, Empowerment, and the Care Economy." *Journal of Human Development* 7 (2): 183–199.

Freeden, Michael. 1996. *Ideologies and Political Theory: A Conceptual Approach*. Oxford: Clarendon Press.

Freeden, Michael. 2003. *Ideology: A Very Short Introduction*. New York: Oxford University Press.

Freeden, Michael, Lyman Tower Sargent, and Marc Stears. 2013. *The Oxford Handbook of Political Ideologies*. New York: Oxford University Press.

Freeman, Dena. 2017. "The Global South at the UN: Using International Politics to Re-Vision the Global." *The Global South* 11 (2): 71–91.

Fricker, Miranda. 2000. "Sex and Social Justice (Book Review)." *Journal of Philosophy* 97 (8): 471.

Friedman, Milton and Rose Friedman. 1980. *Free to Choose: A Personal Statement*. New York: Harcourt.

Friedman, Thomas. 1999. *The Lexus and the Olive Tree*. New York: Farrar, Straus & Giroux.

Fukuda-Parr, Sakiko. 2011. "Theory and Policy in International Development: Human Development and Capability Approach and the Millennium Development Goals." *International Studies Review* 13 (1): 122–132.

Fukuda-Parr, Sakiko and David Hulme. 2011. "International Norm Dynamics and the 'End of Poverty': Understanding the Millennium Development Goals." *Global Governance* 17 (1): 17–36.

Fukuda-Parr, Sakiko, and A.K. Shiva Kumar, eds. 2003. *Readings in Human Development: Concepts, Measures and Policies for a Development Paradigm*. New Delhi: Oxford University Press.

Fukuyama, Francis. 1992. *The End of History and the Last Man*. New York: Free Press.

Galtung, Johan, and Mari Homboe Ruge. 1965. "The Structure of Foreign News: The Presentation of the Congo, Cuba, and Cyprus Crises in Four Norwegian Newspapers." *Journal of Peace Research* 2 (1): 64–90.

Gebremedhin, Abrehet and Devin Joshi. 2016. "Social Justice, Human Rights and Education Policy Discourse: Assessing Nelson Mandela's Legacy." *Education as Change* 20 (1): 172–198.

Geuss, Raymond. 1981. *The Idea of a Critical Theory: Habermas and the Frankfurt School*. Cambridge: Cambridge University Press.

Ghodsee, Kristen. 2010. "Revisiting the United Nations Decade for Women: Brief Reflections on Feminism, Capitalism and Cold War Politics in the Early Years of the International Women's Movement." *Women's Studies International Forum* 33 (1): 3–12.

Ghosh, Shanti. 2006. "Food Dole or Health, Nutrition and Development Programme?" *Economic and Political Weekly* 46 (34): 3664–3666.

Giddens, Anthony. 1990. *The Consequences of Modernity*. Stanford, CA: Stanford University Press.

Goldin, Ian and Kenneth A. Reinert. 2012. *Globalization for Development: Meeting New Challenges*. Oxford: Oxford University Press.

Golub, Philip S. 2013. "From the New International Economic Order to the G20: How the 'Global South' Is Restructuring World Capitalism from Within." *Third World Quarterly* 34 (6): 1000–1015.

González-Cantón, César, Sonia Boulos, and Pablo Sánchez-Garrido. 2019. "Exploring the Link Between Human Rights, the Capability Approach, and Corporate Responsibility." *Journal of Business Ethics* 160 (4): 865–879.

Gray, Kevin and Barry K. Gills. 2016. "South–South Cooperation and the Rise of the Global South." *Third World Quarterly* 37 (4): 557–574.

Group of 77 at the United Nations. n.d. "About the Group of 77." http://www.g77.org/doc/.

Gygli, Savina, Florian Haelg, Niklas Potrafke, and Jan-Egbert Sturm. 2019. "The KOF Globalization Index - Revisited." *Review of International Organizations* 14 (3): 543–574.

Haas, Peter M. 2022. "Stockholm + 50: A Look Ahead in International Environmental Politics." *Environmental Policy and Law* 52 (1): 3–11.

Hall, Jon. 2019. "Role of Nature-based Solutions: A Guidance Note for National Human Development Report Teams." UNDP (UN Development Programme), Human Development Reports Office (HDRO). https://hdr.undp.org/reports-and-publications.

Hamilton, Lawrence. 2019. *Key Contemporary Thinkers*. Cambridge: Polity Press.

Handl, Günther. 2012. "Declaration of the United Nations Conference on the Human Environment (Stockholm Declaration), 1972 and the Rio Declaration on Environment and Development, 1992." *United Nations Audio-visual Library of International Law*. http://www.un.org/law/avl.

Haq, Mahbub ul. 1995. *Reflections on Human Development*. New York: Oxford University Press.

Haq, Mahbub ul. 2003. "The Human Development Paradigm." In *Readings in Human Development*, edited by S. Fukuda-Parr and A. V. Shiva Kumar, 17–34. New York: Oxford University Press.

Haq, Khadija and Richard Ponzio, eds. 2008. *Pioneering the Human Development Revolution: An Intellectual Biography of Mahbub ul Haq*. Oxford: Oxford University Press.

Harpham, Geoffrey Galt. 2002. "The Hunger of Martha Nussbaum." *Representations* 77 (1): 52–81.

Harvey, David. 2007. *A Brief History of Neoliberalism.* Oxford: Oxford University Press.

Haseeb, Muhammad, Tulus Suryanto, Nira Hariyatie Hartani, and Kittisak Jermsittiparsert. 2019. "Nexus between Globalization, Income Inequality, and Human Development in Indonesian Economy: Evidence from Application of Partial and Multiple Wavelet Coherence." *Social Indicators Research* 147 (3): 723–745.

Haug, Sebastian, Jacqueline Braveboy-Wagner, and Günther Maihold. 2021. "The 'Global South' in the Study of World Politics: Examining a Meta Category." *Third World Quarterly* 42 (9): 1923–1944.

Hayek, Friedrich A. 1944/2007. *The Road to Serfdom.* London: Routledge.

Heberle, Renee. 2000. "Book Review: Sex and Social Justice. By Martha Nussbaum." *Journal of Politics* 62 (4): 1225–1228.

Held, David, Anthony McGrew, David Goldblatt, and Jonathan Perraton. 1999. *Global Transformations: Politics, Economics and Culture.* Stanford, CA: Stanford University Press.

Helleiner, Eric. 2014. "Southern Pioneers of International Development." *Global Governance* 20 (3): 375–388.

Hirai, Tadashi. 2017. *The Creation of the Human Development Approach.* Cham: Springer.

Hirai, Tadashi. 2022. "A Balancing Act Between Economic Growth and Sustainable Development: Historical Trajectory through the Lens of Development Indicators." *Sustainable Development* 30 (6): 1900–1910.

Hirsch, Jorge E. 2005. "An index to quantify an individual's scientific research output." *Proceedings of the National Academy of Sciences of the United States of America* 102 (46): 16569–16572.

Horner, Rory and Pádraig Carmody. 2019. "Global North/South." In *International Encyclopedia of Human Geography*, edited by Audrey Kobayashi, 181–187. Amsterdam: Elsevier.

Hovland, Carl I. and Walter Weiss. 1951. "The Influence of Source Credibility on Communication Effectiveness." *Public Opinion Quarterly* 15 (4): 635–650.

Huntington, Samuel P. 1997. *The Clash of Civilizations and the Remaking of World Order.* New York: Touchstone.

Hutchinson, John and Anthony D. Smith, eds. 1994. *Nationalism.* Oxford Readers: Oxford University Press: Oxford and New York.

Ibrahim, Solava. 2006. "From Individual to Collective Capabilities: The Capability Approach as a Conceptual Framework for Self Help." *Journal of Human Development* 7 (3): 397–416.

Ishay, Micheline R. 2012. *The Human Rights Reader*, 2nd edition. Abingdon: Routledge.

IPoA (Istanbul Programme of Action for the Least Developed Countries). 2011. A/CONF.219/3/Rev.1. *United Nations General Assembly.* https://digitallibrary.un.org/record/704838?ln=en.

Falobi, Omololu, ed. 2004. "Beyond the Shadows: Unmasking HIV/AIDS-Related Stigma and Discrimination in Nigeria." *Journalists against AIDS.* https://nigeria-aids.org/wp-content/uploads/2019/12/BeyondTheShadows.pdf.

JAAIDs (Journalists against AIDS). 2023. "About." *Journalists against AIDS.* https://nigeria-aids.org.

Jain, Devaki. 2005. *Women, Development, and the UN: A Sixty Year Quest for Equality and Justice.* Bloomington, IN: Indiana University Press.

JHDC (Journal of Human Development and Capabilities). 2005. "Bibliography on the Capability Approach, January 2004–June 2005." *Journal of Human Development* 6 (3): 421–426.

Jillani, M. S., and Masooda Bano. 2008. "From 'Growth' to 'Growth with a Social Conscience': Haq as an Economic Planner in Pakistan." In *Pioneering the Human Development Revolution*, edited by Khadija Haq and Richard Ponzio. Oxford: Oxford University Press.

Jolly, Richard. 2003. "Human Development and Neoliberalism: Paradigms Compared." In *Readings in Human Development: Concepts, Measures, and Policies for a Development Paradigm*, Sakiko Fukuda-Parr and A.K. Shiva Kumar (Eds.). 106–116. New Delhi: Oxford University Press.

Jolly, Richard, Louis Emmerij, Dharam Ghai, and Frédéric Lapeyre. 2004. *UN Contributions to Development Thinking and Practice.* Bloomington, IN: Indiana University Press.

Jolly, Richard, Louis Emmerij, and Thomas G. Weiss. 2009. *UN Ideas that Changed the World.* Bloomington, IN: Indiana University Press.

Joshi, Devin. 2012. "Varieties of Developmental States: Three Non-Western Paths to the Millennium Development Goals." *Journal of Developing Societies* 28 (3): 355–378.

Joshi, Devin. 2021a. "The Human Development and Capabilities Approach as a 21st Century Ideology of Globalization." *Globalizations* 18 (5): 781–791.

Joshi, Devin. 2021b. "Footprints of a Winning Idea: Three Decades of the Human Development Paradigm (1990–2019)." *Journal of Human Development and Capabilities* 22 (3): 506–516.

Joshi, Devin. 2021c. "A New Conceptualization of the Political Left and Right: One Dimension, Multiple Domains." *Canadian Journal of Political Science* 54 (3): 534–554.

Joshi, Devin, and Roni Kay O'Dell. 2013. "Global Governance and Development Ideology: The United Nations and the World Bank on the Left-Right Spectrum." *Global Governance* 19 (2): 249–275.

Joshi, Devin, and Roni Kay M. O'Dell. 2015. "Wie die Berichte über die menschliche Entwicklung die Welt verändern." *Vereinte Nationen* 63 (1): 257–262.

Joshi, Devin, and Roni Kay M. O'Dell. 2017. "The Critical Role of Mass Media in International Norm Diffusion: The Case of UNDP Human Development Reports." *International Studies Perspectives* 18 (3): 343–364.

Joshi, Devin, and William Smith. 2012. "Education and Inequality: Implications of the World Bank's Education Strategy 2020." In *Education Strategy in the Developing World: A Conversation about the World Bank's Education Policy Revision*, edited by A. Wiseman and C. Collins, 173–202. Bingley: Emerald.

Joshi, Devin, and Rakkee Thimothy. 2019. "Long-Term Impacts of Parliamentary Gender Quotas in a Single-Party System: Symbolic Co-option or Delayed Integration?" *International Political Science Review* 40 (4): 591–606.

Kamtekar, Rachana. 2002. "Reviewed Work(s): Sex and Social Justice: Women and Human Development: The Capabilities Approach by Martha Nussbaum." *The Philosophical Review* 111 (2): 262–270.

Kapur, Devesh, John B. Lewis, and Richard Webb. 1997. *The World Bank: Its First Half-Century*. Washington, DC: World Bank.

Kauffman, Johan. 1968. *Conference Diplomacy: An Introductory Analysis*. New York: A.W. Sijthoff-Leyden Oceana Publications.

Kaul, Inge. 2003. "Choices that Shaped the Human Development Reports." In *Readings in Human Development*, edited by Sakiko Fukuda-Parr and A. K. Shiva Kumar. New Delhi: Oxford University Press.

Kennedy, Emmet. 1979. "'Ideology' from Destutt De Tracy to Marx." *Journal of the History of Ideas* 40: 353–368.

Kennedy, Paul M. 2007. *The Parliament of Man: The Past, Present, and Future of the United Nations*. New York: Vintage Books.

Keynes, John Maynard. 1919/2019. *The Economic Consequences of Peace*. New York: Palgrave Macmillan.

Khan, Haider A. 2021. "Towards a New Socially Embedded Intersectional Capabilities Theory (SEICT) in the 21st Century: Analysis of COVID-19 Policies in South Africa through Socio-economic Modeling and Indigenous Knowledge Base." *Journal of Applied Economic Sciences* 16 (72): 168–184.

Kiani, Adiqa, Noor Mohammad, and Raheem Bux Soomro. 2021. "The Impact of Globalization on Human Development Index: A Case of Pakistan." *Estudios de Economia Aplicada* 39 (2): 1–22.

Kohli, A. 1987. *The State and Poverty in India: The Politics of Reform*. Cambridge: Cambridge University Press.

Kovach, Bill, and Tom Rosenstiel. 2021. *The Elements of Journalism: What Newspeople Should Know and the Public Should Expect*, 4th edition. New York: Crown.

Krishna, Sankaran. 2009. *Globalization and Post-colonialism: Hegemony and Resistance in the Twenty-First Century*. Lanham, MD: Rowman & Littlefield.

Liedke, Jacob and Jeffrey Gottfried. 2022. "US Adults under 30 Now Trust Information from Social Media Almost as Much as from National News Outlets." *Pew Research Center,* October 27, 2022. https://pewrsr.ch/3DF4dn1.

Lipset, Seymour M., Paul F. Lazarsfeld, Allen H. Barton, and Juan Linz. 1954. "The Psychology of Voting: An Analysis of Voting Behavior." In *Handbook of Social Psychology, Vol. 2*, edited by Gardner Lindzey, 1124–1175. Reading, MA: Addison-Wesley.

Lorenzo, David J. 2013. *Conceptions of Chinese Democracy*. Baltimore: The Johns Hopkins University Press.

Maizland, Lindsay. 2023. "Backgrounder: The Taliban in Afghanistan." *Council on Foreign Relations*. Accessed July 11, 2023. https://www.cfr.org/backgrounder/taliban-afghanistan.

Mangin, Virginie. 2022. "Switzerland Tops UN Human Development Index for the First Time." *SWI Swissinfo.ch*, September 8.

Mannheim, Karl. 1936/2015. *Ideology and Utopia: An Introduction to the Sociology of Knowledge*. Mansfield Centre, CT: Martino Publishing.

Manulak, Michael W. 2017. "Developing World Environmental Cooperation: The Founex Seminar and the 1972 Stockholm Conference." In *International Organizations and Environmental Protection: Conservation and Globalization in the Twentieth Century*, edited by Wolfram Kaiser and Jan-Henrik Meyer, 103–127. New York: Berghahn Books.

Marcuse, Herbert. 1964/1991. *One-Dimensional Man: Studies in Ideology of Advanced Industrial Society*. New York: Routledge.

Marklund, Carl. 2020. "Double Loyalties? Small-State Solidarity and the Debates on New International Economic Order in Sweden during the Long 1970s." *Scandinavian Journal of History* 45 (3): 384–406.

Marshall, Katherine. 2008. *The World Bank: From Reconstruction to Development to Equity*. New York: Routledge.

Martill, Benjamin and Sebastian Schindler. 2020. "Introduction: Theory as Ideology in International Relations." In *Theory as Ideology in International Relations: The Politics of Knowledge*, edited by B. Martell and S. Schindler, 1–16. New York: Routledge.

Marx, Karl and Freidrich Engels. 1965. *The German Ideology*. London: Lawrence & Wishart.

Marx, Karl and Freidrich Engels. 1848. *Manifesto of the Communist Party*. In *Marx/Engels Selected Works, Vol. One*, Moscow: Progress Publishers; translated by Samuel Moore (1969): 98–137. Available on the Marxist Internet Archive with Creative Commons Attribution. https://www.marxists.org/archive/marx/works/download/pdf/Manifesto.pdf.

Max-Neef, Manfred. 1992. "Development and Human Needs." In *Real-life Economics: Understanding Wealth Creation*, edited by Paul Ekins and Manfred Max-Neef, 197–213. New York: Routledge.

McCombs, Maxwell. 2004. *Setting the Agenda: The Mass Media and Public Opinion*. Cambridge: Polity Press.

McCombs, Maxwell and Donald Shaw. 1972. "The Agenda-Setting Function of Mass Media." *Public Opinion Quarterly* 36 (2): 176–187.

McNeill, Desmond. 2007. "'Human Development': The Power of the Idea." *Journal of Human Development* 8 (1): 5–22.

McQuail, Denis. 2010. *McQuail's Mass Communications Theory, 6th Edition.* London: Sage Publications.

Meadows, Donella H., Dennis L. Meadows, Jørgen Randers, and William W. Behrens III. 1972. *The Limits to Growth. A Report for the Club of Rome's Project on the Predicament of Mankind.* New York: Universe Books.

Meisler, Stanley. 1995. *United Nations: A History.* New York: Grove Press.

Mercury, The. 1997. "Have-Nots Exist Day to Day on Under $1: UN." *The Mercury* (Hobart), June 13.

Meredith, M. 2005. *The State of Africa: A History of Fifty Years of Independence.* London: Free Press.

Morris, David, and Overseas Development Council. 1979. *Measuring the Condition of the World's Poor: The Physical Quality of Life Index.* New York: Pergamon Press.

Moyo, Lungisani, and Nketsi A. Moqasa. 2017. "News Coverage of HIV/AIDS in Selected South African Newspapers." *Journal of Communication* 8 (1): 28–43.

Murphy, Craig N. 2006. *The United Nations Development Programme: A Better Way?* New York: Cambridge University Press.

Murphy, Gillian H. and Steven Pfaff. 2005. "Thinking Locally, Acting Globally? What the Seattle WTO Protests Tell Us About the Global Justice Movement." In *Political Power and Social Theory*, edited by Diane E. Davis, 151–175. Bingley: Emerald.

Najam, Adil. 2005. "Developing Countries and Global Environmental Governance: From Contestation to Participation to Engagement." *International Environmental Agreements: Politics, Law and Economics* 5 (3): 303–321.

Nation, The. 2021. "Omololu: Unforgettable Journalist, Media Advocate par Excellence." *The Nation*, October 10. https://thenationonlineng.net/omololu-unforgettable-journalist-media-advocate-par-excellence/.

National Education Policy of India (NEP). 2020. "National Education Policy of India." New Delhi: Ministry of Human Resource Development, Government of India.

Newell, Peter. 2002. "Globalisation and Sustainable Development: A Dialogue of the Deaf?" *International Review for Environmental Strategies* 3 (1): 41–52.

Newman, Nic. 2021. *Reuters Institute Digital News Report 2021: 10th Edition.* Reuters Institute for the Study of Journalism and University of Oxford.

Noël, Alain, and Jean-Philippe Thérien. 2008. *Left and Right in Global Politics.* New York: Cambridge University Press.

Norris, Pippa. 1997. "Introduction: The Rise of Postmodern Political Communications." In *Politics and the Press: The News Media and their Influences*, edited by Pippa Norris, 1–17. Boulder, CO: Lynne Rienner.

Norris, John. 2021. *The Enduring Struggle: The History of the US Agency for International Development and America's Uneasy Transformation of the World.* Lanham, MD: Rowman & Littlefield.

Nussbaum, Martha. 1986. *The Fragility of Goodness: Luck and Ethics in Greek Tragedy and Philosophy.* Cambridge: Cambridge University Press.

Nussbaum, Martha. 1999. *Women and Human Development: The Capabilities Approach.* Cambridge: Cambridge University Press.

Nussbaum, Martha. 1999. *Sex and Social Justice.* Oxford: Oxford University Press.

Nussbaum, Martha. 2000. "Women's Capabilities and Social Justice." *Journal of Human Development* 1 (2): 219–247.

Nussbaum, Martha. 2011. *Creating Capabilities: The Human Development Approach.* Cambridge: Harvard University Press.

Nussbaum, Martha and Amartya Sen, eds. 1993. *The Quality of Life.* Oxford: Clarendon Press.

O'Dell, Roni Kay M. 2023a. "Refugee and Migrant Rights: A Human Rights Perspective." In *Holocaust Education Today: Confronting Extremism, Hate, and Mass Atrocity Crimes,* edited by Carol Rittner. Greensburg, PA: Seton Hill University National Catholic Center for Holocaust Education.

O'Dell, Roni Kay M. 2023b. "Global Governance." In *Elgar Encyclopedia of Development,* edited by Matthew Clarke and Xinyu Zhao, 279–283. London: Edward Elgar Publishing.

O'Dell, Roni Kay M. and S. Breger Bush. 2021. *Global Politics: A Toolkit for Learners.* Lanham, MD: Lexington Press.

O'Dell, Roni Kay M., Ariana Scott, Mark Nealon, and Brianna Franzino. 2023. "Training for the United Nations in the Twenty-First Century; Professionalism Training on Leadership, Negotiation, and Gender for Model United Nations Simulations." *International Studies Perspectives,* https://doi.org/10.1093/isp/ekad011

O'Dell, Roni Kay M. and Linda Veazey. 2023. "Is Amnesty International Still a Grassroots, Member-Led Organization? An Assessment of Its Democratic Viability." *Journal of Human Rights Practice* 15 (1): 186–203.

O'Donoghue, Aoife, and Adam Rowe. 2022. "Feminism, Global Inequality, and the 1975 Mexico City Conference." In *Women and the UN: A New History of Women's International Human Rights,* edited by Rebecca Adami and Dan Plesch. New York: Routledge.

Organization for Economic Cooperation and Development (OECD). 2022. *Education at a Glance 2022 OECD Indicators; India.* https://gpseducation.oecd.org/Content/EAGCountryNotes/EAG2022_India.pdf.

Olcott, Jocelyn. 2017. *International Women's Year: The Greatest Consciousness-Raising Event in History.* Oxford: Oxford University Press.

Osborn, Fairfield. 1948. *Our Plundered Planet.* Boston: Little, Brown.

Paglia, Eric. 2021. "The Swedish Initiative and the 1972 Stockholm Conference: The Decisive Role of Science Diplomacy in the Emergence of Global Environmental Governance." *Humanities and Social Sciences Communications* 8 (1): 1–10.

Palmstierna, Hans. 1967. *Plundring, Svält, Förgiftning.* Translated as *Plunder, Famine, and Poisoning.* Stockholm: Rabén & Sjögren.

Peters, Michael A. 2021. "The Early Origins of Neoliberalism: Colloque Walter Lippman (1938) and the Mt. Perelin Society (1947)." *Educational Philosophy and Theory* 55 (14): 1574–1581.

Petty, Richard E., and Duane T. Wegener. 1998. "Attitude Change: Multiple Roles for Persuasion Variables." In *The Handbook of Social Psychology, 4th Edition,* edited by Daniel T. Gilbert, Susan T. Fiske, and Gardner Lindzey. New York: McGraw-Hill.

Pieterse, Jan Nederveen. 2010. *Development Theory, 2nd Edition.* London: Sage.

Piketty, Thomas. 2014. *Capital in the Twenty-First Century* (translated by Arthur Goldhammer). Cambridge, MA: Belknap Press.

Potrafke, Niklas. 2015. "The Evidence on Globalisation." *The World Economy* 38 (3): 509–552.

Potter, W. James. 2013. "Synthesizing a Working Definition of 'Mass' Media." *Review of Communication Research* 1 (1): 1–30.

Potter, Jessica. 2014. "Montreal Gazette." *The Canadian Encyclopedia,* October 17, 2014. https://www.thecanadianencyclopedia.ca/en/article/montreal-gazette.

PPoA (Paris Programme of Action for the Least Developed Countries). 1990. A/CONF.147/18. *United Nations General Assembly.* https://digitallibrary.un.org/record/126889?ln=en.

Rahman, Bushra H. 2014. "Conditional Influence of Media: Media Credibility and Opinion Formation." *Journal of Political Studies* 21 (1): 299–314.

Rahman, Rakan Abed El and Huthifa Fayyad. 2020. "I Want to Spread Peace: Meet Gaza's 11–year-old Rapper."*Video Report; Middle East Eye,* August 23. https://www.middleeasteye.net/video/i-want-spread-peace-meet-gazas-11-year-old-rapper.

Rajamani, Lavanya. 2003. "From Stockholm to Johannesburg: The Anatomy of Dissonance in the International Environmental Dialogue." *Review of European Community & International Environmental Law* 12 (1): 23–32.

Rasgon, Adam and Iyad Auheweila 2020. "'11-Year-Old Scores Viral Rap Hit but Trips on Gaza Politics.'" *New York Times,* August 22.

Rawls, John. 1971. *A Theory of Justice.* Cambridge: Harvard University Press.

Reinhard, Scott and David Zucchino. 2021. "20 Years of Defense, Erased by the Taliban in a Few Months." *New York Times,* August 14. https://www.nytimes.com/interactive/2021/08/14/world/asia/afghanistan-maps-taliban.html.

Rist, Gilbert. 2008. *The History of Development: From Western Origins to Global Faith, 3rd Edition.* London: Zed Books.

Robeyns, Ingrid. 2005. "The Capability Approach: A Theoretical Survey." *Journal of Human Development* 6 (1): 93–114.

Robeyns, Ingrid. 2017. *Wellbeing, Freedom and Social Justice: The Capability Approach Re-Examined.* Cambridge: Open Book Publishers.

Robinson, Nicholas A. 2021. "Depleting Time Itself: The Plight of Today's 'Human' Environment." *Environmental Policy and Law* 51 (6): 361–369.

Rodrik, Dani. 2011. *The Globalization Paradox.* Oxford: Oxford University Press.

Rosati, Clayton. 2018. "Development as Freedom after Flint: A Geographical Approach to Capabilities and Antipoverty Communication." *Journal of Multicultural Discourses* 13 (2): 139–159.

Rupert, Mark. 2000. *Ideologies of Globalization: Contending Visions of a New World Order.* New York: Routledge.

Sabaratnam, Sarah. 2002. "So Free and So Unjust." *New Straits Times*, August 27, p. 11.

Said, Edward. 2003. *Orientalism, 25th Anniversary Edition.* New York: Vintage Books.

Said, Edward. 1993. *Culture and Imperialism.* New York: Knopf.

Sandbrook, Richard, Marc Edelman, Patrick Heller, and Judith Teichman. 2007. *Social Democracy in the Global Periphery: Origins, Challenges, Prospects.* New York: Cambridge University Press.

Scerri, Andy. 2013. "The World Social Forum: Another World Might Be Possible." *Social Movement Studies* 12 (1): 111–120.

Schlesinger, Stephen C. 2005. *Act of Creation: The Founding of the United Nations: A Story of Superpowers, Secret Agents, Wartime Allies and Enemies, and Their Quest for a Peaceful World.* Boulder, CO: Westview.

Stokke, Olav. 2009. *The UN and Development: From Aid to Cooperation.* Bloomington: Indiana University Press.

Sen, Amartya. 1979. "Equality of What?" The Tanner Lecture on Human Values. Stanford, CA: Stanford University.

Sen, Amartya. 1981/2013. *Poverty and Famines: An Essay on Entitlement and Deprivation.* Oxford: Oxford University Press.

Sen, Amartya. 1990. "More than 100 Million Women Are Missing." *The New York Review of Books* 37 (20): 61–66.

Sen, Amartya. 1992. "Missing Women." *British Medical Journal* 304 (6827): 587.

Sen, Amartya. 1993. "Capability and Well-being." In *The Quality of Life*, edited by Martha Nussbaum and Amartya Sen, 30–53. Oxford: Oxford University Press.

Sen, Amartya. 1995. *Inequality Reexamined.* Cambridge, MA: Harvard University Press.

Sen, Amartya. 1999. *Development as Freedom.* New York: Anchor.

Sen, Amartya. 2002. "Response to Commentaries." *Studies in Comparative International Development* 37 (2): 78–86.

Sen, Amartya. 2003a. "Foreword." In *Readings in Human Development, edited by* Sakiko Fukuda-Parr and A. K. Shiva Kumar, vii–xiii. New Delhi: Oxford University Press.

Sen, Amartya. 2003b. "Development as Capability Expansion." In *Readings in Human Development, edited by* Sakiko Fukuda-Parr and A. K. Shiva Kumar, 3–16. New Delhi: Oxford University Press.

Sen, Amartya. 2009. *The Idea of Justice.* Cambridge, MA: Harvard University Press.

Sen, Amartya. 2018. *Collective Choice and Social Welfare: An Expanded Edition.* Cambridge, MA: Harvard University Press.

Sen, Amartya. 2021. *Home in the World: A Memoir.* New York: Liveright.

Seyfang, Gill. 2003. "Environmental Mega-Conferences—from Stockholm to Johannesburg and Beyond." *Global Environmental Change* 13 (3): 223–228.

Singh, Ajit. 2012. "Financial Globalization and Human Development." *Journal of Human Development and Capabilities* 13 (1): 135–151.

Smith, William and Devin Joshi. 2016. "Public vs. Private Schooling as a Route to Universal Basic Education: A Comparison of China and India." *International Journal of Educational Development* 46 (1): 153–165.

SNPA. 1981. *Substantial New Programme of Action for the 1980s for the least developed countries.* A/CONF.104/7/Add.6 PartI). United Nations General Assembly. https://digitallibrary.un.org/record/25122?ln=en.

Steger, Manfred. 2009. *Globalisms: The Great Ideological Struggle of the Twenty-First Century.* Lanham, MD: Rowman & Littlefield.

Steger, Manfred. 2017. *Globalization: A Very Short Introduction.* Oxford: Oxford University Press.

Steger, Manfred and Paul James. 2019. *Globalization Matters: Engaging the Global in Unsettled Times.* New York: Cambridge University Press.

Steger, Manfred. 2020. *Globalisms, 4th edition.* Lanham, MD: Rowman & Littlefield.

Steger, Manfred, James Goodman, and Erin K. Wilson. 2012. *Justice Globalism: Ideology, Crises, Policy.* Thousand Oaks, CA: Sage.

Steil, Benn. 2014. *Battle of Bretton Woods—John Maynard Keynes, Harry Dexter White, and the Making of a New World Order.* Princeton, NJ: Princeton University Press.

Stewart, Frances. 2005. "Groups and Capabilities." *Journal of Human Development* 6 (2): 185–204.

Stewart, Francis, Gustav Ranis, and Emma Samman. 2018. *Advancing Human Development: Theory and Practice.* Oxford: Oxford University Press.

Stiglitz, Joseph E. 2002. *Globalization and Its Discontents.* London: Penguin Press.

Streeten, Paul P., and World Bank. 1979. *Basic Needs: Premises and Promises.* World Bank Reprint Series, No. 62. Washington: World Bank.

Streeten, P. 2003. "Shifting Fashions in Development Dialogue." In *Readings in Human Development,* edited by Sakiko Fukuda-Parr and A. K. Shiva Kumar, 92–105. New York: Oxford University Press.

Sun, Yat-Sen. 1922. *International Development of China*. New York: G.P. Putnam's Sons.

Sun, Yat-Sen. 1938. *The Three Principles of the People* (translated by San Min Chu I). Shanghai: Commercial Press.

Suzuki, Severn. 1992. "Speech at U.N. Conference on Environment and Development." Delivered at the 1992 UN Rio Earth Summit, Rio de Janeiro, Brazil (June 3–14, 1992). https://www.americanrhetoric.com/speeches/severnsuzukiunearthsummit.htm.

Thérien, Jean-Philippe. 2012a. "The United Nations and Human Development: From Ideology to Global Policies." *Global Policy* 3 (1): 1–12.

Thérien, Jean-Philippe. 2012b. "Human Security: The Making of a UN Ideology." *Global Society* 26 (2): 191–213.

Thérien, Jean-Philippe. 2014. "All Human Rights for All: The United Nations and Human Rights in the Post-Cold War Era." *Human Rights Quarterly* 36 (2): 373–396.

Thunberg, Greta. 2019. "Transcript: Greta Thunberg's Speech at the U.N. Climate Action Summit." Speech delivered September 23, 2019. https://www.npr.org/2019/09/23/763452863/transcript-greta-thunbergs-speech-at-the-u-n-climate-action-summit.

Tolle, Eckhart. 2005. *A New Earth: Awakening to Your Life's Purpose*. New York: Plume.

Tsai, Ming-Chang. 2007. "Does Globalization Affect Human Well-Being?" *Social Indicators Research* 81 (1): 103–126.

Tsfati, Yariv, Jesper Strömbäck, Elina Lindgren, Hajo G. Boomgaarden, and Rens Vlieenthart. 2023. "What News Outlets Do People Have in Mind When They Answer Survey Questions about Trust in 'Media'?" *International Journal of Public Opinion Research* 35 (2): edad008.

UN. 1948. *Universal Declaration of Human Rights* (UDHR). New York: United Nations.

UN. 1973. *Report of the United Nations Conference on the Human Environment: Stockholm, 5–16 June 1972*. A/CONF.48/14/Rev.1. New York: UN.

UN. 1976. *Report of the United Nations Conference of the International Women's Year: Mexico City, 19 June–2 July 1975*. New York: UN.

UN. 1987. *Our Common Future: Report of the World Commission on Environment and Development*. (Brundtland Report). A/42/427. New York: United Nations.

UN. 1992. *The Rio Declaration on Environment and Development*. A/CONF.151/5/Rev.1. https://digitallibrary.un.org/record/200866?ln=en.

UN. 1996. *The United Nations and the Advancement of Women: 1945–1996*. Blue Books Series Volume VI. New York: UN.

UN. 2000. *Resolution Adopted by the United Nations General Assembly on September 18, 2000: UN Millennium Declaration*. A/55/2. https://digitallibrary.un.org/record/422015?ln=en.

UN. 2023. *Global Sustainable Development Report (Advance, Unedited Version).* Accessed July 11, 2023. https://sdgs.un.org/gsdr/gsdr2023.

UNAIDS (UN Joint Programme on HIV/AIDS). 2022. "Global HIV & AIDS Statistics—Factsheet." *UNAIDS.* https://www.unaids.org/en/resources/fact-sheet.

UNAIDS. 2023. *The Path that Ends Aids: 2023 UNAIDS Global AIDS Update.* Geneva: Joint United Nations Programme on HIV/AIDS; 2023. Licence: CC BY-NC-SA 3.0 IGO.

UNCTAD (UN Conference on Trade and Development). 2018. *Report on UNCTAD Assistance to the Palestinian People: Developments in the Economy of the Occupied Palestinian Territory.* UNCTAD, July 23, 2018. https://unctad.org/system/files/official-document/tdb65_2_d3_en.pdf.

UNDP (UN Development Programme). 1990–2023. *Human Development Reports.* New York: UN Human Development Reports Office. https://hdr.undp.org/reports-and-publications.

UNESCO (UN Economic, Scientific, and Cultural Organization). 2023. "Press Release: UNESCO Dedicates the 2023 International Day of Education to Afghan Girls and Women." https://www.unesco.org/en/articles/unesco-dedicates-2023-international-day-education-afghan-girls-and-women.

UNESCO. 2021/22. *Global Education Monitoring Report, 2021/2: Non-State Actors in Education: Who Chooses? Who Loses?* https://unesdoc.unesco.org/ark:/48223/pf0000379875.

UNESCO. 2023. "Press Release: UNESCO Dedicates the 2023 International Day of Education to Afghan Girls and Women." https://www.unesco.org/en/articles/unesco-dedicates-2023-international-day-education-afghan-girls-and-women.

UNGA (UN General Assembly). 1968. *Resolution Adopted by the General Assembly on December 3, 1968: Problems of the Human Environment.* A/RES/2398(XXIII). https://digitallibrary.un.org/record/202554?ln=en.

UNGA. 1969. *Resolution Adopted by the General Assembly on December 15, 1969: United Nations Conference on the Human Environment.* A/RES/2581(XXIV). https://digitallibrary.un.org/record/202662?ln=en.

UNGA. 1972. *Resolution Adopted by the General Assembly on December 18, 1972: International Women's Year.* A/RES/3010(XXVII). https://digitallibrary.un.org/record/191761?ln=en.

UNGA. 2015. *Transforming Our World: The 2030 Agenda for Sustainable Development.* October 21 A/RES/70/1. https://digitallibrary.un.org/record/803352.

UNSC (UN Security Council). 2021. "8853rd Meeting Provisional Agenda: The Situation in Afghanistan: S/PV.8853." September 9. https://research.un.org/en/docs/sc/quick/meetings/2021.

Veseth, Michael. 2005. *Globaloney: Unraveling the Myths of Globalization.* Lanham, MD: Rowman & Littlefield.

Waisbord, Silvio. 2009. "Advocacy Journalism in a Global Context." In *The Handbook of Journalism Studies*, edited by Karin Wahl-Jorgensen and Thomas Hanitzsch, 391–405. New York: Routledge.

Wakefield, Melanie A., Barbara Loken, and Robert C. Hornik. 2010. "Use of Mass Media Campaigns to Change Health Behavior." *The Lancet* 376 (9748): 1261–1271.

Wallerstein, Immanuel. 1979. *The Capitalist World-Economy*. New York: Cambridge University Press.

Ward, Michael. 2004. *Quantifying the World: UN Ideas and Statistics*. Bloomington, IN: Indiana University Press.

Way, Wendy. 2013. *A New Idea Each Morning: How Food and Agriculture Came Together in One International Organization*. Canberra: ANU Press.

Weiss, Thomas G. 2012. *What's Wrong with the United Nations and How to Fix It*, *2nd Edition*. Cambridge: Polity Press.

Wodak, Ruth. 2015. *The Politics of Fear: Analysing Right-Wing Popular Discourse*. Los Angeles: Sage.

Yee, Albert. 1996. "The Causal Effects of Ideas on Policies." *International Organization* 50 (1): 69–108.

Young, Iris Marion. 2001. "Nussbaum, Martha C. Sex and Social Justice: Book Review." *Ethics*, July: 819–823.

Yousafzai, Malala. 2013. *I Am Malala: The Girl Who Stood up for Education and Was Shot by the Taliban*. New York: Little, Brown and Co.

Yousafzai, Malala. 2021. *We are Displaced: My Journey and Stories from Refugee Girls Around the World*. New York: Little, Brown and Co.

Yousafzai, Ziauddin and Louise Carpenter. 2018. *Let Her Fly: A Father's Journey*. New York: Little, Brown and Co.

Zimbardo, Philip G. and Michael R. Leippe. 1991. *The Psychology of Attitude Change and Social Influence*. Philadelphia: Temple University Press.

Zinsser, Judith P. 2002. "From Mexico to Copenhagen to Nairobi: The United Nations Decade for Women, 1975–1985." *Journal of World History* 13 (1): 139–168.

INDEX

About the Authors

Roni Kay M. O'Dell is associate professor of political science and Coordinator of the Political Science and Global Studies Programs at Seton Hill University (SHU). Her recent book is *Global Politics: A Toolkit for Learners*, written with Sasha Breger Bush. Her published peer-reviewed articles appear in *International Studies Perspectives*, *Journal of Human Rights Practice*, and *Global Governance: A Review of Multilateralism and IOs*, among others. She is the main advisor for SHU's award-winning Model UN program and is actively involved in organizations that support the UN, which currently includes positions on the Academic Council on the United Nations System (ACUNS) Board and the Human Development and Capability Association (HDCA) Executive Council.

Devin K. Joshi is associate professor of political science in the School of Social Sciences at Singapore Management University and a current recipient of the Lee Kong Chian Fellowship. His research interests include globalization, ideology, and human development. He is co-author of the book *Strengthening Governance Globally: Forecasting the Next 50 Years* and has written more than fifty academic journal articles and book chapters. His articles appear in journals such as *Globalizations*, *International Studies Quarterly*, *World Development*, and *Journal of Human Development and Capabilities*.

www.ingramcontent.com/pod-product-compliance
Lightning Source LLC
Chambersburg PA
CBHW050343270326
41926CB00016B/3586